Juvenile Correctional Reform

SUNY Series in Critical Issues in Criminal Justice

Gilbert Geis, Donald J. Newman, and Terence P. Thornberry, Editors

Juvenile Correctional Reform

Two Decades of Policy and Procedural Change

Edmund F. McGarrell

State University of New York Press

Published by
State University of New York Press, Albany

© 1988   State University of New York

For information, address State University of New York
Press, State University Plaza, Albany, N.Y., 12246

McGarrell, Edmund F., 1956-
    Juvenile correctional reform : two decades of policy and procedural change / Edmund
F. McGarrell.
    p.   cm. — (SUNY series in critical issues in criminal justice)
    "Bibliography of New York State specific references": p. 203
    Bibliography: p. 191
    Includes index.
    ISBN 0-88706-759-X.   ISBN 0-88706-760-3 (pbk.)
    1. Juvenile corrections—United States. 2. Juvenile justice, Administration of—United
States. 3. Juvenile corrections—New York (State)—Case studies.   I. Title.   II. Series.
HV9104.M33 1988
364.3′6′0973—dc19   87-24499
                                                                                      CIP

Contents

Tables

Figures

Preface

This book addresses the divergent reform agendas that have shaped American juvenile justice systems during the last two decades, examining national trends in juvenile justice and intensively investigating the process of change in New York State's juvenile corrections system.

Essentially, this is a study of change. The key question addressed is *how* and *why* has juvenile justice, particularly juvenile corrections, changed during the last twenty years. As such, it most clearly deals with issues of concern to the student of juvenile justice and corrections. In addition, by dealing with the question of change, the book also raises perhaps the most basic question of political science: "who gets and who should get what, how and why in governmental decisionmaking..." (Nagel, Fairchild, and Champagne, 1983:ix).

This study asks: What juvenile justice policies have changed? Who has changed them? Why have they been changed? What has been the effect on juvenile corrections, and ultimately, on youth? Although the questions may appear straightforward, the answers are complex. Thus, in terms of who and why, the study suggests that factors as broad as cultural shifts in prevailing political ideology and as narrow as the individual initiative of an agency head have shaped policy and procedure at specific times. In addition, the shifting roles of federal, state, and local governments and executive, legislative, and judicial branches therein have been apparent, as well as the occasional influence of the media and reform groups.

Beyond these questions of power and influence, the book also provides a case study of an organization in relation to its environment. The organizational sociologist is presented with a picture of an organization, a juvenile corrections agency, struggling to survive during a period of unprecedented and often contradictory (e.g., divert versus punish) external demands for change. The organization at times appears as the pivotal actor in the formation of policy, at times as the reactive implementor of policy, and most commonly, as some combination of lobbyist, policymaker, and administrator.

Whether the primary interest is in juvenile justice, politics, law, or organizations, the book's unifying feature is its focus on change and reform. The book presents the findings of an empirical study grounded in a theory of social reform originally developed in a similar study of the Massachusetts juvenile corrections system (Miller, Ohlin, and Coates, 1977). The analysis provides a test of the theory and an attempt is made to more fully develop the theory by drawing upon the insights of Wamsley and Zald's (1973) political economy approach to organizations.

Thus, this study of juvenile corrections change and reform raises issues not only of interest to the juvenile justice policymaker, reformer, and scholar, but also to the political scientist, social welfare reformer, and organizational sociologist interested in processes of large-scale reform. Because of these diverse interests, some readers may find certain chapters more relevant than others. The first three chapters frame the analysis but from rather different perspectives. Chapter One covers the historical development of American juvenile justice systems with particular attention on the major reform agendas witnessed nationwide since the late 1960s. Chapter Two discusses relevant theoretical and empirical developments in the study of corrections as an "open system." The chapter also reviews a number of studies of criminal law and correctional policy formation. Chapter Three presents the theory of social reform developed in the Massachusetts studies (Miller, Ohlin, and Coates,

1977; Miller and Ohlin, 1985). The chapter also presents the key research questions and the methodology employed to test the theory. Chapters Two and Three will be of most interest to those concerned with the theoretical issues raised in the study. They may be of less interest to readers primarily concerned with the practical impact of reform agendas on the juvenile justice system.

The next four chapters present the findings of the study of the New York State juvenile corrections system. Chapter Four describes the system level changes that have occurred in New York State and places the system in historical and national context. Chapters Five through Seven present the main findings and the analysis of the change process. These chapters are organized around the tenure of the administrators of the state's juvenile corrections system from the late 1960s to 1984. Finally, Chapter Eight presents an analysis of the overall change process and summarizes the empirical support for the theory of social reform. The chapter concludes by placing the study in perspective of national contemporary trends in juvenile justice and within the broad-context of the deinstitutionalization movement and the so-called get tough movement toward crime and delinquency.

Acknowledgements

Deep appreciation is extended to all those "key actors" who graciously gave of their time and thoughts in helping to reconstruct the story of change in the New York State system. Particular thanks to Dr. Ron Simeone and his colleagues within the Bureau of Program Analysis of the Division for Youth.

Several individuals have been helpful since the initial stages of this project. In particular, David Duffee and Timothy Flanagan from the School of Criminal Justice at SUNY Albany, Lloyd Ohlin from Harvard Law School's Center for Criminal Justice, and the late Alden Miller provided invaluable support. In addition, I would like to thank Margaret Farnworth, Harold Pepinsky, and Simon Singer for their comments on the manuscript.

Much of the manuscript was prepared at the Hindelang Criminal Justice Research Center. Kim Schoonmaker and Ramona Peace were particularly helpful in preparing tables and figures as well as typing the original manuscript. Ann Pastore helped with much of the artwork. Kathleen Maguire, Kevin Vaughn, and Kate Jamieson gave much of their time and talent in coding the *New York Times* data. Final preparation here at Indiana University was made considerably easier because of the support of Ellen Dwyer, chairperson of the Department of Criminal Justice, and because of the word processing skills of Gina Lake.

I would also like to thank Gilbert Geis, Donald Newman, and Terence Thornberry for including this in the "Critical Issues in Criminal Justice" series.

Appreciation is also expressed to the editors of *Criminal Justice Policy Review* for permission to reprint Figures 4.2 and 4.3, Table 5.4, and portions of the narrative text in Chapters Five through Eight. These materials originally appeared in the article, "Change in New York's Juvenile Corrections System," *Criminal Justice Policy Review* (1986) 1,2:169-197 (Indiana, PA: Indiana University of Pennsylvania). Thanks also to Flora Rothman, John Jay College of Criminal Justice, for permission to include Table 4.1.

Finally, my unending thanks to Donna, Corey, and Erin, the three who provide all that is good in my life.

Abbreviations

ACLU	American Civil Liberties Union
AFDC-FC	Aid to Families with Dependent Children-Foster Care
DCJS	Division of Criminal Justice Services
DFY	Division for Youth
DOB	Division of the Budget
DOCS	Department of Correctional Services
DOP	Division of Parole
DSS	Department of Social Services
FAA	Federal Aviation Administration
FCC	Federal Communications Commission
JJDPA	Juvenile Justice Delinquency Prevention Act of 1974
JJRA	Juvenile Justice Reform Act of 1976
JO	Juvenile Offender Law
LEAA	Law Enforcement Assistance Administration
NYCDJJ	New York City Department of Juvenile Justice
OJJDP	Office of Juvenile Justice and Delinquency Prevention
PINS	persons in need of supervision
SEC	Securities and Exchange Commission
YDDPA	Youth Development and Delinquency Prevention Administration

Chapter One

Juvenile Justice In Change

In June 1978, a fifteen-year-old youth gained notoriety in New York State when he was sentenced to the maximum allowable five-year sentence for murdering two subway passengers and attempting to murder a third. The case had ramifications beyond the effect on those directly involved, as it was considered to have acted as a "triggering event" in subsequent legislative changes. As discussed in Chapter Six, the sentence was announced during a gubernatorial campaign during which Governor Hugh Carey was being criticized as soft on crime because of his stands against capital punishment and against criminal court jurisdiction for juveniles. While on a campaign flight, the governor was handed a newspaper with a front page article highlighting the above case. The governor reportedly slammed down the newspaper and announced plans to submit legislation that would permanently keep such a youth off the streets. The governor stuck to his pledge and the state passed what some experts called the toughest juvenile statute in the country (Smith et al., 1980).

One reason for the governor's response was his dissatisfaction with the maximum five year sentence. It is interesting to note, however, that if the case had occurred just two years prior, the youth would have faced an eighteen-month indeterminate placement (although the law did include a rarely used provision for a three-year sentence). Further, a youth committing a similar offense several months later could face a minimum five- to nine-year sentence with a maximum sentence of life.

This case, while certainly atypical, is interesting both because of its historical significance and because it raises a number of questions concerning public policy towards juvenile crime. The recognition that a juvenile committing the same act could, within a three-year span, face either an eighteen-month, five-year, or life sentence, raises fundamental questions about juvenile policy. At the very least, one must ask why these policies changed.

In addition to, and as a partial consequence of these policy changes, New York State's juvenile corrections system changed during these years. The policy changes that produced these shifts in available sentences followed a period in which the juvenile corrections system moved from a primary reliance on large institutions to a near-equal mix of institutional and community-based programming. Since the late 1970s, however, a renewed emphasis has been placed on institutions and particularly the development of secure facilities.

These changes in juvenile justice policy are not unique to New York State. Indeed, since the 1960s, American juvenile justice systems increasingly have been called into question. Perhaps more than at any time since the creation of the juvenile court at the turn of the twentieth century, the idea that the state acts as the benevolent guardian of delinquents has been questioned. Demands for reform ranged from complete deinstitutionalization to "cracking down" on serious juvenile crime (Ohlin, 1983). In order to understand these pressures for reform and the consequent effects on juvenile justice practice, both the historical development of the juvenile justice system and the changes in juvenile justice that have occurred on a national level since the 1960s must be examined.

Historical Development

Although the origins extended to European common law and the early American colonial era (Empey, 1979; Rendleman, 1971), the major development of a separate juvenile justice system occurred during the nineteenth and early twentieth centuries. An early development was establishing houses of refuge in the 1820s, facilities intended to house juveniles who otherwise would be sent to adult jails or penitentiaries. During the second half of the nineteenth century the houses of refuge grew into disfavor and were replaced by the newly developed reformatories and industrial schools. The reformatory and industrial school movement proved popular and by the turn of the century most non-Southern states had built such institutions. These years also witnessed the expansion of probation and of placing out practices, the latter referring to practices whereby troublesome urban youths were sent to live with farm families. The culmination of the trend toward a separate system of justice for youths was the development of the juvenile court in Chicago in 1899 and the subsequent spread of the juvenile court model to the rest of the country.

A rich body of historical literature has developed tracing the evolution of the penitentiary, house of refuge, asylum, reformatory, and the juvenile court. Some of this literature focuses on the development of total institutions and deals with the growth of a separate juvenile justice system as part of this broader development (Foucault, 1979; Rothman, 1971, 1980; Ignatieff, 1978); while other studies focus more directly on the development of the juvenile justice system in particular (Mennel, 1973; Platt, 1969, 1974; Schlossman, 1977; Hawes, 1971; Fox, 1970; Pickett, 1969). This literature provides not only historical documentation of these institutions' emergence and growth, but also insights into the social and political forces behind the process.

Traditional or orthodox explanations for developing these total institutions, and juvenile institutions in particular, emphasize the evolutionary progression from traditional forms of corporal punishment to the development of correctional institutions, separate juvenile institutions, and eventually a separate juvenile justice system (Hawes, 1971; Pickett, 1969; Mack, 1909). This process was brought about through the efforts of humanitarian philanthropic and religious reformers, concerned first with the use of barbarous corporal punishment and later with conditions of the jails, penitentiaries, and juvenile institutions. Along with concern for the conditions of legal punishment, the reformers were concerned with the plight of poor children growing up in the disorganized large cities during this period of increasing immigration, urbanization, and industrialization. Reformers became interested in developing institutions and programs to remove children from inadequate families and provide proper educational and moral training. Such a response was necessary to save these children from a life of poverty and crime. The reform agenda was influenced in the late eighteenth and early nineteenth centuries by the Enlightenment philosophers such as Beccaria and Bentham, and later in the nineteenth century by the tenets of Social Darwinism and positivistic criminology's emphasis on both hereditary and environmental causes of crime. The development of the separate juvenile justice system, similar to parallel reforms in the areas of adult corrections, education, and social welfare, is thus seen as a humanitarian, consensual, and functional response to the problems of rising juvenile crime and youth misconduct precipitated by the disorganized character of life in the rapidly growing urban centers.

In the 1960s and 1970s, several historical analyses of the rise and development of juvenile justice institutions questioned traditional, orthodox explanations of this development (Platt, 1969, 1974; Rendleman, 1971; Fox, 1970; and in relation to the development of the penitentiary in England and France, see Ignatieff, 1978; Foucault, 1979). These revisionist historians also saw this process as evolutionary, but rather than as a progressive movement from corporal punishment to humanitarian reform institutions, this process was seen as the further extension of social and legal control over subordinate classes. The revisionist account also stresses the importance of social structural changes caused by immigration, urbanization, and industrialization, but interprets the reform movement as the effort of the social and political elite to control the poor, urban, "dangerous" classes. Rather than portraying reformers as humanitarians, they are seen either as elite oppressors or as tools of the dominant classes.

Later writings criticized the revisionist interpretation as reductionist (Ignatieff, 1981; Mennel, 1983; Hagan and Leon, 1977). The assertion that the development of the penitentiary and the juvenile justice system was the product of a rational conspiracy fails to recognize the actual complexity of the process (Ignatieff, 1981; Mennel, 1983; Schlossman, 1977; Empey, 1979). Speaking of accounts regarding the development of the penitentiary system, Ignatieff (1981:156) scored revisionist portrayals for " . . . overschematizing a complex story and for reducing the intentions behind the new institution to conspiratorial class strategies of divide and rule." While control intentions are not denied, the process is best understood as the result of complex social structural changes occurring at the political, economic, cultural, and religious levels. Furthermore, rather than being the sole product of either humanitarian or elite efforts, the development of the penitentiary, house of refuge, reformatory, and juvenile court, was the product of compromise and political and legal debate revolving around basic issues of both humanitarian reform and security and order.[1]

Despite the debate among orthodox, revisionist, and antirevisionist accounts over the motives and functions of these new institutions, several insights of relevance to the study of change in the juvenile justice system can be noted. First, the development of the separate juvenile justice system clearly cannot be understood apart from the broad social structural changes brought about by the processes of immigration, urbanization, and industrialization. Second, while revisionist historians interpret the role of social science as merely providing legitimacy to control activities (Platt, 1969, 1974), changes in social thought and theory, ranging from the Enlightenment philosophers of the eighteenth century to the theories of Social Darwinism and positivistic criminology of the late nineteenth century, definitely played a role in the process of change occurring in the developing correctional and juvenile justice systems. Third, the reform process was driven by the involvement of several interest groups including philanthropists, religious activists, women's organizations, and newly emerging child care and social welfare professionals. Fourth, this development reflected a process of conflict, debate, and compromise. While orthodox accounts emphasize the consensual nature of reform and revisionist accounts emphasize conspiratorial domination, case studies from both frameworks provide evidence of such debate and conflict (Hawes, 1971; Pickett, 1969; Platt, 1969). Thus, a review of the historical literature indicates that the separate juvenile justice system was the product of a complex of social forces that led to this new legal apparatus for the control of delinquency and youth misconduct.

1900–1960

Following the 1899 creation of the juvenile court in Chicago, the juvenile court movement quickly spread throughout the nation. By 1910, twenty-two states had created juvenile courts. By 1925, all but two states had juvenile courts; by 1945, all the states had juvenile courts (President's Commission on Law Enforcement and the Administration of Justice, 1967a; Mennel, 1973). During the early years of the juvenile courts, a number of challenges to the lack of constitutional safeguards in the new courts were initiated through the appellate process. However, the informality of the juvenile courts was upheld as the appellate courts in forty states denied these constitutional challenges (Faust and Brantingham, 1979; see also Lemert, 1970). Not until the 1960s were procedural dilemmas resolved in favor of requiring more safeguards (Empey, 1982). Support for the juvenile court model was evidenced by the findings of the Wickersham Commission in the early 1930s (National Commission on Law Observance and Enforcement, 1931). The commission found that although the juvenile court suffered from inadequate resources, the basic model was clearly the solution to the problem of juvenile delinquency and misconduct. Indeed, the "awesome superparent" that was the juvenile court, continued to enjoy widespread support until the 1960s (Empey, 1982).

The 1900–1960 period also witnessed the growth of juvenile corrections institutions, particularly training schools utilizing the cottage plan. Unfortunately, in contrast to the rich historical accounts of the development of juvenile and other total institutions in the nineteenth century, much less has been written on the development of juvenile institutions during the first half of the twentieth century.[2] Despite this lack of research on the dynamics behind the development of juvenile correctional institutions, several relevant points can be noted. First, while such institutions grew throughout the period, growth was particularly significant in the post-World War II period (National Advisory Committee on Criminal Justice Standards and Goals, 1976). Second, these institutions were developed according to a rehabilitation model characterized by indeterminate sentences, diagnostic centers, and specialized treatment personnel (Empey, 1982). Third, the treatment technologies adopted by these institutions reflected the thinking of the social and behavioral sciences of the times. In the early twentieth century, the works of psychiatrists such as Healy and Bronner were particularly influential (Mennel, 1973). Psychotherapy was adopted, at least symbolically, in many juvenile institutions. During the post World War II period, influenced by Edwin Sutherland's emphasis on differential association and group delinquency, as well as by the group oriented work of Kurt Lewin, a number of well-known experimental treatment programs were developed utilizing group therapy approaches (Shichor, 1980; Duffee, 1980a).[3] This period also witnessed the development of differentiated services, including rural camps and farms, vocational and educational programs, and home visitation programs. Despite these changes, the general consensus appears to be that the change that occurred in juvenile correctional institutions during 1900 and 1960 reflected a growth pattern to meet the demands of an expanding population and that very little change actually occurred in the basic structure or functioning of these institutions (Bartollas, Miller, and Dinitz, 1976; Empey, 1982; Mennel, 1973).

This period also witnessed several developments reflecting a basic community orientation. Although probation preceded the creation of the juvenile court, it was probation's link to the juvenile court that actually legitimized and provided impetus for the further development of probation (Mennel, 1973; Empey, 1982). Additionally, Shaw, McKay, and their colleagues at the University of Chicago stressed the importance of the community as both the source of juvenile delinquency and the proper locus of delinquency prevention efforts (Shaw and McKay, 1942). The outgrowth of their work was the Chicago Area Project (Kobrin, 1959). The theoretical underpinning of this project was similar to that of the nineteenth-century reformers in that it, too, attributed delinquency to the social disorganization of urban communities. However, rather than preventing delinquency by removing children from these communities, the Chicago Area Project's prevention efforts emphasized community organization and development.

Thus, the juvenile justice system became firmly established as the legitimate institution for responding to juvenile delinquency and misconduct during 1900 and 1960. Challenges to the informality of the court were unsuccessful. Perceived limitations of the juvenile court and correctional institutions were attributed to insufficient resources, not concept. Juvenile corrections institutions grew and, as was the case in the nineteenth century, adopted the technology of the dominant belief systems of the day (Street, Vinter, and Perrow, 1966). Finally, probation services and the idea of community-oriented prevention efforts took hold during these years.

1960–mid–1970s

The first signs of change for the traditional juvenile justice system arose during the early 1960s with developments at both the state and federal levels. During these years, several states, including California and New York, substantially revised their juvenile codes to provide many of the procedural safeguards later guaranteed in the Supreme Court cases of *Kent, Gault,* and *Winship*.[4] In both states, the revisions followed a period that witnessed an increase in appellate court cases involving the juvenile court, criticism of the lack of procedure of the juvenile courts, and special commissions established to study the problems of the juvenile court (Lemert, 1970; Paulsen, 1963; Schinitsky, 1962).

At the federal level, "the advent of the 1960s marked a historic watershed in the federal role in the delinquency control problem" (Kobrin and Klein, 1983:24). Increased juvenile arrests and juvenile court cases, increased public concern over crime, and criticism of the juvenile justice system combined with the Kennedy Administration's activist approach to elevate juvenile delinquency and juvenile justice to a national concern. Early in the administration's tenure, the President's Committee on Juvenile Delinquency and Youth Crime was created. The committee was heavily influenced by *strain theory,* which placed the cause of delinquency on a defective social structure that failed to provide youth with sufficient legitimate opportunities (Cloward and Ohlin, 1960). The policy implications of this perspective downplayed the importance of traditional individual casework approaches and emphasized the need to reintegrate youth into the community. The initial effort to implement these ideas was embodied in the Juvenile Delinquency and Youth Offenses Control Act of 1961.[5] The Act identified school dropout, unemployment, and family problems as the major sources of delinquency, called for intensive and coordinated private and government efforts to deal with delinquency, and provided grant money and technical assistance to state and local service providers. An early project that served as a model for these federal initiatives was the Mobilization for Youth program in New York City, which attempted to prevent deliquency through the coordination and mobilization of youth services and welfare institutions. These efforts, which located the delinquency problem in the broader problem of poverty, were later subsumed under the more general Great Society and War on Poverty programs (Miller and Ohlin, 1985).

Despite these efforts, reported offenses and arrests continued to rise during the 1960s. President Johnson appointed the President's Commission on Law Enforcement and the Administration of Justice in 1965 to examine the problem of crime and delinquency. The commission issued its report in 1967 (President's Commission on Law Enforcement and the Administration of Justice, 1967b). The report dealing with juvenile delinquency continued to emphasize the need to deal with the social structural sources of delinquency (President's Commission on Law Enforcement and the Administration of Justice, 1967a). Furthermore, the commission voiced concern over the limitations of rehabilitation efforts and noted the gap between the ideal juvenile justice system envisioned by its founders and the actual system in operation. The commission, therefore, recommended additional resources for the juvenile justice system. However, unlike earlier national crime commissions (National Commission on Law Observance and Enforcement, 1931) and traditional calls for reform, the additional resources were not offered as a panacea to cure the delinquency problem. Rather, only with reform of basic political, economic, and social structures could progress be made in the effort to combat delinquency.

The commission also expressed the additional concern that the juvenile justice system actually may be contributing to the delinquency problem. Drawing on the tenets of *labelling theory* (Lemert, 1967), the commission warned that the stigmatizing effects of official processing may actually intensify delinquent behavior. Thus, in addition to addressing the primary, root causes of delinquency, the commission recommended that juvenile justice systems adopt a noninterventionist, or hands-off approach. Specifically, the commission urged policies of decriminalization, diversion, and deinstitutionalization. Furthermore, the commission recommended providing due process safeguards for those juveniles processed in the system.

The commission's due process concerns were concurrently supported by the Supreme Court in the *Gault* case, and later in the *Winship* case. The commission's emphasis on nonintervention was given further credence with the 1973 report of the Nixon Administration's National Advisory Commission on Criminal Justice Standards and Goals (1973). The National Advisory Commission questioned the utility of the juvenile justice system and stressed the need for diversion. As with the 1967 commission, the National Advisory Commission viewed large training schools as ineffective, if not harmful, and criticized correctional systems for failing to reintegrate offenders into the community.

The policy proposals of the 1967 commission, and later of the 1973 National Advisory Commission, were given impetus through the federal government's Youth Development and Delinquency Prevention Administration (YDDPA) created in 1968. YDDPA's mandate was to provide funds to develop local youth programs and to encourage diversion through the development of Youth Service Bureaus (Kobrin and Klein, 1983).

Federal efforts in the delinquency area were expanded in 1974 with passage of the Juvenile Justice and Delinquency Prevention Act of 1974 (JJDPA). The Act created the Office of Juvenile Justice and Delinquency Prevention (OJJDP) as the single federal agency with responsibility in the delinquency area and created a program of formula grants designed to encourage deinstitutional-ization of status offenders and to eliminate the commingling of juveniles and adults in local jails. The Act clearly demarcated the federal resolve to encourage the states to implement the major policy initiatives urged by the national commissions (Kobrin and Klein, 1983).

State and local implementation of the commission recommendations appears uneven. To a significant extent, status offenders have been removed from secure detention centers and institutions (Handler and Zatz, 1982; Kobrin and Klein, 1983; Krisberg and Schwartz, 1983). On the other hand, evidence suggests that status offenders have been encapsulated in other control systems (Austin and Krisberg, 1981; Klein, 1979; Spergel, 1976; Coates, Miller, and Ohlin, 1978), and that status offenders have been relabelled as juvenile delinquents (Klein, 1979; Schneider, 1984). While the number of diversion programs have proliferated, to a large extent they have continued to be administered by the justice system (Dunford, 1977; Lemert, 1981). Further-more, as with the deinstitutionalization of status offenders, critics have main-tained that diversion programs have merely widened the net of social control (Austin and Krisberg, 1981; Cohen, 1979; Klein, 1979). Finally, despite notable exceptions,[6] most states have limited deinstitutionalization to status offenders, large noncommunity-based institutions have remained the dominant type of juvenile correctional facility, and most states have retained juvenile court jurisdiction over status offenders (Vinter, Downs, and Hall, 1975; Empey, 1982).

The specific nature of the federal policy initiatives of the 1960s and early 1970s was clearly influenced by the emerging theories and empirical findings of social science. The influence of strain or opportunity theory (Cloward and Ohlin, 1960; see also Cohen, 1955), was clearly reflected in the approach of the Kennedy and Johnson Administrations to the problems of juvenile delinquency and poverty. Likewise, labelling theory (Lemert, 1967; Becker, 1963; Schur, 1971) clearly influenced the national commission reports (President's Commission on Law Enforcement and the Administration of Justice, 1967b; National Advisory Commission on Criminal Justice Standards and Goals, 1973).

In addition to these theoretical developments, empirical studies of juvenile and adult correctional institutions and treatment programs raised serious questions about the effectiveness of these institutions and programs. Numerous studies of the internal workings of both adult (Clemmer, 1958; Sykes, 1958; Schrag, 1954; Sykes and Messinger, 1960) and juvenile correctional institutions (Polsky, 1962; Rose, 1959; Ohlin and Lawrence, 1959) demonstrated the presence of an apparent ubiquitous inmate subculture in opposition to the staff and evidence of widespread exploitation. Such findings raised fundamental questions about the rehabilitative potential of traditional institutions. Furthermore, actual studies of the effectiveness of various treatment programs failed to demonstrate an effective treatment approach (Robison and Smith, 1971; Kassebaum, Ward, and Wilner, 1971; Bailey, 1966).

Such findings raised serious questions about the traditional reliance on correctional institutions for the rehabilitation of offenders. These findings were particularly critical for the juvenile corrections system, which symbolically represented the treatment approach. These studies not only highlighted the gap between the ideal and actual systems, but raised fundamental questions about the actual potential of the traditional juvenile justice model. The lack of effectiveness findings were also highly congruent with the dominant theoretical paradigms of the day. Strain theory's emphasis on root causes and labelling theory's focus on the negative effects of official processing, both could lead to predictions of either no effect or a negative effect of traditional correctional approaches. While the "nothing works" argument seems to have been influential in the policy proposals of deinstitutionalization and diversion emanating from the 1967 and 1973 national commissions, they would also lie behind very different proposals influential in the 1970s.

Mid-1970s–early 1980s

The criticism of the juvenile justice system expressed in the Supreme Court cases and the presidential commission reports did not abate in the 1970s. Juvenile arrest rates continued to rise through the 1960s and early 1970s despite the seemingly massive federal efforts to control juvenile delinquency. The "nothing works" conclusion received further support with the findings of Lipton, Martinson, and Wilks (1975; see also, Martinson , 1974).[7] While the sources of disillusionment remained much the same as in the 1960s, the policy proposals changed.

The theoretical basis for these policy proposals was found in the writings of so-called Neoclassical theorists who argued for a return to the classical principles of deserts based proportionality and a utilitarian emphasis on deterrence. One group of Neoclassical theorists, typically labelled as proponents of the deserts or justice model, urged that in light of the abuses perpetuated under the guise of the rehabilitative model and in light of the inability to rehabilitate, the state should abandon the therapeutic paradigm and focus instead on administering justice in a fair manner (American Friends Service Committee, 1971; Morris, 1974; Fox, 1974; Fogel, 1975; Von Hirsch, 1976). The essential point of the deserts model is that in view of our inability to treat, the only defensible policy is to administer justice in an equitable manner. Key elements of reform based on the justice model include sharp restrictions on discretion and the use of proportionate sentencing based on the seriousness of the offense and the prior record of the offender. Of course, such proposals are incompatible with the juvenile justice system and could seemingly only be implemented through major overhaul of the system.

A second group of theorists, falling under the rubric of the Neoclassical school also rejected the rehabilitative model; but instead of focusing on deserts, placed primary emphasis on the need to prevent crime through punishment. This work, often associated with van den Haag (1975) and Wilson (1975), focused on rising crime rates and the perceived leniency of the criminal and juvenile justice systems and urged that the main goal of the justice system should be to promote order and community protection through deterrence and incapacitation (see also Boland and Wilson, 1978). As with the deserts model, the policy implications of this crime control model are apparently incompatible with traditional juvenile justice. Punishment is intended to meet society's need to deter and incapacitate, not to address the offender's individual needs. Once again, implementing such reforms seems to require major modifications in juvenile justice philosophy and practice.

While at first glance the two models may appear incompatible (deserts theorists seeking to restrict state control, crime control theorists seeking to expand state control), elements from each model have been combined in a number of policy proposals that, if implemented, would significantly alter the traditional juvenile justice system. Several of the recommendations associated with the Neoclassical school include the following: (1) lowering the age of accountability; (2) abolishing or radically changing the juvenile court; (3) making punishment proportionate to the seriousness of the offense and seriousness of the prior record; (4) uniform/determinate sentences; (5) harsher penalties; (6) removing status offenders from the court's jurisdiction (Empey, 1982; Erickson, 1979).

The policy proposals were reflected to varying degrees in the recommendations of three prestigious advisory groups, the National Advisory Committee on Criminal Justice Standards and Goals (1976); the Juvenile Justice Standards Project of the Institute of Judicial Administration–American Bar Association Joint Commission (1977a, b); and the Twentieth Century Fund Task Force (1978) on youth crime. While differences are found among the three reports, several common features are representative of a new approach to juvenile justice and mark a significant departure from the traditional philosophy of the juvenile justice system. Of most significance is the fact that all three reports consider the seriousness of the offense and prior record as prime considerations in reaching an appropriate disposition. This marks a significant shift from the long-held belief of an individualized disposition based on the needs of the youth with little regard to the actual act committed. No longer is the state's response based on youths' needs; now it is based wholly, or at least significantly, on the basis of present offense and prior record. This change in philosophy is indicative of the thinking of both deserts based and punishment based theorists of the Neoclassical school.

On other issues, however, the advisory groups were less willing to abandon the basic tenets of a separate juvenile justice system. This is particularly true of the National Advisory Committee (1976) which stressed the need for a family court model that would meet youth's needs by focusing on such problems within the context of the family. The Committee followed that suggestions of the earlier Presidential Commissions (President's Commission on Law Enforcement and the Administration of Justice, 1967a; National Advisory Commission on Criminal Justice Standards and Goals, 1973) by retaining the basic juvenile court but emphasizing the need for procedural safeguards. The National Advisory Committee also stressed community-based dispositions, with absolute restrictions on institutional placements of status offenders and institutionalization considered as a last resort placement.

The reports of the Institute of Judicial Administration–American Bar Association (1977a, b) and the Twentieth Century Fund Task Force (1978) place less emphasis on youth's needs and more fully reflect the writings of Neoclassical theorists, particularly the deserts model. The rehabilitation model is rejected and doing justice is offered as the ascendant goal of the juvenile justice system. Recommendations include eliminating jurisdiction over status offenders and adopting determinate sentences proportionate to the offense and prior record.

The writings of the Neoclassical theorists and the National Advisory Committee reports were apparently influential as legislation was passed in a number of states in the late 1970s and early 1980s seemingly reflective of these recommendations. Perhaps most faithful to the deserts model was the revised code of the state of Washington (Serrill, 1980; Castellano, 1986). With its revisions, Washington eliminated juvenile court jurisdiction over status offenders and created a determinate sentencing scheme featuring sentences proportionate to the offense and prior record. Other elements of the Washington code seemed to reflect the punishment model, as community protection was prioritized as the top goal of the juvenile justice system and prescribed periods of incarceration were increased.

The Washington legislation seems to be indicative of trends in a number of states. Although eliminating jurisdiction over status offenders appears to be atypical (Empey, 1982), several states have passed legislation that, to varying degrees, reflect deserts-based concerns of determinacy and proportionality and utilitarian concerns of deterrence and incapacitation. For example, California and Florida have made it easier to waive juvenile cases to adult court by enacting presumptive waiver provisions. Tennessee, Kentucky, and South Carolina have lowered the age of waiver, while Illinois, Indiana, Louisiana, and Oklahoma have created lists of offenses excluded from the jurisdiction of the juvenile court (Krisberg et al., 1986). A similar approach is evident in the statutory provisions of New York State and Vermont, which provide automatic transfer of targeted offenses to adult court. In addition to increased reliance on the adult criminal courts, several states have sought to provide criminal court provisions in the juvenile courts. Thus, Colorado, Idaho, and New York State have provided mandatory minimum periods of incarceration for juveniles. Furthermore, prosecutors, traditionally absent from the juvenile court, have become increasingly involved in juvenile court proceedings (Krisberg et al., 1986; Rubin, 1985). Increased prosecutorial involvement is not merely found at the adjudication and disposition stages, but in states such as Colorado, Florida, North Carolina, and Washington, it is found as early as the intake stage. Juvenile court scholar H. Ted Rubin notes, "The future appears clear: the prosecutor is becoming the most powerful functionary in the juvenile justice system" (Rubin, 1985:246).

In addition to these policy changes at the state level, changing views toward juvenile justice are clearly evident at the federal level. With the 1980 election of Ronald Reagan, discussion of the desirability of the four Ds—decriminalization, diversion, due process, and deinstitutionalization—disappeared. Rather, the argument emanating from the executive branch was that the proper focus of the juvenile justice system should be on isolating and punishing the repeat or violent juvenile offender. Alfred Regnery, OJJDP administrator under the Reagan Administration, states "Chronic offenders pose the greatest threat to society and the greatest challenge to juvenile justice programs across the country" (1985:2). Regnery continues, "Criminals should be treated as criminals . . . there is no reason that society should be more lenient with a sixteen-year-old first offender than a thirty-year-old first offender" (1985:4). In its effort to influence state juvenile policy, Attorney General Edwin Meese recently announced the development of an OJJDP-sponsored model juvenile code. Among the key provisions of the deserts-based code is the recommendation of mandatory determinate sentences based on the seriousness of the offense and prior record ("OJJDP Project Offers States 'Just Deserts' Juvenile Code," *Criminal Justice Newsletter,* 1986:1–3).

Clearly, both federal executive branch recommendations and state legislation lowering the age of criminal responsibility and increasing available sentencing lengths reflect the punishment concerns of retribution, deterrence, and incapacitation. As such, juvenile justice policy has tended to move away from the limiting principles of the Advisory Commissions (see, for example, Institute of Judicial Administration–American Bar Association, 1977a). Overall the tendency in the late 1970s and early 1980s with respect to juvenile delinquents, particularly serious juvenile delinquents, has been to extend state control over juveniles who violate the law (Hamparian *et al.,* 1982; Smith *et al.,* 1980; Ohlin, 1983; Empey, 1982).

Summary and Contemporary Assessment

The history of corrections, and juvenile corrections in particular, is a history of successive reforms (Empey, 1982; Platt, 1969; Duffee, 1980a).[8] Dissatisfaction with dominant correctional philosophy and practice leads to new ideologies and technologies that, in turn, fall into disfavor. Thus, dissatisfaction with corporal punishment led to the development of the penitentiary, dissatisfaction with housing juveniles with adults led to development of the house of refuge and training school, dissatisfaction with traditional court processing led to the creation of the juvenile court, dissatisfaction with the once-heralded correctional technologies of psychotherapy and group therapy led to a movement away from institutions and toward the community, and finally, dissatisfaction with the community movement led to a return to institutionalization, at least for some youths.

Several lessons of importance to this study of change can be taken from this history of reform. First, the process of change in juvenile corrections cannot be understood in isolation from broader social changes. For example, the processes of immigration, urbanization, and industrialization in the nineteenth century and the social and legal activism of the 1960s clearly influenced correctional reform in these eras. Furthermore, correctional ideology and technology seems reflective of the dominant belief system of the day and the writings of the social and behavioral sciences—witness the solitary and the congregate system of the early penitentiaries, placing-out practices, psychotherapeutic approaches, community organization, diversion and deinstitutionalization, and deterrence and incapacitation. Unfortunately, with the exception of the historical accounts of the origins and early development of correctional institutions and the juvenile court, little is known about the sociopolitical dynamics underlying these change processes. From the historical studies, several interest groups, including child care professionals, philanthropists, organized women's groups, and religious groups become involved. In addition, early developments seemed to be the products of political conflict and debate. To move beyond these limited observations, however, an intensive analysis of the way these broad social and political forces impact at the state and local level is needed. For instance, while recognition of the general conservative swing in the mid-1970s might lead one to expect more "adult-like" handling of juvenile offenders, it provides no understanding of why the state of Washington adopted a determinate juvenile code while other states retained traditional indeterminate schemes. Additionally, recognizing the prominence of the deinstitutionalization goal in the 1960s and 1970s tells little of why California adopted the probation subsidy or why Massachusetts closed its training schools while juvenile corrections systems in many states remained largely unchanged. The key point is that while attention to broad social and political shifts can suggest likely directions of juvenile justice reform, it provides little understanding of the variation among states in juvenile justice reform. Unfortunately, few studies exist that provide insight into these issues.

One exception to this statement is the work of Lloyd Ohlin and his colleagues at Harvard Law School's Center for Criminal Justice. These researchers engaged in a twelve-year intensive analysis of the Massachusetts juvenile corrections system. A key focus of the study was analysis of the political dynamics behind Jerome Miller's closing of the Massachusetts training schools in the early 1970s (Miller, Ohlin, and Coates, 1977). Closing the training schools and developing a community-based system of youth corrections was, perhaps, the most radical reform of a correctional system ever undertaken in the United States. As will be discussed in Chapter Three, Ohlin and his colleagues developed a theory of social reform based on their study of the Massachusetts reform. The theory provides one of the first comprehensive models for explaining how and why systems like a juvenile corrections system change and resist change.

The present study represents an attempt to build upon and move beyond the Massachusetts studies. The study focuses on the process of reform and counterreform in the New York State juvenile corrections system from the late 1960s to the mid-1980s. New York State juvenile corrections provides a fascinating site for such study because the state's juvenile justice system can be seen as both reflecting nationwide trends and being a forerunner of such trends. For example, New York State's Family Court Act of 1962 presaged the U. S. Supreme Court by providing due process safeguards to juveniles later mandated by the court. Furthermore, as will be seen in Chapter Four, New York State was at the forefront of the deinstitutionalization movement as a number of training schools were closed and community-based settings opened in the 1970s. Finally, New York State has led the way toward the focus on serious juvenile crime by adopting provisions for automatic transfer of juveniles to adult court and stiffer penalties within the juvenile court. Thus, because New York State has undergone both liberal and conservative reform, it provides an excellent opportunity to update the pioneering work of the Harvard research team.

The need for this type of intensive analysis of the change process in juvenile corrections seems particularly strong at this time in the ongoing development of American juvenile justice. The debate between advocates of the reform agenda of the early 1970s (i.e., decriminalization, diversion, and deinstitutionalization) and advocates of the reform agenda of the 1980s (i.e., determinacy, deterrence, and incapacitation) "rages" (Krisberg *et al.*, 1986:34). This study offers insight into how this debate is likely to be played out at the state level. As such, we can begin to learn of the relationship between national-level debate and state-level policy and practice. Such insights are crucial for the correctional administrator, legislator, or youth rights advocate hoping to influence juvenile corrections policy and practice. Finally, for the scholar interested in the dynamics of social reform, this study provides an initial step in testing the Massachusetts theory in another state and in relation to conservative as well as liberal reform.

Chapter Two

Open Systems and Policy Change

This study focuses on the process of change in juvenile corrections. As such, the study deals with issues considered in several disciplines including sociology, political science, and public administration. Literature from each of these disciplines is related both to the theoretical model utilized in this study and to the research findings. The present focus, however, is on placing the study within the context of contemporary correctional theory and research that urges the adoption of an open-systems perspective, and within the context of criminal law and correctional policy formation.

Corrections as an Open System

Traditionally, correctional research has focused to a considerable extent on the internal operations and internal social system of the prison (Clemmer, 1958; Sykes, 1958; Goffman, 1961; Polsky, 1962) and on evaluation of correctional programs (Robison and Smith, 1971; Kassebaum, Ward, and Wilner, 1971; Bailey, 1966; Lipton, Martinson, and Wilks, 1975). Such an approach, at least with respect to the focus on internal operations and the internal social system, is emblematic of a closed-systems approach to organizations that treats the organization as an independent enterprise insulated from its environment (Trist, 1961). Since the early 1960s, however, several researchers have broadened the analysis by approaching the study of corrections from the complex organizations perspective. This body of research is particularly relevant to this study because it focuses on the prison's relationship to the larger society and the environment's impact on internal correctional structures and processes.

One of the first publications to utilize this broadened framework was the collection of papers on the social organization of the prison published by the Social Science Research Council (Cloward, 1960). Of particular relevance are the works by Cressey, McCleery, and Ohlin.

Cressey (1960) analyzed the dysfunctions and contradictions involved in the transformation of custodial-oriented prisons to treatment-oriented prisons. Although the bulk of the analysis focused on the internal contradictions related to change in goals, Cressey noted the importance of the larger society in this change process. Indeed, he argued that the observed internal contradictions are directly attributable to the demands of the larger society that charge the prison with responsibility for implementing a program based on the seemingly mutually exclusive goals of treatment and punishment. Cressey (1960:88) noted, "There is societal resistance to changing prisons into places of treatment as well as societal stimuli to change." These conflicting societal attitudes are considered a key obstacle to the transformation of the prison into a treatment institution. Cressey does little to further address this organization-environment relationship, but his work is important because it recognizes the environment's key role in the prison's internal structure and process.

McCleery's studies of a Hawaiian prison also highlighted the importance of correctional goals and the prison's relationship to the environment. McCleery's (1960) initial analysis involved a study of power relations within the social system of the prison during a period when a rehabilitation-oriented warden succeeded a custodial-oriented warden. During this transformation, a liberal interest group emerged and engaged in a contest with the traditional custodial force for control over prison operating procedures. The emergence of the liberal group, which gained formal control over policy, and the introduction of rehabilitation policy proved disruptive and conflictual for staff and inmates. Furthermore, although formal policy changed, the actual operating procedures retained a custodial emphasis. Like Cressey (1960), McCleery's study illustrated the importance of policy and goals, the potential conflict over policies and goals, and the change-resistant nature of the prison. This study also illustrated the presence of conflicting internal interest groups. However, it was not until a follow-up study that the importance of the external environment emerged as a key factor in these internal process (McCleery, 1968).

McCleery's (1968) interest in a follow-up study was kindled by a 1960 riot in the Hawaiian prison. In looking at the prison, McCleery noted several developments since his initial study, which increasingly placed the prison in the larger arena of state politics. Foremost was the move to statehood and the subsequent shift from an appointed executive to an elected governor, thereby removing what had been a traditional buffer between state bureaucratic agencies and the public. Along with these broader shifts came a reorganization of correctional services which placed the correctional system under the Department of Social Services. In this increasingly politicized forum, disaffected internal interest groups were able to gain access to sympathetic external groups. The access of the custodial interest group to external interest groups, coupled with the loss of autonomy resulting from the administrative placement of the prison under the Department of Social Services, eroded the authority of the prison's warden. This erosion of authority directly contributed to the custodial staff's failure to quell the riot. Following the riot, the politicalization of corrections continued with the warden and the director of the Department of Social Services pitted against one another for control over prison policy. In addition, the governor and the parole board became increasingly involved in the prison policy formation process. These developments meant that the warden could no longer focus exclusively on internal policies, procedures, and relationships, but, instead, was now forced to focus on these key external relationships. Reflecting on this politicalization process, McCleery (1968:147) noted that " . . . administering society's sense of justice . . . " is an inherently political process intertwined with state-level politics. Particularly in times of crisis, the prison system becomes caught in a power struggle between competing forces seeking to impose their own administrative definition of the state of corrections.

Ohlin's (1960) analysis extended Cressey's (1960) work by not only acknowledging the conflicting societal demands but also explicitly focusing on the network of internal and external interest groups in which these demands are translated into policy influences. Similar to McCleery, Ohlin's (1960:135) thesis is that the structure and process of a correctional institution is the product of " . . . a network of competing or cooperating interest groups located inside and outside the correctional agency." Indeed, "interest groups constitute the basic organizational structure which gives form and content to correctional activities" (1960:148). Interest groups typically become involved in issues of most direct relevance, however, as McCleery observed, involvement is heightened and particularly important during periods of change. During these periods, typically associated with scandal or crisis, interests are threatened leading to mobilization of interest groups. External interest groups such as legislators, the governor, reform groups, and the media and internal interest groups such as custodial, treatment, and administrative factions form loose coalitions " . . . to enforce the broad mandates of prison management which would serve their common interests" (1960:114). It is during these times, as a consequence of the struggle over mandate, that the correctional organization is most vulnerable to externally imposed change.

In a subsequent article, Ohlin (1974) further explicated the environment's role for correctional agencies. Because the agency is dependent upon the environment for basic resources such as personnel, facilities, funds, and clients, the agency is vulnerable to external influence. This dependence restricts the autonomy of the correctional agency and acts as a constraint on correctional policy and program. Typically, the agency exists in relative anonymity with internal and external interest groups in a structure of accommodation. However, when problems reach the public crisis stage, this structure of accommodation breaks down. As he noted in his previous article, disparate interest groups form loose coalitions during these periods and engage in a struggle over the desired goals of the correctional agency. Furthermore, although the environment always acted as a constraint on available policy choices, during periods of crisis, the environment can emerge as a major force for change.

Ohlin (1974) noted that the resolution of these crises can have long-range implications for the correctional agency. The resolution often involves adopting an organizational mandate and appointing a new administrator. Also, the process involves shifts in internal staff relations, reallocation of authority, redefinition of role relationships, and shifts in external relationships.

Zald (1968) was one of the first to emphasize the importance of the external environment for juvenile correctional institutions. Zald noted the limits of applying the Weberian rational bureaucratic model to the analysis of large scale organizations and, instead, followed Selznick's (1949; 1957) approach by studying the "organizational character" of juvenile correctional institutions. This approach combines the analysis of goals and relationships to the external community with the traditional analysis of internal structure. Zald noted that juvenile correctional organizations are charged with multiple and possibly conflicting goals under conditions of variation in resources, personnel, and clientele. Like McCleery and Ohlin, Zald stated that the goals may become the subject of conflict between internal and external interest groups seeking policies most supportive of their own interests.

The environment's impact, although intricately tied to the goal-setting process, goes beyond this process. The correctional organization, like all organizations, " . . . exists in a matrix of intricate relations with the larger society and must meet certain standards in order to exist" (Zald, 1968:232). The correctional agency is dependent on state, professional, and lay associations for legitimacy; the legislature for budgetary allocations; and the police and courts for clientele. External relationships also develop in relation to evaluation of the correctional agency. The agency, like " . . . any large-scale organization must satisfy the needs of others in the society by its output if it is to continue in existence" (Zald, 1968:234). However, evaluation is problematic due to the conflicting nature of correctional goals and the difficulty in assessing rehabilitative effects.

Like most analyses of the prison, Zald also focused on the internal structure of the prison and viewed the internal social system as comprising three sets of relationships: staff-staff, staff-client, and client-client. However, unlike most studies of these internal relationships, Zald argued that these relationships cannot be viewed in isolation from the prison's setting in the larger society; they are all affected by the nature of correctional goals and relations with the environment.

Street, Vinter, and Perrow's (1966) study of six juvenile correctional institutions built on many of these themes and explicitly examined the impact of correctional goals on internal structures and processes. Street, Vinter, and Perrow began with the fundamental premise that as people changing organizations, juvenile correctional institutions operate with indeterminant and uncertain technologies. One consequence is that these organizations develop a " . . . heavy dependence upon belief systems . . . " (1966:7).

Operating from these premises, Street, Vinter, and Perrow examined the impact of variation in correctional goals on organizational structure, staff perspectives, and inmate behavior. Goal formulation is the primary task of the correctional executive. In playing this role, the executive acts as the key link between external demands and internal operations. Because the correctional organization is dependent on a differentiated group of external agencies and interests for basic resources (legitimacy, funding, clientele, personnel), the administrator must balance technological requirements with external demands. The executive must " . . . formulate goals effective inside while legitimate outside" (Street, Vinter, and Perrow, 1966:49). The goal-setting process is thus structured by both technological (effectiveness) and political (legitimacy) concerns. To further complicate matters, this process is not static but dynamic, with the goal-setting process and programmatic changes having feedback effects on external interests.

The main focus of the Street, Vinter, and Perrow study was of the impact of variation in goals on the internal correctional system. The six facilities were categorized according to three basic goal configurations—obedience and conformity, reeducative/developmental, and treatment—and, indeed, the internal organizational structure and staff and inmate relations varied by goal sets. The crucial point, in terms of this study, is that the Street, Vinter, and Perrow study further highlights the importance of the relationship between the correctional environment and correctional goals and the impact of goals on internal correctional structures and relationships. As such, the work is similar to that previously discussed in that it points to the limitations of adopting the traditional closed-system perspective for understanding the correctional enterprise.

Duffee (1975; 1980a) extended this line of analysis in studies of correctional policy, change in a minimum security prison, and Pennsylvania halfway houses. Duffee drew upon the work of Cressey; McCleery; Street, Vinter, and Perrow; and others, by applying an open-systems perspective to the study of correctional systems. This perspective explicitly recognizes the importance of external relations on correctional goals, policy, and internal structure, as well as the complex and dynamic interplay of external and internal structures and relationships.

Duffee noted that the unclear objectives and uncertain technologies of a public human service agency such as a correctional agency have important implications. The lack of clear objectives often results in organizational goals representing "core cultural symbols" (1980a:65). The lack of a clear technology tends to tie internal structure more closely to changing external demands. Furthermore, the agency tends to be " . . . evaluated in terms of its mission rather than in terms of the consequences of its performance" (1980a:66). The very nature of organizational goals and technologies thus opens the agency to external influence and necessitates analysis and management that focuses on environmental relations.

Duffee (1980a) empirically demonstrated the importance of correctional environments in relation to the interorganizational relationships of halfway houses attempting to reintegrate offenders. The halfway house study involved an analysis of problem resolution of halfway house residents (1980a:309–313). Duffee and his colleagues found that most of the problems resolved were done so through the efforts of community agencies or friends or relatives—not through the efforts of halfway house staff or residents. Additionally, they found that halfway houses with formalized interactions with community agencies were most effective in resolving the problems of the majority of released offenders. These findings suggest that agencies outside the correctional system, i.e., within the system's environment, may be most effective in providing needed services to offenders (at least released offenders), and that the correctional agency's relationships with these agencies may be a key variable in securing these needed services. These findings suggest that not only may external relations be important in the policy formation process, but also that the environment and environmental relations may be a potential source of resources for the correctional agency.

Summary

These studies suggest several key themes. The observations of Cressey, McCleery, and Ohlin, represented a new analytic approach to the study of the correctional institution. These authors explicitly recognized the correctional environment's important role on internal prison operations and suggested that the traditional analysis of the internal prison in isolation from its environment was incomplete. Zald; Street, Vinter, and Perrow; and Duffee built upon and extended these observations by placing the study of the correctional institution within the framework of the sociological analysis of complex organizations.

This shift toward an expanded or open-system view of corrections seems to be the product of two related developments. First, the shift parallels developments in the broader sociological analysis of complex organizations that moved from analysis of internal technologies, structures, and social systems (e.g., Taylor, 1911; Blau, 1955; McGregor, 1960) to a broader conceptualization that considers not only internal structures but external relationships and the interplay of the two (e.g., Selznick, 1949; Thompson and McEwen, 1958; Aldrich, 1979; Katz and Kahn, 1966; Hall, 1982). This trend toward an open-systems view of organizations seems to be the product of the recognition of the increased importance of organizational environments in postindustrial society (Terreberry, 1968).

Both the correctional literature currently reviewed and the more general literature on complex organizations suggest the importance of an open-systems analytic approach for understanding the structure and process of the correctional enterprise. Such an approach is particularly important for the study of change in the correctional system. Street, Vinter, and Perrow (1966) and Duffee (1975; 1980a) have stressed, as have students of organizational change generally (Selznick, 1949, 1957; Thompson and McEwen, 1958; Katz and Kahn, 1966; Terreberry, 1968), the crucial role of environmental pressures in generating change in correctional systems. Clearly, the study of the broad policy changes of one state's juvenile correction system requires systematic analysis of these organization-environment relations.

The Dynamics of State-Level Legal and Policy Change

The preceding section highlights the need to consider organizational environments when analyzing correctional systems. These studies suggest that environments may be particularly important as forces of change. However, the correctional literature is somewhat limited for current purposes. First, most of these studies focus on single institutions. This study considers change in one state's entire juvenile corrections system. Second, while many of these studies stress the environment's importance in the goal-setting and policy-formation processes, very few explicitly examine organization-environment relationships.

One area where correctional organization-environment relationships occur is in the formulation of state-level criminal justice policies. One approach to gaining insight into these environmental relationships is to consider the literature related to the structure and dynamics of criminal law and correctional policy formation.

One of the first studies of the legislative politics involved in changing the criminal law was Heinz, Gettleman, and Seeskin's (1969) analysis of amendments of the Illinois criminal code. Heinz, Gettleman, and Seeskin focused on six legislative bills, four that passed and two that did not. They found that the several interest groups involved in the legislative process varied according to several characteristics. One such characteristic was the permanency of the groups' involvement in criminal justice issues. Three categories of interest groups were identified with regard to the permanency dimension. *Ad Hoc groups* were formed in relation to a particular bill affecting group interests; *recurrent groups* were permanently in existence but only involved in a specific issue (e.g., National Rifle Association); and *principal groups* were " . . . permanent organizations for which the criminal law is a principal and continuing area of concern" (1969:283). Interest groups also varied according to whether they were public or private agencies, prosecution or defense oriented, and external or internal to the political decisionmaking system (1969:282–291).

In addition to the description and characterization of these interest groups, Heinz, Gettleman, and Seeskin provide insight into the structure of the decisionmaking process. One of the interesting findings is that the criminal lawmaking process seemed to be dominated by a small group of key decisionmakers. The authors noted, " . . . the legislative politics of criminal law in Illinois seems to be characterized by the *de facto* delegation of decisions to a small group or groups, and by deference in the decisions of the full legislature to the small group or groups—a deference based, we think, on expertise, seniority, and political power (not necessarily in that order)" (1969:334). This group, dominated by white, male, prosecutor-oriented lawyers, constituted an elite. This elite group performed a gatekeeper role as it was at this level that options were set and issues framed. Indeed, "to get an issue before the legislature over the active opposition of the elite we have identified would be extremely difficult" (1969:336–337). At this level, interest groups could most effectively press for their interests. The legislature tended to acquiesce to the elite's recommendations. This process tended to minimize conflict and secure consensus on "agreed-upon" bills. Consequently, the bills that passed did so by wide margins.

The significance of the Heinz, Gettleman, and Seeskin study is that it is one of the first to provide insight into the structure of the criminal law formation process. However, as with most studies of the lawmaking process, the findings are of questionable generalizability due to the limits imposed by the focus on a single jurisdiction at one point in time. However, consideration of these findings in relation to similar studies in other jurisdictions may provide a more general perspective of the structure and dynamics of the law formation process.

Roby's (1969) analysis of the revision of New York State's statute on prostitution reveals some similar findings to those of Heinz, Gettleman, and Seeskin (1969). The passage of the revised prostitution statute was somewhat different, however, in that it was part of a comprehensive revision of the state's penal code. In this case, the legislature delegated responsibility for penal code revisions to a Penal Law Revision Commission comprised entirely of lawyers and heavily represented by district attorneys. The commission's proposed statute, which made prostitution a violation rather than a crime and reduced the maximum penalty from a one-year jail term (or three-year reformatory sentence) to a fifteen-day jail sentence, was passed without comment by the legislature as part of the revised penal code. Thus, as was the case in Illinois (Heinz, Gettleman, and Seeskin, 1969), the law formation process involved legislative delegation to a small group of lawyers (see also Ingraham, 1980), the recommendations of whom formed the basis of an agreed-upon bill that was passed without controversy by a consensus.

Unlike the Heinz, Gettleman, and Seeskin study, Roby's study also included an analysis of the initial implementation of the law and the consequent attempts to revise the law. Following passage, opposition to the prostitution statute arose and was expressed by the New York City Police Department and business interests, particularly hotel owners. The opposition was based on an alleged influx of prostitutes in the Times Square area. In response to this perceived influx and the controversy over police due process violations committed during a "sweep" of prostitution arrests, a New York City Mayor's Committee was appointed to consider the merits of the law. The committee attributed the alleged increase in prostitution to the leniency of the new statute and recommended the law be amended to reclassify prostitution a misdemeanor. The police department introduced a bill to the state legislature that followed the committee's recommendation to make prostitution a misdemeanor and included provisions to expand the loitering statute to include prostitution. The proposed bill amending the prostitution statute was considered by the Senate Codes Committee which voted against the bill, thereby preventing it from reaching the floor of the entire legislature. Formally, the Senate Codes Committee reasoned the law had not been in effect long enough for adequate evaluation and that a one-year sentence was unwarranted and might lead to jail overcrowding. Informally, Roby reported that all sixteen members of the Senate Codes Committee were lawyers who were reluctant to make revisions to the proposals of the respected and supported Penal Law Revision Commission.

Roby also noted that different interest groups had varying involvement and varying influence at different stages of the lawmaking process.[1] For instance, women's rights groups were able to influence the Penal Law Revision Commission to include provisions making the male patron equally culpable under the prostitution statute. The commission had a dominant and persistent influence over the legislature. Business interests and the police were minimally involved in the initial development of the revised statute, but they were able to generate sufficient interest following enactment of the law to have the Senate Codes Committee seriously consider abandoning the revised statute. Also, although the police were unsuccessful in the legislative arena, they were able to influence significantly the actual effect of the law by refusing to enforce the new section making patrons culpable. Thus, Roby suggests that the network of interests shaping the law formation process vary at the different stages from initial consideration to legislative passage and ultimately implementation.

One further study pertaining to interest-group involvement in the formation of criminal justice policy is Berk and Rossi's (1977) study of correctional elites in three states. Unlike the previous studies that examined interest group involvement in relation to specific pieces of legislation, Berk and Rossi focused on the individuals and groups generally involved in state-level correctional policy formation. Interviews in which respondents were asked to rate the relative influence of various groups and officials on correctional policy, indicated that the governor, legislative committee and party leaders, and corrections officials are the key groups influencing policy. The authors tentatively suggest that state correctional policy may be dominated either by a legislative faction, consisting of key committee and party leaders, or by an executive faction, consisting of the governor and corrections officials.

As was the case with the earlier studies (Heinz, Gettleman, and Seeskin, 1969; Roby, 1969), the basic picture of a small group of political insiders controlling policymaking once again emerges. While the basic configuration is similar, the Berk and Rossi study, more so than the earlier studies, highlights the important role of correctional administrators. While this is doubtless a product of their explicit focus on correctional policymaking rather than more general penal code revisions, the finding is important for this study of juvenile corrections policy change. Additionally, the authors point out that this basic configuration of key actors is the structure in place during periods of routine policy formation. During periods of crisis or for particularly controversial issues, the decisionmaking structure indeed may be different.

Several additional studies take a broader approach to changes in state-level criminal law and criminal justice policy by focusing not only on interest group involvement in the legislative process, but also the developments that led to the issue reaching the legislative stage and the broader social processes influencing the legal change.

One such study is Lemert's (1970) analysis of the development and 1961 passage of the California juvenile code. Lemert sought to explain the processes leading to the revolutionary legal change embodied in the new juvenile code. The code was considered revolutionary in that while it continued to stress the goal of individualized treatment, it explicitly rejected the tradition of procedural informality and required basic procedural safeguards.

Lemert worked under the assumption that most legal change is evolutionary and incremental and that the legal system resists change. This resistance is attributed to the legal system's reliance on precedent, to personal interest, and to the dominance of the highly specialized and homogeneous legal profession. Because most legal change is evolutionary and the system is change resistant, the dynamics of revolutionary change are particularly interesting.

Drawing on Kuhn's (1970) theory of scientific revolutions, Lemert posited that revolutionary legal change is the product of accumulating anomalies, produced through awareness of the discrepancy between legal ideals and realities, which lead to the questioning of dominant paradigms. The accumulation of anomalies alone, however, is insufficient to ensure change. Rather, anomalies must be converted into issues that become " . . . the focus of discussion, value conflicts, and social action" (1970:88).

In California, the accumulation of anomalies began with growing awareness of the discrepancy between the treatment-oriented ideals of the juvenile court and the actual practices of the courts. This was evidenced in the growing number of appeals of juvenile cases during the 1950s. The conversion of anomalies into issues occurred in the context of growing concern for the legal rights of court related juveniles. Lemert noted that the legal rights focus was not specific to juveniles or to California, but rather it was part of a nationwide trend toward clarification of procedural issues in the courts (1970:97).

The initial pressure for change was not generated by widespread discontent or public opinion but rather by a small group of judges, chief probation officers, officials of the juvenile corrections agency (California Youth Authority), and several college professors. This group's voiced discontent led the governor to appoint a Study Commission on Juvenile Justice in 1957 comprised of prominent attorneys and several professors. The commission was receptive to those urging procedural safeguards and issued a report with a number of statutory proposals including right to counsel, record of hearings, and provisions for detention hearings.

Organized opposition arose when the proposals were drafted into a Senate bill. The most significant opposition came from criminal justice professionals, particularly juvenile court judges, probation officers, and the police. However, the opposition of the probation officers and the police was somewhat mitigated because several provisions within the revision package were attractive to each of these groups. In addition, because no strong organization representing juvenile court judges existed, judicial opposition tended to be unorganized and expressed by individual judges. On the other side, proponents of the juvenile code were a small but well-organized group with clear and articulate goals and access to key politicians. Administrators of the California Youth Authority, although initially part of the small group instigating procedural reform, did not become actively involved at this stage. Although still considered sympathetic to reform, the need to maintain organizational relationships with the system of judges, probation officers, and the police precluded a strong advocacy role.

The Senate Judiciary Committee held hearings on the commission's recommended bill and ultimately voted in favor of it. Ironically, the inadvertent testimony of juvenile court judges describing court practices was considered a key factor in the committee's support for the bill. Committee members noted that the testimony dramatically demonstrated the lack of, and disregard for, procedural rights in the juvenile courts. With the support of the Senate Judiciary Committee, the juvenile code, with the provisions for counsel, recorded hearings, and detention hearings, was passed by the legislature.

Lemert's study illustrates several important points. First, the legislative change is placed within the context of broader legal trends, in this case, national trends toward clarification of procedural rights. Second, as with the earlier studies, the juvenile code is viewed as the product of a political struggle engaged in by several groups seeking to control policy in a particular issue area. In this case, a small but well-organized group ideologically committed to the introduction of procedural safeguards was pitted against the unorganized and fragmented efforts of juvenile justice professionals. These two groups lobbied for the support of the Senate Judiciary Committee to whom the legislature had seemingly delegated decisionmaking control over the juvenile code. The dramaturgical demonstration of procedural irregularity during committee hearings was considered key in gaining support for the new code. Once the committee endorsed the code, the legislature as a whole supported it.

While this description of the actual lobbying and passage of the code is similar to the previously mentioned studies, Lemert's study places the process in a broader historical context. Lemert reported that for years criticism of the lack of procedure in juvenile court had been expressed by various groups and individuals. It was not until the 1950s, however, bolstered by national trends (clarification of procedural rights) and state-level criticism (growth of appeals), that these concerns were raised to the issue level of state political decisionmakers. Without reaching this stage, the interest group contest would not have occurred.

Galliher and Basilick's (1979) study of Utah's adoption of liberal drug laws provides further insights into the dynamics of legal change. In 1969, Utah became one of the first states to make possession of marijuana a misdemeanor. At the same time, penalties for other drugs were increased. In 1971, sentences for all drug possession charges were decreased. In addressing the question of why the morally conservative Utah legislature would adopt such a reform approach, Galliher and Basilick offered an explanation very similar to Lemert's. They suggested that legal change can only be understood within a broad context, which takes into account the structural characteristics that provide the milieu for change. The two key structural conditions affecting change in Utah were the nationwide concern with drug use in the 1960s and the homogeneous nature of Utah's population. The first factor, coupled with increased media attention on drug use in prominent Utah newspapers, was important in making drug use a public issue. Utah's homogeneous population meant that the targets of drug use laws were not perceived as a threatening symbolic minority but rather the targets were "our kids" (1979:294). As an attorney lobbying in 1971 for reduced penalties stated, "The 1969 legislature was taking our high school kids and putting them with men who were rapists and big drug dealers. These criminals were treated the same as our sons and daughters" (1979:292). Because of the population homogeneity, the tough penalties typically were not enforced.

Within this structured context, advocates for reduced penalties, primarily a Governor's Advisory Committee and a State Bar Committee, met with little opposition from traditional conservatives who realized the stiff penalties were not, and probably should not, be enforced.

Galliher and Basilick argued that an understanding of legal change requires a focus on both broad structural characteristics and more immediate interest-group activity, which they termed triggering events. As such, their approach is very similar to Lemert's. Applying the Galliher and Basilick model to California's juvenile code revision, the national trend toward procedural safeguards can be seen as providing the structural context for change. The efforts of the reform group and the dramaturgical demonstration of procedural abuse within the Senate hearings were the triggering events that shaped the actual change made possible by the structural changes.

Messinger and Johnson's (1978) study of the 1976 adoption of the California Determinate Sentencing Law places a similar emphasis on both broad social changes and more immediate interest-group activity. Furthermore, as with Lemert, the authors distinguish between evolutionary and revolutionary legal change. They wrote, "The law is constantly changing, but the change is usually evolutionary and incremental. Occasionally, a statute or judicial decision breaks abruptly with the past, announcing not only a set of new rules but also a new philosophical approach, indicating a change in the way the opinion leaders of a society are thinking about a long-standing problem" (1978:13). The California Determinate Sentencing Law, which involved the state's shift from an indeterminate sentencing scheme (offender oriented, administrative release discretion, rehabilitative, long parole supervision) to a determinate sentencing scheme (offense oriented, fixed sentence, punishment, reduced parole supervision) represented a new philosophical approach to sentencing—that is, a revolutionary change.[2]

Interest in sentencing reform appeared to have been stimulated by the broad social changes of the 1960s, particularly the emphasis on civil rights. One apparent consequence was the growth of prisoner's rights groups that, in turn, provided a forum for expressions of dissatisfaction with the abuses perpetuated under the indeterminate sentencing scheme. In 1974, a staff member of a Senate Committee on Penal Institutions began consulting with criminal justice professionals and found a great deal of dissatisfaction with the current sentencing system. This led to a working paper draft proposing narrowed ranges for criminal sentences. The working paper then served as the basis for open hearings in which criminal justice professionals and prison reform groups expressed dissatisfaction with the current system. At the same time, several state appellate court decisions struck down current sentencing practices. These court decisions were considered very significant in persuading key decisionmakers, particularly the governor and his staff, that change was needed.

The initial fixed-sentencing bills were criticized by law enforcement groups, such as district attorneys, as too soft, and by civil rights groups, such as the American Civil Liberties Union (ACLU) as too harsh. However, during the course of legislative hearings and negotiations, a coalition of traditional liberals, dissatisfied with the abuses of the indeterminate system, and conservatives, dissatisfied with the uncertainty of punishment under the indeterminate system, formed in favor of the determinate sentencing proposals. The main opponents of the reform were criminal court judges. However, as Lemert found in relation to juvenile court judges in the early 1960s, the judges tended to be too poorly organized to present a unified opposition bloc. Consequently, in 1976, California passed the Determinate Sentencing Law.

Thus, Messinger and Johnson's study once again emphasizes the point that major legal change is the product of broad social and cultural changes, in this case, the increasing focus on civil rights, as well as more immediate triggering events, such as the liberal and conservative coalition and the appellate court decisions.

Berk, Brackman, and Lesser's (1977) study of changes in the California penal code from 1955 to 1971 provides a somewhat different perspective on penal code revision because of the long timeframe, the inclusion of all changes in the code, and the utilization of both qualitative and quantitative indices of change. Berk, Brackman, and Lesser reported that two loose coalitions of interest groups dominated the change process: a law enforcement coalition, primarily comprised of district attorneys and the police, and a civil liberties coalition, comprised of groups such as the ACLU, the American

Friends Service Committee, and prison reform groups. These two coalitions tended to coexist in a pattern of accommodation in which the legislative process represented not a zero-sum contest but rather an arena in which the needs of both coalitions could be fulfilled. This structure of accommodation was reflected in findings that changes in the penal code reflected trends toward criminalization of increasing types of behavior, increasing penalties, and additional resources for criminal justice professionals, but also increasing resources for defendants and offenders. An exception to this pattern of accommodation was observed in the mid-to late 1960s when criminal justice debate became increasingly conflictual and polarized as the law enforcement coalition apparently reacted to the perceived liberal climate. However, rather than a shift to law and order legislation, the increased politicalization led to legislative logjams.

These findings of a structure of accommodation are similar to points Ohlin (1974) makes in relation to correctional interest groups and may indicate that the typical or usual pattern of relationships among criminal justice interest groups is one of accommodation leading to incremental policy change. Ohlin and Lemert suggest that during times of crisis, the structure of accommodation breaks down, and the system is open for fundamental change.

One additional finding of interest is that Berk, Brackman, and Lesser found *Los Angeles Times* crime-related editorials an excellent predictor of change in the penal code. The authors presented data indicating the relationship is not spurious, although they do raise the possibility that both the editorials and the legislation were influenced by the opinions of powerful elites. They suggested that the *Times* attention placed crime and justice issues " . . . on the political agenda by affording them legitimation and wide public exposure . . . and rearrang[ing] political priorities in ways that moved the whole gamut of criminal justice issues higher up the list of legislative business" (1977:291). They noted, however, that the mechanisms through which the editorials exerted influence over legislators and the legislative process remain unknown.

The Berk, Brackman, and Lesser finding of the correlation between media attention and penal code revision is interesting because it provides systematic empirical support for a relationship that had been suggested in other studies but often based on anecdotal or impressionistic observations. For instance, Ohlin's (1960; 1974) studies of change within correctional systems pointed to the potential role of the media in policy and organizational change. As noted in the earlier discussion, Ohlin argued that during periods of crisis, correctional agencies are most open to change. The media's importance in this process relates to the role of publicity in the development of crisis and scandal. Indeed, "[W]ithout preparation and participation by the mass media only a major catastrophe could create this type of public crisis for a correctional organization" (1974:1010). Media coverage can focus attention on the correctional organization, mobilize interest groups, and create pressure on policymakers to respond to the issues.

Fishman (1978) and Cook (1981) both illustrated how the media can play a role in placing particular crime and justice issues on the policy agenda. Both of their studies focused on the media's creation of a crime wave against the elderly during the mid-1970s. Fishman, who analyzed New York City newspapers and television news shows, found that the heightened media attention led to an outcry from elected officials, the formation of specialized police units, and the development of legislation to deal with this newly perceived problem. Cook, who examined the rise of crime against the elderly as a national issue, found that the dramatic rise in media attention, by documenting the apparent scope of the problem and bringing the issue to the public, played a crucial role in placing the issue on the national policy agenda and ultimately in the passage of legislation and funding of programs.

Several studies have noted the importance of the media's reporting of sensational crimes on policymaking. Travis's (1982) study of Oregon's adoption of parole guidelines and Gottleib's (1985) study of the enactment of public danger laws governing pretrial release both found that media coverage of sensational, although isolated, crime incidents was crucial in the passage of such laws (see also Messinger and Johnson, 1978).

Finally, Hagan's (1980) review of studies of law formation in the areas of delinquency and probation, alcohol and drugs, and prostitution and sexual psychopath also supports the contention that media attention play a role in developing crime and justice policies. Hagan reported a number studies from all these substantive areas that found passage of legislation to be accompanied by considerable media publicity. Hagan noted, however, the difficulty of assessing the causal significance of media effects on public policy. Of particular difficulty is the issue of separating media effects on policy from those factors that led to the media attention itself.

The Berk, Brackman, and Lesser study importantly provides systematic empirical support for these studies that have alleged a relationship between media attention and legal change. While Hagan's points on the difficulty of interpreting the causal significance of the relationship are well taken, these studies suggest that the media may play a role by placing the crime issue on the public policy agenda, as well as acting as a triggering event (sensational cases).

Summary

These studies provide significant insight into the structure and dynamics of state-level criminal justice policymaking, at least to the lawmaking aspect of policy formation. Lemert (1970), Galliher and Basilick (1979), and Messinger and Johnson (1978) all stress the importance of considering the broad social and cultural processes that create the context for change. Examples of factors operating at this level include U. S. Supreme Court decisions, nationwide trends in the appellate courts to clarify procedural issues, the civil rights movement of the 1960s, and the growth of drug abuse as a social issue in the 1960s. These factors, coupled with (and perhaps leading to) more immediate interest-group activity, played a crucial role in placing particular crime and justice issues on the public policy agenda.

Once on the agenda, the analytic focus was on interest-group activity. Although differences were found among the studies and discerning whether these differences are due to differences among the researchers or to state variation is difficult, several points common to the studies can be made. First, criminal justice legislation tends to be controlled by a small group to whom the legislature defers responsibility for criminal justice matters. This group tends to consist of key legislators, particularly criminal justice committee heads and party leaders, and the governor and staff. The study most directly concerned with correctional policy included top correctional administrators in this group (Berk and Rossi, 1977). Similar groups have been identified in other policy domains and have been labelled policy subsystems (Cobb and Elder, 1983). For most issues, conflict was worked out at this subsystem level and resulting legislation was enacted on a relative consensus basis.

These studies also indicate considerable interest-group activity. Furthermore, a number of studies identified two loose coalitions of interest groups variously labelled as liberal-conservative, civil rights-law enforcement. These coalitions primarily comprised permanent interest groups, including criminal justice professionals, legal groups such as bar associations, and the ACLU and reform groups. Other interest groups, termed recurrent groups, tended to become involved when proposed legislation could potentially affect group interests. An example is the association of hotel owners who became involved in the attempted revision of the prostitution statue (Roby, 1969).

The typical pattern of interest group involvement was described as a structure of accommodation. Legislation was not considered a zero-sum contest, negotiation and compromise were more common than conflict and policy change tended to be incremental. Within the structure, actual involvement of individual groups varied with different issues and at different stages of the same issue. While this structure of accommodation may be the typical pattern of decisionmaking, at times the structure breaks down and becomes conflictual. Evidence demonstrates that the system is open to more fundamental change at these times.[3]

Since the early 1960s, a number of scholars have argued that an understanding of correctional systems, and particularly an understanding of correctional change, requires analysis of the relationships between the correctional system and its environment. This view is supported by both studies of the historical development of the juvenile justice system and studies of criminal lawmaking. As seen in the preceding sections, the literature from both of these areas stresses the importance of environmental factors such as broad social and cultural changes and interest-group activity. These studies suggest that an attempt to understand state-level change in the policy and program of a juvenile correctional system requires a theoretical and methodological approach that focuses on these organization-environment relationships. In the following chapter, a theoretical and methodological model derived from this framework is presented.

Chapter Three

Theoretical Model and Methodology

During the early 1970s, some of the most radical changes in the corrections field occurred in the Massachusetts juvenile corrections system. Following a series of scandals involving the state's training school system, the director was forced to resign and was replaced by Jerome Miller. Miller instituted a series of reforms and eventually closed the entire training school system. In its place, Massachusetts developed a community-based system of youth corrections (Miller, Ohlin, and Coates, 1977; Bakal and Polsky, 1979).

During this period, Harvard Law School's Center for Criminal Justice engaged in a comprehensive study of the process of change in the Massachusetts system. Through this study, a theory of large-scale change processes and a model for the analysis of such change were developed (Miller, Ohlin, and Coates, 1977).

The Massachusetts Study

In viewing the change that occurred in the Massachusetts system, Miller, Ohlin, and Coates (1977) found that reform in youth corrections involved a struggle among interest groups over the preferred goals of the system. This debate centered around the choice of one of two basic positions advocated for youth corrections. Miller, Ohlin, and Coates conceptualized these two positions as the "institutionalization-normalization continuum." At a basic level, the institutionalization position prescribes the role of youth corrections as providing . . . security and control and/or punishment. . . " while the normalization position prescribes ". . .therapy and/or community linkage. . ." (Miller, Coates, and Ohlin, 1980). The study of change becomes an analysis of the struggle over goals and the resulting impact of these struggles on a change-resistant corrections system. While viewing Massachusetts's struggle, Miller, Coates, and Ohlin developed their theory of change and the model for studying the process of change. The theory of change provides a set of testable hypotheses from which predictions can be made both about the course of the change process and the impact of the struggle on the youth corrections process itself. The model for study allows one to describe and analyze this struggle and to assess the change actually produced in the corrections process.

The Theory of Change

Through its development, the theoretical model has undergone several refinements. The original model, presented in 1977 (Miller, Ohlin, and Coates, 1977), focused on the major coalitions or interest groups relevant to the policymaking area, the interactions among these interest groups, and their impact upon the formal decisionmakers and the corrections process itself.

Miller, Ohlin, and Coates found that the proper focus of analysis for understanding and explaining the process of change included both the correctional process itself and the political arena in which correctional policy is determined. Diagrammatically, the focus of analysis appears like that in Figure 3.1.

Figure 3.1   The Field of Analysis

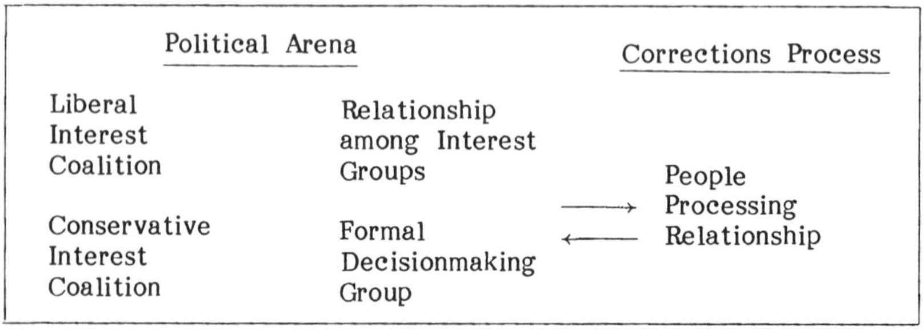

Political Arena		Corrections Process
Liberal Interest Coalition	Relationship among Interest Groups	
		People Processing Relationship
Conservative Interest Coalition	Formal Decisionmaking Group	

The process of change was seen as the result of the interaction of the corrections process and the political arena, i.e., the interactions of relationships identified in Figure 3.1.

The five sets of relationships consist of the Liberal Interest Coalition, the Conservative Interest Coalition, the Formal Decisionmaking Group, the Relationship among Interest Groups, and the People Processing Relationship. The Liberal and Conservative Interest Coalitions refer to those groups of individuals, including legislators, judges, members of the youth corrections system, and citizen groups, working for and against proposed changes in the youth corrections system. The Formal Decisionmaking Group comprises those ultimately responsible for decisions affecting " . . . budgets, appointments and jobs, contracts, and changes in fiscal authority . . . related to youth corrections" (Miller, Ohlin, and Coates, 1977:28–29). Included is the legislature, the governor's office, and various units in the state government (e.g., Division of the Budget). The Relationship among Interest Groups refers simply to the relations among the various interest groups in which the corrections process (People Processing Relationship) is a central concern. The People Processing Relationship refers to the actual youth corrections process.

The five relationships are described by a set of categorical variables. The relationships are then linked together by five empirical principles that were inductively derived in the study. The study was then structured around qualitative analysis of each of the principles. The authors found that the five empirical principles provided an explanation of the change process in Massachusetts.

In subsequent analyses, Miller and Ohlin (1985) extended their work through attempts to model social control and change in communities. In doing so, the key locus of change shifted beyond the juvenile corrections system to a broad conceptualization of institutionalized adult social control in the community. Miller and Ohlin found that the model of change developed in the earlier work was applicable to the community study, but also that with several refinements the model could provide a sharper conceptualization of social control and change.

The revised model begins with the premise that the institutionalized social control network dealing with youths can be conceptualized as a political change process at four levels or systems of intervention. These four related systems, diagrammatically presented in Figure 3.2, include the mobilization generating system, the policy generating system, the control generating system, and the behavior generating system. The systems are linked through influence

Figure 3.2 Generating system model of correctional change

<u>Mobilization Generating System</u> → <u>Policy Generating System</u> → <u>Control Generating System</u> → <u>Behavior Generating System</u> → <u>Behavior System</u>

Actors-All those who influence constituents

Actors-Constituents and Partisans (voters, interest groups)

Actors-Politicians/ Formal Decision- Making Group

Actors-Juvenile Corrections staff

Actors-Youths

Doing what-Influenc- ing constituents to take action con- cerning corrections

Doing what-Influenc- ing politicians to implement policies reflecting dominant ideologies

Doing what-Developing set of policies to guide juvenile corrections system

Doing what-Attempting to influence youth to increase desired behavior, decrease undesired behavior

Doing what-Living in community

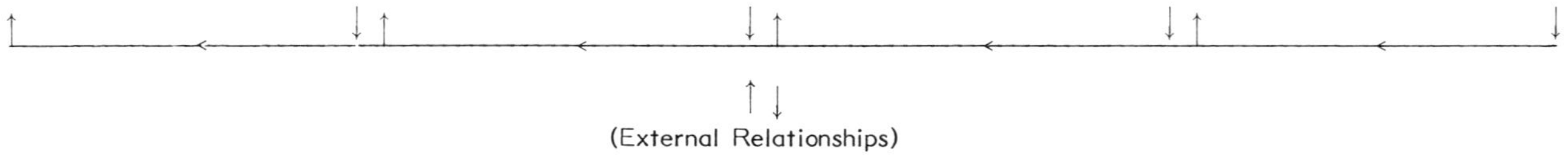

(External Relationships)

processes. The key focus for the analyst is the way groups within each system attempt to influence one another and the way each system influences the corresponding system. The mobilization generating system, the initial system in the influence process, comprises all those forces that generate pressures or influences on the actors in the next system, the policy generating system. The actors in the policy generating system, partisan constituents including the liberal and conservative interest coalitions, generate pressure or influence on the members of the control generating system to implement policies reflecting the views and ideologies of the dominant interest groups. At the control generating level, politicians, the Formal Decisionmaking Group, are involved in attempts to develop policies to guide actors at the behavior generating level. That is, politicians are attempting to establish policies to guide the authorities and staff at the service delivery level. Labelled the behavior generating system, this level comprises adults in relationships with youths in which the adults are attempting to induce preferred behavior on the part of the youth. The behavior generating system thus represents the formal system of social control in interaction with youths, comprising not only juvenile corrections officials, but also a host of other actors involved in the social control of youth. These groups include other criminal justice officials, families, schools, churches, employers, and social welfare agencies (however, because the focus of this research is on the correctional system's role in this social control network, attention is restricted to correctional programs). A fifth system is also presented in Figure 3.2 to represent the ultimate target of all these generating systems, youths in the community. This final system is not seen as the determined product of the generating systems, but rather the target of these systems. That is, the youth's behavior in the community is, at least formally, the target of this network of institutionalized social control. Miller and Ohlin (1985) explicitly recognize that youth's behaviors are affected by influences other than those considered as part of the institutionalized system of social control, e.g., peer relationships.

One important point should be noted. Figure 3.2 may create the image that the relationships between the generating systems are rather static or fixed and that influence processes flow along a linear path from the mobilization system to youth behavior. Such an image is inaccurate. These relationships are not fixed; rather they are dynamic. For instance, the actors involved in the overall process may be part of different generating systems. Top correctional administrators are typically part of the control generating system, acting as formal decisionmakers attempting to establish policies to govern staff-youth interactions, as well as part of the policy generating system, acting as partisans attempting to influence the decisions of politicians regarding correctional policy. Correctional staff are involved in the behavior generating system through their interactions with youth. At the same time, they may be involved through their union at the policy generating level in attempting to influence policies. The key point is that the generating systems framework is not an attempt to force structure on what seems to be a dynamic and complex process, rather the generating systems provide a means to conceptualize the wide range of influence processes and network of interests that give shape to the correctional system at any given time. Furthermore, to say that youth behavior is the ultimate target of these generating systems should not be taken to imply that this overall system is a rationally organized system concerned only with influencing youth behavior. Clearly, the literature on people-processing organizations indicates that these organizations will have multiple interests (Hasenfeld, 1983). Rather, treating youth behavior as the ultimate goal acts as a heuristic device for conceptualizing the juvenile corrections arena.

Miller and Ohlin's (1985) revised conceptualization is very similar to the earlier model (Miller, Ohlin, and Coates, 1977). For instance, the Liberal and Conservative Interest Coalitions identified in the earlier model are now included as key actors in the policy generating system. The Formal Decision-makers are the key actors of the control generating system. The Relationship among Interest Groups is represented in the control generating system, and the People Processing Relationship comprises the behavior generating system. Of course, as mentioned above, there is an explicit recognition that the roles of individual actors and groups are not fixed but are dependent upon the behavior engaged in.

The main distinction between the two models is that where the earlier model recognized the key actors and groups as a set of relationships, the newer model conceptualizes these relationships within a set of related systems. In doing so, the systemic nature of the juvenile correctional arena is articulated and made explicit.

Another key feature is that the series of related generating systems explicitly recognizes the political nature of juvenile corrections. In analyzing the range of reports generated by the Massachusetts case study, including those of inmate violence and subcultural development within facilities, comparisons of institutional and community-based facilities, studies of policy change, and studies of social control in the community,[1] Miller and Ohlin (1985) found that all of these correctional processes involved influence processes, one group trying to influence another. Thus, both the politics of policy formation and attempts at social control of youth are processes whereby individuals and groups try to influence one another.

The generating systems are linked by the five empirical principles identified in the earlier study of the correctional change process (Miller, Ohlin, and Coates, 1977). The empirical principles underlie the explanation of the process of change observed in Massachusetts and provide predictive hypotheses with which to guide analysis in other settings. These empirical principles, which guide this analysis, will be considered more fully in subsequent discussion.

In summary, the generating system model provides the tools to conceptualize and describe the entire arena of juvenile corrections, from interest group pressure to youth behavior. The empirical principles provide the means to describe and analyze the course of change. The model focuses on both the structure and process and the interaction of structure and process in the juvenile corrections system. Thus, the model is considered a system model, one that provides a complete picture of the system at any given time, and more importantly, one that provides a theory of the way the system changes over time.

Relationship of the Model to Other Frameworks

Miller, Ohlin, and Coates (1977:47–87) related their theoretical model to a broad range of sociological theories—conflict, process, social structure, and structural functional theories (see also Miller and Ohlin, 1985:119–144). Discussing each theory is redundant. However, considering several works from disparate fields that seem to adopt similar models of change in human service agencies might be useful.

A distinctive feature of the Massachusetts model is the explicit attempt to focus on the entire sociopolitical field or arena of juvenile corrections. This approach differs from many analyses that treat criminal justice as a well-ordered, rational system, isolated from external influences. Miller, Ohlin, and Coates reject such an approach and instead focus on all those influence patterns, from mobilization of interest groups to staff-youth relationships, that affect the shape of youth corrections. In doing so, they have taken an approach suggested by critics of traditional analyses of criminal justice who have stressed the importance of the sociopolitical environment (Duffee, 1980b; Wright, 1981).

This type of approach is also suggested by several implementation analysts who have studied policy implementation in a variety of issue areas. These analysts reject the assumptions of early students of implementation, i.e., the assumption of a rational implementation structure in which policymakers enunciate policy and staff at the service delivery level implement. Rather, the public policy sector is viewed as a loosely coupled structure characterized by bargaining and conflict in which the match between policy and program is problematic rather than assumed (Berman, 1978; Elmore, 1978, 1979–80).

The Miller and Ohlin model is also quite similar to the social systems model presented by Seidman (1983). The social system model is offered as a "heuristic framework for the consideration of social interaction" (1983:13). In Seidman's model, the individual is affected by social intervention programs through linkage with the delivery system. The delivery system is linked to an administrative exosystem, which is "comprised of persons charged with overall responsibility for administering the various programs that will presumably solve the 'problem'" (1983:14). The administrative exosystem is, in turn, linked to the donor exosystem, which is "composed of legislative, judicial, and executive subsystems in the governmental arena, occasionally philanthropic organizations, or also in the private sector, boards of directors of business and human service corporations" (1983:14). The donor exosystem sets broad policies for the administrative and delivery systems. All of these systems are embedded in the larger macrosystem.

These systems closely correspond to the generating systems in the Miller and Ohlin model. One distinction is that the generating systems encompass the link between the systems. Thus, the behavior generating system comprises the link between the organism and the delivery system; the control generating system comprises the link between the administrative and donor exosystems and the delivery system; and the policy generating system comprises the link between interest groups and the donor exosystem.

The advantages Seidman attributes to the social system framework are equally applicable to the generating system model.

> First it is clear that there are a variety of stakeholders, and while each has a stake in multiple systems and subsystems, some subsystems exert more powerful influences over organisms' behavior than do others. Second, it helps us identify between which systems direct transactions occur . . . . Third, it highlights the importance of the delivery system for the successful implementation since it is the only direct linkage between the administrative exosystem and the recipient system. Fourth, successful implementation requires the support or at least cooperation of other systems (1983:15–16).

A conceptualization similar to Miller and Ohlin's (1985) generating system model and Seidman's (1983) social system model has been used by

McCarthy and Zald (1977) in their analysis of social movements. These authors note that social movements consist of social movement organizations, i.e., the organizations that attempt to implement specific goals and a social movement industry. The social movement industry is the collectivity of social movement organizations. Social movement industries are also part of a larger system, the social movement sector. Thus, just as Miller and Ohlin conceptualize the formal social control arena comprising several embedded systems, so do McCarthy and Zald conceptualize the social movement arena.

This notion of embedded systems is also prominent in Churchman's (1968) approach to systems theory. Furthermore, like Miller and Ohlin, Churchman notes that individual actors often play roles in different systems. Thus, similar to the correctional administrator playing a role in the organization's production system *and* boundary system (see Duffee, 1980a), the manager of an industrial concern is likely to be involved in both internal management *and* external politics.

Finally, the Miller and Ohlin model is consistent with much of the literature reviewed in the previous chapter. Clearly, it focuses on the environment of the corrections agency. Indeed, the correctional agency's systemic relationships with the environment are explicitly articulated and hypothesized as the key to change. In addition, including the mobilization and policy generating systems focuses attention on both the broad social and cultural factors and the interest-group activity deemed important in the studies of the historical development of juvenile justice and the studies of criminal lawmaking.

The Model Applied to the Present Study

Key Research Questions

The theory developed in the Massachusetts study was the product of a number of related studies of the Massachusetts juvenile corrections system. One of the project's ultimate goals was to discern what configurations of service delivery systems most effectively provides combinations of opportunities and controls that lead to increased patterns of desired behavior and decreased patterns of undesired behavior among youths. While the ultimate dependent variable was youth behavior (institutional violence, subcultural development, recidivism), the most proximate and manipulable system variable considered to affect youth behavior was the staff-youth relationship. Thus, the Massachusetts study's major focus was on the factors that affect the staff-youth relationship and the way variation in this relationship affects youth behavior.

This study's focus is more narrow. Since the late 1960s, New York State's juvenile corrections system has gone through several shifts in its relative use of institutional versus community-based programming. This change process is the focus herein. The major research questions to be addressed include:

1. HOW HAS NEW YORK STATE'S JUVENILE CORRECTIONS SYSTEM CHANGED DURING THE PERIOD FROM THE LATE 1960s TO 1984?

To address this question, the study attempts to document the trend in New York State's relative use of institutional- versus community-based settings for delinquent youths. In effect, this is the dependent variable of the study as the bulk of the analysis focuses on the factors influencing over time variation in the use of institutional- versus community-based programs. This is a more limited focus than that of the Massachusetts study, which linked changes from institutional- to community-based programs with variation in staff-youth relationships and youth behavior. However, the emphasis is justified on at least two grounds. First, the question of how and why human service programs change over time is a significant research question in itself. Second, although the impact of broad policy and program shifts on staff-youth relationships and youth behavior remains an empirical question beyond the scope of this study, such shifts clearly set constraints on the service delivery system and affect youths' lives.

These trends in program emphasis are documented in Chapter Four.

2. WHAT ARE THE KEY POLICY DECISIONS THAT ACCOUNT FOR THE CHANGES IN NEW YORK STATE'S JUVENILE CORRECTIONS SYSTEM?

On the basis of the Massachusetts study as well as this study, several key policy decisions clearly altered the fundamental shape of each state's juvenile corrections system. Thus, much of the focus herein is on identifying these key policy decisions.

The term *key policy decision* refers to those "critical decisions" (Selznick, 1957) that have shaped the institutional development and overall mission of the system. The term includes both discrete decisions, such as a legislative act, and more general policy decisions, such as deinstitutionalization.

3. WHAT ARE THE DYNAMICS BEHIND THESE KEY POLICY DECISIONS?

Having identified the key policy decisions, the next step involves analysis of the decisions' dynamics, which involves identifying the key actors involved in policy decisions, the tactics employed influencing policy, and other factors that seem to influence policy.

4. WHAT ADDITIONAL FACTORS AFFECT OR INFLUENCE CHANGES IN THE JUVENILE CORRECTIONS SYSTEM?

Initially, the main focus of the study was on the above three questions. However, early in the interviewing process it became apparent that a host of related factors were important because of their influence on policy decisions and their direct influence on the juvenile corrections system. These were factors that could not be considered state-level policy decisions, nor could they be linked to specific actors within the policy arena. Examples of such factors include the U. S. Supreme Court decisions concerning due process rights of juveniles and changes in court processing of youths.

These four research questions are approached through the framework developed in the Massachusetts study, which involves two main analytic tasks: conceptualizing the entire arena of juvenile corrections and applying the empirical principles to the process of change.

The Juvenile Corrections Arena

One of the key features of the Massachusetts study is that it emphasizes the importance, and provides the means, to "map" the entire arena in which juvenile corrections policy is determined. Another major goal herein is to develop such a map of New York State's juvenile corrections arena.

Two features of the present research require modification of the Massachusetts model in relation to the conceptualization of the correctional arena. The first restriction is that this study does not include analysis of staff-youth relationships or youth behavior. The second restriction is imposed by methodological considerations. As discussed subsequently in the methodological section, pretesting of the interview instrument indicated that respondents had difficulty answering some of the more focused, closed response items, apparently due to the study's retrospective nature. The schedule was revised so that the questions on influence processes were addressed in a more open-ended format. One result was that it became difficult to measure all the variables for each generating system for the entire timeframe. Thus, the generating scheme was not utilized in mapping the correctional arena. It should be noted, however, that all the groups and actors involved in the policy arena are included in the analysis. The distinction is that the relationships between these groups and actors are not aggregated to the system level. Thus, in terms of conceptualizing the corrections arena, the modified format is more akin to the earlier model (Miller, Ohlin, and Coates, 1977), which focused on the set of relationships indicated in Figure 3.1.

In terms of the level of analysis, the actual focus shifts between two different levels according to the issue being addressed. When dealing with issues of the overall change process, the focus of analysis is on the organization, i.e., the juvenile corrections agency and its environment. Alternatively, when dealing with specific policy decisions the focus of analysis is on the more generalized policy community.

As noted in Chapter Two and emphasized in the Massachusetts study, research suggests that major forces of change often emanate from the correctional environment. Thus, in addressing issues of system change, major attention is on environmental forces of change (e.g., external policy decisions) and the relationship between the correctional agency and its environment. At this level of analysis, the approach is very similar to Wamsley and Zald's (1973) political economy model of public organizations. The political economy model stresses the need to focus on these organization-environment relations in order to understand the change process. Indeed, the Wamsley and Zald model is used in the analysis of change both to help clarify the analysis and to help assess the generalizability of the Massachusetts model to different public organizations.

The second level of analysis does not exclude the juvenile corrections agency but rather includes the agency, particularly top administrators, within the policy community. At this level, the focus is not on a focal organization and its environment but on an interorganizational network of groups involved in the formation of corrections policy. This network is the policy community. The notion of a policy community is a broad conceptualization that "defines the outer bounds of influence in an [issue] area . . . " (Milward, 1982:466). Included are all the groups and individuals identified as having influenced, or having attempted to influence, the juvenile corrections system. The policy community comprises two general sets of actors: those who seek to influence policy decisions and those who ultimately make policy decisions. In Miller, Ohlin, and Coates's (1977) terms, the first group comprises the Liberal and Conservative Interest Coalitions; the second, the Formal Decisionmaking Group. This second set of actors, those responsible for actually making a particular policy decision, are variously labelled as a policy subsystem (Cobb and Elder, 1983) or decision network (Milward, 1982). The policy subsystem is an empirical phenomenon determined by identification of those actually involved in the policy decision.

The two levels of analysis are not inconsistent; rather, the level used is the one most appropriate for the particular research issue. For instance, when addressing policy decisions or related issues that are resolved at the policy community level, the policy community itself is the most appropriate level of analysis. When dealing with broader patterns of change, the level of analysis shifts to organization-environment relationships (of which the relationship to the policy community is a key to change).

Theoretical Principles

Having structured the analysis by focusing on the policy community and the organization-environment relationships, the next task is to begin assessing the utility of the Miller, Ohlin, and Coates (1977) theory for explaining the process of change in New York State. In doing so, the focus is on applying the five empirical principles. These include:

> 1. *Sequencing.* The process of change involves shifts in both internal, aspired choices (what one wants to do) and external, available choices (what one can do). Change is most likely to occur when there is congruence between aspired choices and available choices.

This is a general change principle applicable at the individual, group, or organizational level. The 1977 model emphasized the importance of congruence between external and internal forces of change (Miller, Ohlin, and Coates, 1977). The 1985 model emphasized the importance of congruence between aspired choices (internal dimension) and available choices (external dimension) (Miller and Ohlin, 1985).

Numerous examples suggesting the validity of the sequencing principle can be found in criminal justice literature. At the individual level, correctional technologies have been criticized for overemphasizing internal change strategies, e.g., therapy, while ignoring external strategies, e.g., provision jobs, housing (President's Commission on Law Enforcement and Administration of Justice, 1967b). At the organizational level, studies of juvenile deinstitutionalization suggests that change is most likely when internal adaptation is congruent with external demands. Handler and Zatz's (1982; see also Lerman, 1984:102–104) study of local level deinstitutionalization of status offenders found that federal funds (external) had the greatest impact where local officials (internal) already had favorable attitudes toward deinstitutionalization. Similarly, at the state level, Downs (1976) found that the ideology and priorities of the director of the juvenile corrections agency (internal), coupled with agency autonomy and environmental group activity (external), were significant predictors of variation in state rates of deinstitutionalization.

The sequencing principle receives theoretical support in Wamsley and Zald's (1973) political economy model of public organizations. Wamsley and Zald argue that the structure and process of public organizations and, importantly, the process of change are products of internal and external factors operating at both the political and economic levels. Political factors include those affecting the very existence of the organization or the overall structure or domain of the system. At the organizational level, these include factors such as the overall goals and the functional niche of the organization. At the economic or technological level, attention focuses on factors affecting task accomplishment and basic service delivery. These include factors such as service technologies, the rate of placement of juveniles from the courts, and state-level fiscal policies.

Zald's (1970) study of the transformation of the Young Men's Christian Association (YMCA) from an evangelical organization to a general service organization illustrates the principles of the framework. The YMCA's change was shown to be the product of external economic forces, the demand for general services, and internal political shifts, service-oriented interest groups gained control of policy over evangelical-oriented interest groups. The combination of political and economic forces was the key to change.

Miller and Ohlin's (1985) emphasis on aspired and available choices roughly corresponds with the political economy model. Aspired choices reflect a political goal choice. Available choices reflect economic factors— available technologies, fiscal realities. Both models recognize that these forces are interrelated.

Initial interviewing in New York State indicated that the forces identified as influencing correctional change could be classified according to the political economic categorization. Thus, the classification was adopted in this study. As a predictive theoretical statement, one should expect change, particularly fundamental change, at both the policy community and organizational levels to be the product of a combination of internal and external, political and economic factors.

> 2. *Inertia and Crises.* A system such as the juvenile corrections
> system is characterized by bureaucratic inertia. Change is most likely
> to occur during periods of crisis that open the system to the possibility
> of change.

This principle is based on the fundamental assumption that organizations are characterized by inertia and resist change. The validity of this principle is attested to by organizational theorists (Stinchcombe, 1965; Kaufman, 1971; Hannan and Freeman, 1977; Katz and Kahn, 1966). These theorists have noted a number of factors both internal and external to the organization that foster organizational inertia. Among the internal factors are sunk costs in existing technologies, personnel selection and training patterns that reinforce stability, political coalitions that resist change, individual and group habit, existing norms and belief systems, and historical precedent. External factors include legal barriers, existing interorganizational relations, and legitimacy constraints (radical change may threaten support).

The second aspect of this principle holds that during times of crisis inertial forces are weakened and the system is open to change. Miller, Ohlin, and Coates (1977) base their assumption of the importance of crises on the findings from Massachusetts and from Ohlin's (1960; 1974) earlier studies of correctional change. The McCleery (1968) and Lemert (1970) studies reviewed in Chapter Two also suggested the importance of crisis periods in correctional change. In another area of criminal justice, Sherman (1983) has argued that the criticism generated by critical events can unfreeze law enforcement policies and procedures and create the opportunity for change in police agencies.

Crises have also been suggested as important factors in other areas of public change. Kemp's (1984) study of budgetary allocations for the Securities and Exchange Commission (SEC), the Federal Communication Commission (FCC), and the Federal Aviation Administration (FAA) found that scandals and accidents significantly affected budgetary support. Likewise, Steinberg's (1982) study of the development of laws governing wage and hour standards found that crises were important factors in reform legislation. Rieselbach (1983) has also noted that legislative change is often in response to perceived crises.

These findings are placed in context by Cobb and Elder (1983; see also Anderson, 1984). These authors argue that a crisis can elevate an issue out of the large pool of issues facing policymakers at any given time. The crisis places an issue on the policy agenda. Because of inertia, fundamental change is unlikely unless the issue reaches this agenda stage.

Many of the above-cited studies suggest that crises are a necessary but not sufficient cause of change. In this respect, we should see an interrelationship between the crisis principle and the sequencing principle. That is, the effects of the crisis should be accounted for in shifts along internal and external political and economic dimensions.

3. *Key Swing Groups.* In conflicts between liberal and conservative interest groups, there are key swing groups, typically

political actors, who are essential allies for either side to win. Shifts in position of these key swing groups can be important factors in change.

Miller, Ohlin, and Coates (1977) argue that certain individuals and groups play a key swing role in political contests among Liberal and Conservative Interest Coalitions. The notion of a small group of key decisionmakers whose support is necessary for major legislation or policy change was suggested in a number of the studies of criminal lawmaking reviewed in Chapter Two. Key actors included legislative party leaders, chairs of relevant legislative committees, and the governor. Berk and Rossi (1977) included correctional administrators in this group in matters of correctional policy. These studies seem to have identified the small group of political actors labelled by political scientists as the policy subsystem (Cobb and Elder, 1983) or decision network (Milward, 1982). This group consists of the key decisionmakers who in effect control policy in a given issue area.

Two essential notions are inherent in the key swing group principle. The first is power. The policy subsystem, from which a key swing group may emerge, comprises those actors with sufficient power to heavily influence, if not determine, the policy decision.

The key swing group principle, however, goes beyond power relations. Within the policy community, Miller, Ohlin, and Coates (1977) identify the two interest coalitions and a group labelled the Formal Decisionmaking Group. The Liberal and Conservative Interest Groups are likely to be locked into fixed ideological positions. Members of the Formal Decisionmaking Group, the key political decisionmakers (i.e. the policy subsystem), are less likely to be locked into such ideological positions. This group can thus play the crucial swing role in political contests between competing interest groups. Consequently shifts among the Formal Decisionmaking Group can lead to significant policy change.

> 4. *Responsiveness of Interest Coalitions.* Both the internal structure and the external goals and tactics of the Liberal and Conservative Interest Coalitions are likely to be affected by change in formal correctional policy or in patterns of service delivery.

This principle and the one that follows are useful for investigating the process of change over time. The Liberal and Conservative Interest Coalitions are loose coalitions that may mobilize at times when juvenile corrections issues reach the visible stage of state-level decisionmaking. The coalitions are affected by the outcome of the policy process. The coalition whose interests are reflected in policy change is likely to become less involved in the juvenile corrections arena. Alternatively, the coalition whose interests were defeated is likely to become more active and, perhaps, respond with extreme tactics. One corollary of this principle is that the seeds of counterreform are planted with every significant policy decision.

> 5. *Short- and Long-Run Effects of Extreme Tactics.* Extreme tactics, while important in instigating change, can "use up" coalition power by alienating the formal decisionmakers.

Miller, Ohlin, and Coates (1977) note that the use of extreme tactics may be important in instigating change. They offer the example of Jerome Miller's public repudiation of a state legislator who had been questioning the reform effort. While Miller's tactics seemed to be effective in promoting change (as opposed to limiting the scope of reform through compromise), the long-range effect was that such tactics alienated the Formal Decision-making Group, Miller was forced to resign, and pressure for counterreform arose.

O'Brien (1975) noted this phenomenon in studies of community organization related to the poverty movement. Radical groups were often successful in promoting change because they were willing to use unconventional tactics and tended to work outside the realm of "respectable" organizations. One of the reasons these groups could adopt this role was that they were unconcerned with their own survival needs (financial and legitimacy). However, this lack of concern with survival needs meant that these groups tended to be short-lived. Furthermore, their use of unconventional or extreme tactics seemed to lead policymakers to dismiss these groups once the immediate issue was addressed.

This principle thus raises two research questions. Are extreme tactics necessary for significant policy change (theory predicts they are)? Are groups utilizing these tactics dismissed from serious consideration in further policy issues (theory predicts they will be excluded)?

These five principles form the core of the theory of change. In the next section the methodology used to collect the data for this study will be discussed. The subsequent section will present the analytic approach used to assess the utility of the theory for explaining the process of change in New York State.

Methodology

Data Sources

This project utilized a variety of sources of data, relying primarily on archival records and interviews. The review of archival materials attempted to include all documents related to juvenile justice, juvenile corrections, and juvenile delinquency in New York State during 1960 to 1984. The intent of the archival review was to chronicle the changes that had occurred in New York State's juvenile corrections system during these years and to develop an overall picture of the change process. Sources utilized in this review included statutory and case law, legislative and gubernatorial records, agency documents, and other private agency reports, articles, etc. Additional archival data were compiled through a yearly review and content analysis of articles about juvenile crime and juvenile justice included in the *New York Times Annual Index* during 1968 and 1984. The choice of the *New York Times* was dictated by the fact that respondents mentioned it as one of the New York City newspapers that influenced policy development in the mid-1970s and by the availability of the Index.[2] The intent was to include all articles dealing with juvenile crime or some aspect of the juvenile justice system. This review provided background information on specific issues and incidents and, more importantly, a systematic indicator of media attention in one prominent newspaper over the course of the time period.

The primary source of data for this study was a series of key participant interviews with individuals involved in influencing or formulating juvenile corrections policy in New York State from the late 1960s to 1984. These key participants included initiators of policy or program change, targets of these influence attempts, and informed observers.

1. IDENTIFYING KEY PARTICIPANTS

No comprehensive list of key political actors involved in juvenile corrections in New York State exists. Thus, conventional sampling procedures were precluded. The method used to identify potential participants was the method known as *snowball sampling*. Initial respondents were identified by having been in obvious policymaking positions during various periods of the overall timeframe. The interviewing then progressed through a snowball procedure in which each respondent was asked to identify key individuals and groups active in various policy issues. This resulted in interviews with fifty-eight respondents.[3] Respondents included current and former key actors from the governor's office, legislators and their staffs, administrators of relevant state agencies, practitioners from the juvenile justice system, and representatives of citizen advocacy groups.

The criteria for terminating the snowball procedure was that interviewing would stop when at least one individual from all the various groups mentioned had been interviewed. At the final stages, the same individuals were named over and over and attempts to add respondents provided either redundant information or interviews with individuals only tangentially involved in juvenile corrections.

2. INTERVIEW FORMAT

The interview focused on two main areas of concern. The first was to develop a picture of the policy networks involved in the formulation of juvenile corrections policy during the overall time period. The second was to identify additional factors influencing the juvenile corrections system and to provide a general assessment of the impact of the policy changes on the system.

The portion of the interview instrument focusing on policy networks was adapted from an instrument developed by Miller (1983) to test the revised model of change. This section of the interview was semistructured around four basic questions:

1. *Who* was actively concerned about these issues?
2. *Whom* were they trying to influence?
3. *What* were their goals?
4. *How* did they try to achieve these goals and with what success?

The interview began by asking respondents to identify the key policy decisions (legislative, administrative, or judicial) that seemed to have affected the shape of the juvenile corrections system. Once these policy decisions were identified, each decision was dealt with individually. A subset of questions asked about the respondent's (or organization's) stand on the issue, which individuals or groups they tried to influence, and whether any individual or group tried to influence the respondent (or their organization). Additional questions asked respondents to identify other key individuals or groups that were attempting to influence policy and the groups whom they were trying to influence. These questions provided answers to the first two questions listed above, who was involved and whom they were trying to influence. From these questions a set of initiators and targets, links in the policy network, were identified for each policy decision.

At this point, another subset of questions asked respondents about each of these links. This subset of questions addressed the initiators goals, i.e., what they wanted the target to do, what the initiators' tactics were, and whether the target did what the initiator wanted.

It was in relation to the questions about influence tactics that Miller's (1983) interview instrument was modified. Pretesting indicated that Miller's closed-ended questions were too focused for events and processes that had occurred in the past. Thus, the instrument was adapted by asking a single open-ended question of how the initiator attempted to influence the target. The open-ended structure seemed to allow respondents to work through their recollection of events.

After all the links for all the policy decisions were covered, respondents were asked whether other key policy issues arose that were not resolved by formal policy decisions. For issues so identified, the same set of subquestions were asked concerning who was involved, tactics, and outcomes. This facilitated comparisons of issues that resulted in formal policy decisions with issues that did not result in formal policy.

The final item related to the policy network asked respondents to suggest other key actors that should be interviewed. This facilitated the snowball procedure.

The remaining items of the interview instrument were more general. The first of these was an item that was added after pretesting. During the initial interviews respondents were consistently pointing to additional factors that seemed to have influenced the system. These were factors that could not be attributed to specific individuals or groups within the policy community and included factors such as changes in court processing of youths and changes in thought following the Supreme Court decisions on due process rights of juveniles. The item used to identify these factors asked respondents, "In addition to the actions of key actors we've been discussing, are/were there other factors affecting juvenile corrections?"

The final item asked respondents to summarize the way these policy decisions and related factors had influenced the juvenile corrections system.

Analytic Approach

This research effort seeks to accomplish three main goals. The first is to describe and document the changing nature of the New York State juvenile corrections system. The second is to examine the dynamic forces that seem to account for the system change. The third is to assess the utility of Miller, Ohlin, and Coates's (1977) five empirical principles for explaining this change process. In relation to this last goal, the study takes the form of a successive or confirmatory case study in the theory building process (Campbell, 1979; Glaser and Strauss, 1967).

A major analytic technique is to display these networks in the form of annotated sociograms. The sociograms provide a graphic presentation of the actors within the policy community and policy subsystem, influence tactics, and the outcomes of specific policy decisions or issues. Miles and Huberman (1984:21) have noted that one of the problems of analyzing and verifying qualitative data is that the traditional method of presenting such data, narrative text, is "cumbersome," "dispersed," "poorly structured," and "bulky." The value of matrix presentations is that they provide a data reduction and data display technique that facilitates the organized and systematic assembly of the data. Thus, the analysis will attempt to follow the Miles and Huberman (22) dictum, "You know what you display."

Perhaps the key strength of the present study is the time dimension. The approximate twenty-year time period facilitates comparisons between different policy decisions and over time. Furthermore, the study allows comparison of the dynamics of both liberal and conservative reform. The emphasis on comparisons is intended to maximize the strength or dependability of the findings within the limitations imposed by the data and the single jurisdiction setting. The emphasis on comparison also allows the development of a " . . . box score of hits and misses" concerning support for theoretical implications and thus follows Campbell's (1979:61) suggestions for increasing the rigor of successive qualitative case studies.

LIMITATIONS

A key threat to the validity of the findings is the retrospective nature of the interviews. As a way of addressing this threat, only findings that have been corroborated by two or more respondents are presented. Where discrepancies arose, follow up phone calls were used for clarification. Additionally, archival materials were checked for consistency with respondent's reports. The comparison of interview data with the archival records thus provided a form of triangulation.

A further step to corroborate the findings involved providing key participants with the initial findings of the study and asking them to comment on the findings. Participants were provided a copy of a Working Paper (McGarrell, 1985), which presented the descriptive findings of the study. In addition, they were asked to comment on the findings generally and on the annotated sociograms presenting the data on key policy decisions and issues. Although there was a poor response rate to this mailing (n=13), those who responded strongly endorsed the validity of the findings.

A more general concern has to do with interpretation of the findings on correctional change. Studies of implementation demonstrate the frequent lack of association between enunciated policy and actual practice (Pressman and Wildavsky, 1973; Rose, 1972). In light of these findings, one must be careful not to draw overly broad inferences on change at the service delivery level based on changes in policy and the broad level population changes emphasized in this study (see Duffee and Klofas, 1983). For example, as will be discussed in subsequent chapters, status offenders have been removed from the New York State training schools. However, no indication is found of whether these youths are now engaged in programs that actually increase community linkages, whether additional services have been provided, or whether alternative forms of social control have arisen (see Spergel, 1976; Coates, Miller, and Ohlin, 1978). The point is that inferences about programmatic change based on policy change are problematic. While policy sets constraints on the system and makes real differences in the lives of juveniles (i.e., a policy keeping a child within his community versus a rural institution, or a policy providing a fourteen-year-old child with a ten-year sentence as opposed to an eighteenth-month sentence, certainly make a difference to the youth), the issue of the impact of policy change at the service delivery level remains an empirical question.

Summary

The theory of change developed in the Massachusetts study provides a means to conceptualize the juvenile corrections arena and predictive principles with which to analyze the process of change. In subsequent chapters, this model will be used to address the four main research questions: How has the New York State juvenile corrections systems changed during the period from the late 1960s to 1984? What are the key policy decisions that have accounted for the changes in the system? What are the dynamics behind these key policy decisions? What additional factors have affected the changes in the system? The first question is the subject of Chapter Four. The other three questions, together with the assessment of the applicability of the five empirical principles, are the subjects of the remaining chapters.

Chapter Four

Changing Characteristics of New York State's Juvenile Corrections System

New York State's juvenile corrections system has undergone significant change during the years from the late 1960s to 1984. Following a period of reductions in institutional populations and increases in community-based programs, the state experienced significant growth in the number of secure facilities, the number of youths housed in secure settings, and the total residential population. This chapter documents these changes. A related goal is to place the New York State system in historical and national context. Thus, a discussion of the historical development of New York State's juvenile justice system precedes the section on recent changes in the corrections system. The final sections attempt to compare, briefly, key aspects of New York State's system with other state systems and to consider trends in arrests and court processing of juveniles in New York State.

Historical Development[1]

The origins of New York State's juvenile justice system trace at least to the 1820s when legislation was passed allowing the placement of juveniles younger than age sixteen convicted of a crime or charged as vagrant with the Society for the Reformation of Juvenile Delinquents in New York City.[2] This legislation was followed by the opening of the New York House of Refuge in 1825, the first such facility in the nation. Throughout the remainder of the nineteenth century the movement toward a separate justice system designed for juveniles spread to the rest of the state as legislation applied the sixteen-year-old juvenile/adult age distinction statewide and several more juvenile facilities were opened.[3]

At the turn of the century, New York State quickly followed the lead of the Chicago Juvenile Court with the establishment of the Manhattan Children's Court in 1902. The juvenile court model rapidly spread to the rest of the state, and in 1922 children's courts were established statewide through the New York Children's Court Act.[4] Additionally, development of juvenile institutions continued with the opening of the New York State Training School for Girls at Hudson in 1904 and the Training School at Warwick in 1932.

The years following World War II were significant in terms of the development of the juvenile corrections system. A number of training schools and centers were developed during the 1950s and 1960s. The capacity of these public facilities, operated under the auspices of the Department of Social Services (DSS), greatly increased during these years. These years also saw the initial involvement of the state in local delinquency prevention as the State Youth Commission was created in 1945 to provide localities with financial and technical assistance in developing and expanding delinquency prevention programs. In 1960, the State Youth Commission became the Division for Youth (DFY) and was given the additional responsibility of developing residential and nonresidential experimental programs for youths aged between fifteen and seventeen as alternatives to the state's training schools.

In 1962, following several years of study, the state created the Family Court system through passage of the Family Court Act.[5] In addition to creating the Family Court itself, the Act contained a number of provisions that shaped the development of juvenile justice in New York State during the 1960s and 1970s. First, New York became the first state to statutorily distinguish the category status offenders, persons in needs of supervision (PINS), from juvenile delinquents. Second, the state retained its distinction as one of only a few states to employ the sixteen-year-old age limit for original criminal court jurisdiction. Third, the Act provided the statutory right to counsel in juvenile cases as well as other due process protections later extended nationwide through a series of Supreme Court cases.

By the mid-1960s, New York State had a well-established Family Court system, a training school system run by a large state bureaucracy with a capacity for handling more than 2,000 youths, and a small experimental agency running separate facilities and distributing funds for local delinquency prevention programs. The development of the system from the late 1960s to the present is the subject of the next section.

Figure 4.1 summarizes the key developments in the historical evolution of New York State's juvenile justice system. One should note that the developments in New York State parallel those occurring on a nationwide basis as discussed in Chapter Two.

Profile of a Changing Juvenile Corrections System

In 1970, the New York State juvenile corrections system consisted of four-teen training schools and centers housing approximately 2,000 youths. These fourteen training schools, administered by DSS, ranged from small seventeen- and eighteen-bed facilities to large congregate institutions housing more than 300 youths. Two of the training schools, one housing approximately ninety boys and another smaller facility for girls, were considered secure facilities. In addition, approximately 600 juveniles were held in rural camps, urban homes, and small treatment centers administered by DFY. (In 1971, the training schools were transferred from DSS to DFY.) Although many of the training schools and rural camps engaged youths in the local community, only the urban homes, Youth Development Centers, and several small residential treat-ment centers could be considered community-based.[6] Youths confined in the training schools, camps, and community-based facilities included both adjudicated juvenile delinquents and PINS. Juveniles were committed to these facilities for an initial period of eighteen months, although placement could be extended on a yearly basis until age eighteen.[7] The state agency responsible for the facilities had absolute discretion on when to release.

As Figure 4.2 indicates, the juvenile corrections system underwent fairly dramatic changes in the basic configuration of its residential population. Both the total residential population and the population within noncommunity-based facilities (training schools, residential centers, and camps) dramatically declined in the early 1970s. These overall reductions, and those in noncommunity-based populations specifically, were accomplished by the closing of a number of the large congregate training schools and reductions in the size of the remaining facilities. At the same time these changes were occurring, the population within community-based facilities increased. Whereas in 1970 approximately 90 percent of the residential population was held in noncommunity-based facilities and 10 percent in community-based facilities, by 1977 the proportions had changed to approximately 54 percent

Figure 4.1 Key events in the development of New York State's juvenile justice system, 1824-1984

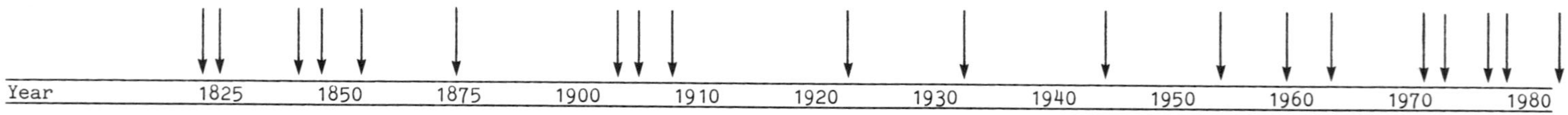

Year   1825   1850   1875   1900   1910   1920   1930   1940   1950   1960   1970   1980

Legend

1. 1824 Legislation authorizes placement of juveniles (younger than 16 years of age) convicted of a crime or charged with vagrancy with the Society for the Reformation of Juvenile Delinquents in New York City (N.Y. Laws 1824, c. 126).

2. 1825 New York House of Refuge opened for care of juveniles placed with Society for the Reformation of Juvenile Delinquents. First such facility in the United States.

3. 1840 Legislative authorization for placement of juveniles in House of Refuge is extended statewide (N.Y. Laws 1840, c. 100).

4. 1848-1849 Western House of Refuge at Rochester opened.

5. 1851 Dobbs Ferry Juvenile Asylum opened.

6. 1875 Legislation authorizes magistrates to place juveniles in houses of detention instead of adult jails (where separate facilities are available) (N.Y. Laws 1875, c. 464, sec. 2).

7. 1902 Manhattan Children's Court established.

8. 1904 New York State Training School for Girls at Hudson opened.

9. 1905-1910 Children's courts or separate children's parts established in Rochester, Buffalo, New York City, Syracuse, and New Rochelle (N.Y. Laws 1906, c. 317; 1909, c. 570; 1910, c. 659, c. 676, c. 559). Legislation provides that juveniles older than seven and younger than 16 years of age who commit a noncapital offense are not guilty of a crime but of juvenile delinquency (N.Y. Laws 1905, c. 655; 1907, c. 417; 1909, c. 478).

10. 1922 Children's Court Act establishes separate children's courts statewide (N.Y. Laws 1922, c. 547).

11. 1932 New York State Court of Appeals establishes standards of due process for children's courts. Court applies less rigorous standards than those applied in criminal court (<u>People</u> <u>v.</u> <u>Lewis</u>, 260 N.Y. 171, 183 N.E. 353 (1932)).

12. 1932 New York State Training School at Warwick opened.

13. 1945 Temporary New York State Youth Commission established (N.Y. Laws 1945, c. 556).

14. 1950s-1960s Period of growth in the institutional capacity juvenile corrections system. Eleven new training schools and centers are opened with a capacity of approximately 1,700 beds. The Division for Youth also adds approximately 600 beds through its development of experimental programs during the 1960s.

15. 1960 Division for Youth is established. Supersedes New York State Youth Commission (N.Y. Laws 1960, c. 881).

16. 1962 New York Family Court Act adopted (N.Y. Laws 1962, c. 686).

17. 1971 State training schools and centers are transferred from the Department of Social Services to the Division for Youth (N.Y. Laws 1971, c. 947).

18. 1973 New York Court of Appeals prohibits commingling of juvenile delinquents and status offenders in training schools (<u>In Re</u> <u>Ellery C.</u>, 32 N.Y. 2d 588, 300 N.E. 2d 424, 347 N.Y.S. 2d 51 (1973)).

19. 1976 Legislation prohibits placement status offenders in training schools (N.Y. Laws 1976, c. 515, 516).

20. 1976 Juvenile Justice Reform Act of 1976 adopted (N.Y. Laws 1976, c. 878).

21. 1978 Juvenile Offender Law adopted (N.Y. Laws 1978, c. 481).

22. 1982 Recodification of Article 3 of Family Court Act dealing with Family Court procedure in juvenile delinquency proceedings (N.Y. Laws 1982, c. 920).

and 46 percent, respectively. Furthermore, while annual data on DFY youths placed in foster care beds are unavailable, data that do exist indicate that the number of youths placed in foster care increased during the mid-1970s from traditional levels of approximately 250–300 to approximately 400. Considering foster care placements with the community-based population further illustrates the trend toward increased reliance on community-based placements.

In addition to the overall population changes, several other characteristics of the system changed during the mid-1970s. Status offenders could no longer be placed in either the training schools or secure centers. The population of secure centers rose slightly to approximately 150 in 1978 when two small facilities were opened. One further change that had developed by 1978 had to do with length of placements. Youths found to have committed one of a select number of serious offenses could be given a restrictive placement of three or five years with limits placed on DFY's discretion to release.

As illustrated in Figure 4.2, the late 1970s and early 1980s were a further time of change. By 1982, the total residential population had significantly increased. The number of youths in noncommunity-based programs had increased from a low point of less than 700 in 1977 to more than 1,400. The number in community-based programs modestly declined from around 550 in 1977 to approximately 470 in 1982. The proportion of youths in noncommunity-based and community-based facilities changed from 54 percent and 46 percent respectively in 1977, to 74 percent and 26 percent in 1982. Perhaps the most dramatic change was in the rise in the number of youths in secure facilities. In 1982, more than 500 youths were confined in secure facilities compared to approximately 150 in 1978. Related to the increase in secure placements were changes in sentencing practices. Youths committing serious offenses now faced possible sentences of seven, ten, fifteen years and even life. Facility size remained fairly stable with the largest facility housing 160 youths, two facilities with just in excess of 100 youths, and the rest with fewer than 100 youths. Since 1982, this growth in the secure centers and in the noncommunity-based facilities has levelled off and slightly declined while the number of youths in community-based settings has remained relatively stable.

Figure 4.3 presents budgetary data on DFY allocations from fiscal year 1971–72 to 1984–85. Although these data are imperfect indicators of program emphasis, they do reflect the same general trends witnessed in the population data.[8] These data indicate that the proportion of the total DFY budget devoted to noncommunity-based residential services steadily declined from

1971–72 (69 percent) to 1977–78 (44 percent). From this point, the proportional allocation was relatively constant until 1981–82 when increases in secure services allocations caused an increase in the overall noncommunity-based allocation. As with the population data, a slight reversal of this trend was seen in the last fiscal year. Allocations to community-based services steadily increased from 1971–72 (12 percent) to 1977–78 (27 percent). A decline was evidenced from this time until fiscal year 1981–82. Since that time, community-based allocations have increased slightly. Finally, the expansion of the secure services component is reflected in the budgetary allocations from 1979–80 to 1983–84. The most recent data, however, indicate a decline in secure services allocations.

Thus, over the course of the last fifteen or sixteen years, New York State's juvenile corrections system has undergone significant change. These changes are reflected in the population data in Figure 4.2 and the budgetary data presented in Figure 4.3 During these years, the number of youths removed from their communities and placed in public residential facilities has decreased. Additionally, the size of facilities has been reduced. Juveniles adjudicated as persons in need of supervision have been removed from the training schools. The number of youths placed in community-based settings has also increased since 1970. On the other hand, the number of secure facilities has significantly increased, as has the number of youths confined in secure facilities since 1978. At the same time, the number of youths placed in community-based settings has decreased from the levels of the mid-1970s. Finally, a number of youths find themselves serving longer periods of confinement than would have been possible in the early 1970s.

It is this process of change that the subsequent analysis attempts to explain. However, before moving to these sections it is important to briefly consider how New York State's juvenile justice system compares to other states' systems and to consider trends in juvenile arrests and court processing.

New York State's Juvenile Justice System in National Context

Several characteristics distinguish New York State's juvenile justice system from those of other states. Most important is the sixteen-year-old age distinction for criminal court jurisdiction. In New York State, all youths sixteen years of age and older are criminally responsible as adults and are processed in adult criminal court. Thus, the Family Court, New York State's juvenile court, deals only with youths age fifteen and younger. New York

Figure 4.2 New York State Division for Youth year-end residential population, by year and facility classification, 1970-1984[a]

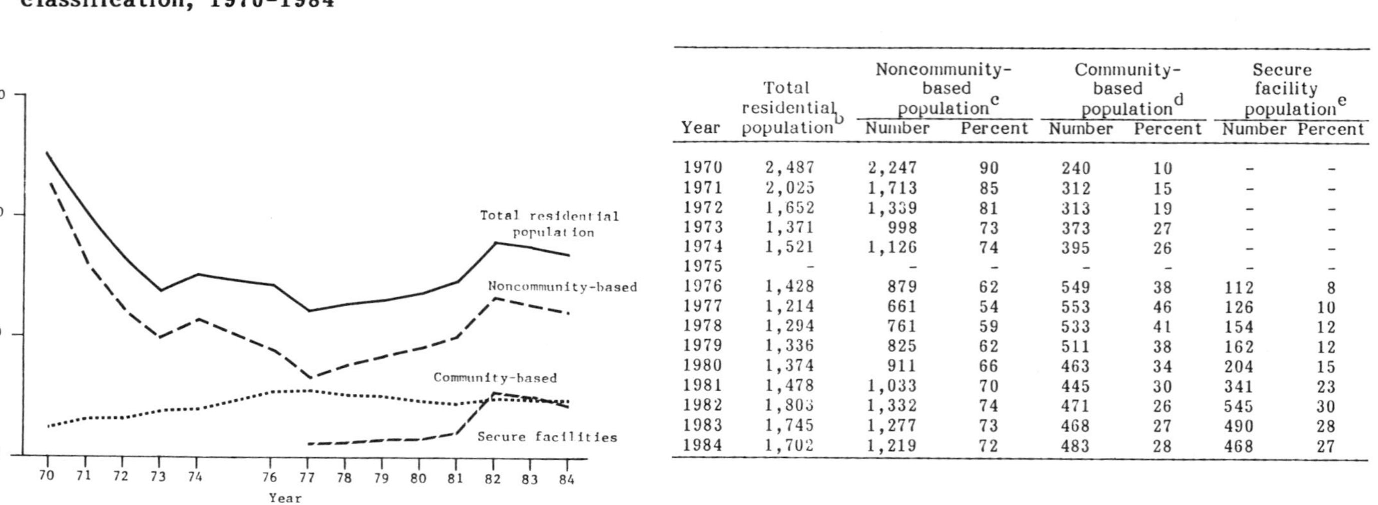

Year	Total residential population[b]	Noncommunity-based population[c]		Community-based population[d]		Secure facility population[e]	
		Number	Percent	Number	Percent	Number	Percent
1970	2,487	2,247	90	240	10	–	–
1971	2,025	1,713	85	312	15	–	–
1972	1,652	1,339	81	313	19	–	–
1973	1,371	998	73	373	27	–	–
1974	1,521	1,126	74	395	26	–	–
1975	–	–	–	–	–	–	–
1976	1,428	879	62	549	38	112	8
1977	1,214	661	54	553	46	126	10
1978	1,294	761	59	533	41	154	12
1979	1,336	825	62	511	38	162	12
1980	1,374	911	66	463	34	204	15
1981	1,478	1,033	70	445	30	341	23
1982	1,803	1,332	74	471	26	545	30
1983	1,745	1,277	73	468	27	490	28
1984	1,702	1,219	72	483	28	468	27

[a]The data in this figure should be interpreted cautiously and treated as estimates rather than absolute figures because of inconsistencies in reporting and changes in the classification of programs. However, the data are consistent with data reported in other archival sources (such as data for average daily population, admissions, and capacity). Thus, the data seem to present a reasonably reliable picture of the general trends in the population levels of these programs.

[b]Consists of the noncommunity-based population and the commmunity-based population. Note that the significant decreases in total residential population during the mid-1970s were accompanied with increases in DFY nonresidential programs such as foster care and day services.

[c]For 1970-74 includes training schools, special residential centers, and camps. From 1976-84 these programs were classified as Level I secure centers, Level II limited secure centers, Level III centers, centers, and camps. Note that the separately enumerated secure facilities are included in this category.

[d]Includes urban homes, youth development centers, and short-term adolescent resident treatment centers. Does not include foster care because annual data were not available.

[e]The secure centers are included in the category noncommunity-based programs. Prior to the designation of secure facilities as part of the Juvenile Justice Reform Act of 1976, the Goshen and Brookwood facilities, with a combined capacity of 135-160 beds, were considered DFY's secure care facilities.

Source: Data provided by New York State Division for Youth, Statistics and Survey Unit.

Figure 4.3 New York State Division for Youth budgetary allocations as percent of total state purposes budget, by year and allocation category, fiscal years 1971-72 to 1984-85[a]

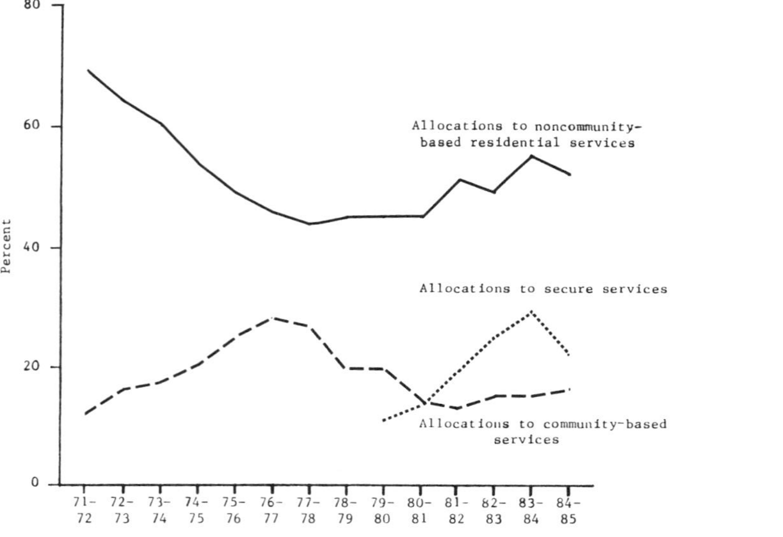

Year	Non community-based[b]	Community-based[c]	Secure services[d]
71-72	69	12	–
72-73	64	16	–
73-74	60	17	–
74-75	54	20	–
75-76	49	25	–
76-77	46	28	–
77-78	44	27	–
78-79	45	19	–
79-80	45	19	11
80-81	45	14	13
81-82	51	13	19
82-83	49	15	25
83-84	55	15	29
84-85	52	16	22

[a]As with the population data in Figure 4.2, these data should be interpreted cautiously. The budgetary data are imperfect indicators of program emphasis. However, when considered in conjunction with the population data the two sets of data present a similar picture of program trends.

[b]For fiscal years 1971-72 to 1978-79, includes training schools, special residential centers, and camps. For fiscal years 1979-80 to 1984-85, these programs were classified as secure facilities and limited secure/noncommunity-based programs. Note that the separately enumerated secure facilities are included in this category.

[c]For fiscal years 1971-72 to 1978-79, includes urban homes, youth development centers, short-term adolescent resident training centers, and foster care. Data for foster care were not available on an annual basis during these fiscal years. Foster care allocations were estimated based on the percentage allocation for those years when data were available. For fiscal years 1979-80 to 1984-85, the above programs were included in the category community-based services.

[d]Allocations for secure facilities as a distinct category were not available prior to fiscal year 1979-80. Allocations for secure facilities are included in the noncommunity-based category.

Source: _New York State Executive Budget_ and data provided by the New York State Division for Youth, Budget Division.

is one of only a handful of states that has applied this low minimum age of initial criminal court jurisdiction (Hamparian et al., 1982). One consequence is that the juvenile court has jurisdiction over a smaller pool of youths than is the case in most states.

One additional characteristic that distinguishes New York State's system from most other states is that, traditionally, New York has not allowed waiver of juveniles to criminal court. One major reason is that juveniles typically subject to waiver provisions, sixteen- and seventeen-year-olds, are already in criminal court. This distinction was modified in 1978 with the enactment of the Juvenile Offender (JO) Law. This law, which is discussed in detail in Chapter Six, places thirteen- to fifteen-year-olds committing targeted serious offenses in criminal court. The law also provides what has been termed a *reverse waiver* provision whereby juveniles can be returned from criminal court to juvenile court.

The fifteen-year-old age distinction also has implications for the juvenile corrections system. Only youths fifteen years of age or younger at the time of their offense are eligible for placement with DFY. Sixteen- and seventeen-year-old youths processed in criminal court are placed under the jurisdiction of the adult Department of Corrections.[9]

New York State's young age of criminal responsibility is a fundamental characteristic that distinguishes the system from the juvenile justice systems of most other states. Any discussion or analysis, and particularly any comparisons with other states, must be done in cognizance of this trait.

Juvenile Arrest and Court Processing Trends

This section presents data on trends in the legal processing of juveniles during the study period. Included are arrest data and court processing data. These data provide indicators of client flow to DFY. Fluctuation in client flow may represent a significant economic change in the agency's environment.

Arrests[10]

Tables 4.1 and 4.2 present juvenile arrest data. Table 4.1 presents felony and misdemeanor arrests of juveniles in New York City. These data are presented because state arrest data are only available for 1975 through 1984. The New York City data cannot be considered valid indicators of statewide arrest trends, but they are important because more than 50 percent of statewide juvenile arrests and nearly 80 percent of juvenile arrests for violent crimes are from New York City (New York State DFY, *Masterplan,* 1984).

Table 4.1   Juvenile arrests, by classification of offense and year, New York City, 1961-83

NOTE: These data were compiled by the New York Coalition for Juvenile Justice and Youth Services from the annual reports of the New York City Police Department, Youth Services Section.

Year	Juvenile Arrests (Age 7-15)	
	Felony	Misdemeanor
1961	6,227	3,354
1962	7,195	3,838
1963	7,769	3,523
1964	8,342	4,001
1965	8,440	3,426
1966	8,177	3,051
1967	9,063	3,350
1968	9,346	4,379
1969	9,788	5,213
1970	10,073	4,932
1971	10,422	4,337
1972	12,772	5,343
1973	14,837	5,638
1974	16,764	6,256
1975	17,226	6,419
1976	16,877	5,590
1977	16,188	4,396
1978	15,920	3,729
1979	14,630	3,158
1980	12,762	3,315
1981	11,556	3,188
1982	9,392	2,588
1983	8,357	2,346

Source: Data provided by the New York Coalition for Juvenile Justice and Youth Services, New York, New York.

These data indicate that both felony and misdemeanor arrests of juveniles in New York City increased between 1961 and 1975. Since 1975, these types of juvenile arrests have declined, with a fairly dramatic decline in the early 1980s.

A similar picture of the post-1974 trends is presented in Table 4.2. These statewide data indicate that total juvenile arrests fluctuated with no consistent pattern of increase or decrease between 1975 and 1982. Only in the last two years has a decline been seen. Arrests of juveniles for serious index crimes were in excess of 40,000 between 1975 and 1978, but have consistently declined since that time. Arrests for violent crimes have also decreased, particularly in the 1980s. Finally, arrests for property crimes, while relatively constant between 1975 and 1979, have declined in the 1980s.

Table 4.2   Juvenile arrests, by classification of offense and year, New York State, 1975-84

| | | Juvenile Arrests (Age 7-15) | | |
| | | Serious crime[a] | Violent crime[b] | Property crime[c] |
Year	Total			
1975	94,329	41,688	8,905	32,783
1976	113,714	42,268	7,777	34,491
1977	110,290	40,895	7,467	33,428
1978	93,184	41,017	7,587	33,430
1979	93,759	38,840	7,578	31,262
1980	90,372	35,269	6,809	28,460
1981	111,052	35,407	6,788	28,619
1982	90,351	30,075	5,924	24,151
1983	83,704	27,334	5,290	22,044
1984	83,035	26,217	5,205	21,012

[a] Includes violent crimes and property crimes.
[b] Includes murder, non-negligent manslaughter, forcible rape, robbery, and aggravated assault.
[c] Includes burglary, larceny-theft, motor vehicle theft, and arson.

Source: New York State Division of Criminal Justice Services, _Crime and Justice, Annual Report_, _1975_, pp. 96-97; _1976_, pp. 100-101; _1977_, pp. 102-103; _1978_, pp. 118-119; _1979_, pp. 109-110; _1980_, p. 133; _1981_, p. 129; _1982_, pp. 127-128; _1983_, pp. 129-130; _1984_, pp. 158-159 (Albany, N.Y.: New York State Division of Criminal Justice Services).

New York City and State data seem to be consistent with nationwide juvenile arrest trends (Strasburg, 1984). These data sources indicate that juvenile arrests increased in the 1960s and early 1970s, peaking in the mid-1970s. Since that time, arrests have levelled off and even declined.

Court Processing

Table 4.3 presents data on juvenile delinquency and PINS petitions filed in Family Court and Family Court placements in the state's juvenile corrections facilities. These data indicate that total petitions increased between 1963 and 1970, declined in the early 1970s, and increased once again. Petitions peaked in 1978 at more than 29,000 and remained at high levels before declining in 1983 and 1984. On the other hand, PINS petitions increased from 1963 to 1970 and have fluctuated with no apparent pattern since that time.

Family Court placements to juvenile corrections facilities declined in the late 1960s and early 1970s. The 831 placements in 1972 represented a 57 percent decrease from 1964, the peak year for placements. From 1973 to 1982 placements increased, peaking in 1977–78 and 1981–82. As a percent of total petitions, placements have generally followed the same pattern. In the early 1960s approximately 9 to 10 percent of petitions resulted in a placement. This proportion dropped to 4 or 5 percent in the mid-1970s and has since risen to 6 or 7 percent. Placements of delinquents followed a similar pattern to total placements although the peak years for such placements have occurred in the late 1970s and early 1980s. As a percent of total delinquency petitions, the proportion of placements declined in the late 1960s and early 1970s and peaked in the 1980s. On the other hand, PINS placements have steadily declined throughout these years. Whereas in 1964 there were 708 such placements, in 1984 there were only 100. Similarly, the percent of PINS petitions resulting in a placement has declined from 9 to 10 percent in the early to mid-1960s to 1 percent in the most recent years.

In addition to receiving juveniles from the Family Courts, since 1978 the juvenile corrections system has received a number of juveniles from the adult criminal courts. These are juveniles processed under the provisions of the 1978 Juvenile Offender Law (discussed in Chapter Six). Table 4.4 presents data on the number of arrests of juveniles under this law and the number of such youths actually sentenced to the juvenile corrections system. These data indicate that the number of arrests peaked in 1981 at slightly more than 1,600 and have since declined to approximately 1,260. The number of such youths actually sentenced to state juvenile corrections facilities steadily increased from 1979 to 1982 and has since declined. The proportion of those arrested who are actually placed peaked at 22 percent in 1982 and 1983.

The observed fluctuation in these court processing data suggest that this variation could be an important factor in the process of change in the juvenile corrections system. Consequently, these data will be reexamined in subsequent chapters. Unfortunately, issues related to the reasons for this variation in court processing are beyond the scope of this study. While factors such as demographic shifts, rates of youth offending, and police and court practices are likely to be affecting these trends, the issue remains an empirical

Table 4.3 Number of Family Court juvenile petitions and number and percent of juveniles placed in New York State juvenile corrections facilities, by type of petition and year, 1963–84

	Petitions			Placement in State Juvenile Corrections Facilities[b]					
Year[a]	Total	Juvenile delinquency	PINS	Total	Percent total petitions	Juvenile delinquents	Percent delinquency petitions	PINS	Percent PINS petitions
1963	17,761	11,357	6,404	1,517	9	953	8	564	9
1964	19,444	12,414	7,030	1,948	10	1,240	10	708	10
1965	18,978	11,806	7,172	1,812	10	1,143	10	669	9
1966	20,267	12,340	7,927	1,708	8	1,025	8	683	9
1967	22,237	13,076	9,161	1,636	7	937	7	699	8
1968	24,552	14,267	10,285	1,574	6	928	7	646	6
1969	24,042	13,158	10,884	1,369	6	697	5	672	6
1970	24,320	13,734	10,586	1,174	5	644	5	530	5
1971	22,994	13,267	9,727	918	4	571	4	347	4
1972	20,514	12,980	7,534	831	4	569	4	262	3
1973	23,007	14,736	8,271	1,001	4	692	5	309	4
1974[c]	13,690	9,130	4,560	543	4	395	4	148	3
1975	26,218	17,645	8,573	1,044	4	721	4	323	4
1976	25,778	18,175	7,603	1,032	4	862	5	170	2
1977	27,507	18,447	9,060	1,615	6	1,308	7	307	3
1978	29,335	19,741	9,594	1,742	6	1,479	7	263	3
1979	27,898	17,880	10,018	1,230	4	1,013	6	217	2
1980	26,717	17,340	9,377	1,404	5	1,221	7	183	2
1981	26,591	16,642	9,949	1,632	6	1,431	9	201	2
1982	26,007	16,210	9,797	1,897	7	1,754	11	143	1
1983	24,756	14,752	10,004	1,489	6	1,379	9	110	1
1984	18,121	10,075	8,046	1,296	7	1,196	12	100	1

[a]For the years 1963 to 1973, these data are for the judicial year July 1 through June 30. The 1974 data are for the six-month period July 1, 1974 through Dec. 31, 1974. Data for the years 1975 to 1984 are for the calendar year.

[b]From 1963 to 1971, these include placements in DSS training schools and in DFY facilities. In 1971, the training schools were transferred to DFY. Hence, data for 1971 to 1984 reflect placements to DFY.

[c]The 1974 data are for the six-month period July 1, 1974 through Dec. 31, 1974.

Source: Table constructed from data presented in New York State Judicial Conference, Report of the Administrative Board of the Judicial Conference of the State of New York, 1965, pp. 248-255; 1966, pp. 328-335; 1967, pp. 310-317; 1968, pp. 400-407; 1969, pp. 294-301; 1970, pp. 342-349; 1971, pp. 386-393; 1972, pp. 396-403; 1973, pp. 432-439; 1974, pp. 412-415, 420-423; 1975, pp. 126-129, 136-139; 1975b, pp. 104-107, 114-117; 1976, pp. 148-151, 158-161; 1977, pp. 156-159, 166-169; 1978; 1979, pp. 85, 86, 90, 91; 1980, pp. 83, 84, 88, 89; 1981, pp. 94, 95, 99, 100; 1982, pp. 97, 98, 102, 103; 1983, pp. 160-163, 167-170; 1984, pp. A-32-A-35, A-44-A-47; 1985, Tables A-22, A-23, A-30, A-31.

Table 4.4 Number of Juvenile Offender arrests and number and percent sentenced to New York State juvenile corrections facilities, 1978-84

Year	Arrests	Sentenced to Juvenile Corrections Facilities	
		Number	Percent
1978[a]	581	2	0.3
1979	1,583	84	5
1980	1,485	164	11
1981	1,613	231	14
1982	1,421	311	22
1983	1,263	274	22
1984	1,266	192	15

[a]Sept. 1, 1978 to Dec. 31, 1978.

Source: New York State Division of Criminal Justice Services, Juvenile Offenders in New York State: 1983 Report, p. 6; and data provided by New York State Division of Criminal Justice Services and New York State Division for Youth, Statistics and Survey Unit.

question. Despite this limitation, the court data loom as an important factor determining the rate of client flow to the juvenile corrections system.

The process of change in New York State's juvenile corrections system has been described and placed in historical and comparative perspective. The remaining chapters more intensively address this process of change and attempt to deal with the question of why the system has changed as it has.

Chapter Five

Diversifying the Juvenile Corrections System: The Luger Years (1966–1974)[1]

In 1970, New York State found itself with two separate public agencies responsible for running facilities for court-related youth. The larger and older of these was DSS which was responsible for administration of the state's fourteen training schools and centers. Along with the training school system, delinquents and status offenders could be placed with the New York State DFY. From 1960, when DFY was created by assuming the responsibilities of the State Youth Commission, to 1971, DFY created a number of programs for court-related youth aged fifteen to seventeen who entered at DFY's discretion. These programs provided less secure settings than the traditional training schools and included rural camps, residential centers, group homes, and day services programs.

Mandate for Change

Throughout the latter 1960s and early 1970s, several factors seemed to coalesce and lead to change in New York State's juvenile justice system. These factors included developments at the national, state, and local levels.

At the national level, the series of Supreme Court cases (*Kent, Gault, Winship*[2]) dealing with the juvenile justice system called into question the lack of procedural safeguards for juveniles and signalled the need to examine critically the juvenile justice system. The President's Commission on Law Enforcement and Administration of Justice (1967a) further chronicled the failings of the traditional juvenile justice system and called for a number of reforms of the system.

At the state level, several citizen's advocacy groups studied the state's training school system and issued reports critical of the training schools and DSS's administration of the schools. The reports cited instances of brutality and abuse and concluded that the training schools were excessively costly and failed to rehabilitate. Additionally, DSS found itself the subject of several lawsuits brought by the New York City Legal Aid Society alleging excessive use of solitary room confinement in the training schools.[3]

At the local level, these criticisms of institutionalization in general, and New York State's training schools in particular, seemed to have an effect on placement practices within the Family Court. While no systematic data on judicial attitudes exists, both legislative studies and respondents reported that Family Court judges began to view the training schools as a place of last resort. At the same time, the growth of DFY from a capacity of forty beds in 1960 to more than 600 in 1971 and the development of locally run community-based programs (through the Mobilization for Youth Program) led to a number of alternative placement options for Family Court judges.

These changes in Family Court sentencing practices are reflected in Tables 5.1, 5.2, and 5.3. Table 5.1 shows that both the total number of placements to juvenile corrections facilities and the percent of petitions resulting in a placement declined from 1967 to 1972. The decline was principally accounted for by the annual decline in placements to the training schools from 1964 (1,908) to 1973 (316). Table 5.1 indicates a slight increase in placements to DFY facilities in 1969 and 1970. However, the increase is not large enough to account for the decline in training school placements, thereby suggesting that Family Court judges were either dismissing a greater proportion of petitions or utilizing community-based options. Tables 5.2 and 5.3 indicate that this trend was true for both youths processed as status offenders (PINS) and juvenile delinquents. The percentage of PINS and delinquent petitions resulting in placement in juvenile corrections facilities, and training schools in particular, declined in the late 1960s and early 1970s. These trends are also reflected in the training schools' admission data in Table 5.4.[4] The initial drop in training school placements established a circular process (see Figure 5.1) that became a significant policy input in the early 1970s. Because the training schools had large physical plants, significant fixed costs were involved in keeping the facilities open despite the reduced number of youths. With reduced populations but constant costs, the rate for maintaining an individual youth in a training school drastically increased. Because the state and localities shared costs for maintaining a youth in a training school on a fifty/fifty basis, the per diem rate charged back to the localities increased (see Table 5.4). The increasing per diem rate created a further disincentive for localities to place youths in the training schools. This, in turn, further reduced placements and further increased the per diem rate. The training schools increasingly were seen as an excessively expensive placement option.

The decreasing populations and increasing costs of the training schools became particularly important in 1971 as the state experienced the first major fiscal crisis in modern times. The fiscal crisis led to overall budget reductions and "a startling reduction in the size of the state's workforce in the spring of 1971" (New York State Division of the Budget, 1981:147). At a time when all state agencies were asked to take cuts, the training schools became a logical place to look for budget reductions. As a result, the governor's office ordered DSS to close two training schools. The closing of the 330-bed New Hampton school for boys and the eighty-bed Wynantskill school for girls became the first in what was to be a series of reductions in the state's training school capacity over the next several years.

Transfer of the Training Schools

The closing of these two training schools was not to be the only significant event in the juvenile corrections system during 1971. The criticism of the training schools proved to be only one of many criticisms of DSS and the social welfare system in general. This crisis led Governor Nelson Rockefeller to propose a complete reorganization of the state's social welfare system. One part of this reorganization involved the transfer of the training schools from DSS to DFY.[5]

A number of factors influenced the decision to transfer the training schools (see Figure 5.2). First, the training schools were always considered an appendage of DSS, in no way central to its core mission. As one DSS administrator stated, the training schools were "like the tail on the dog." Second, the criticisms of the training schools by the advocacy groups and the lawsuits brought by the Legal Aid Society created a desire within the governor's office to "do something" with the training schools. This feeling was exacerbated by the crisis in the overall social welfare system. One official put it, "DSS had headaches on headaches; removing the training schools was a way of removing one of the headaches." The decision was made more attractive by the availability of DFY. DFY, because of its emphasis on prevention programs, small open facilities, and community-based programs, enjoyed a more favorable reputation among the advocacy groups and juvenile justice

Table 5.1 Number of Family Court juvenile petitions and number and percent of juveniles placed in New York State juvenile corrections facilities, by type of placement and year, 1963-73

		Placements					
Year[a]	Petitions[b]	Total	Percent of total petitions	Training schools	Percent of placements	DFY facilities	Percent of placements
1963	17,761	1,517	9	1,494	98	23	2
1964	19,444	1,948	10	1,908	98	40	2
1965	18,978	1,812	10	1,783	98	29	2
1966	20,267	1,708	8	1,677	98	31	2
1967	22,237	1,636	7	1,601	98	35	2
1968	24,552	1,574	6	1,545	98	29	2
1969	24,042	1,369	6	1,302	95	67	5
1970	24,320	1,174	5	1,125	96	49	4
1971	22,994	918	4	730	80	188	20
1972	20,514	831	4	481	58	350	42
1973	23,007	1,001	4	316	32	685	68

[a]These data are for the judicial year July 1 through June 30. Thus, 1963 data are for the period July 1, 1963-June 30, 1964.
[b]Includes PINS and juvenile delinquency petitions.

Source: Table constructed from data presented in New York State Judicial Conference, Report of the Administrative Board of the Judicial Conference of the State of New York, 1965, pp. 248-255; 1966, pp. 328-335; 1967, pp. 310-317; 1968, pp. 400-407; 1969, pp. 294-301; 1970, pp. 342-349; 1971, pp. 386-393; 1972, pp. 396-403; 1973, pp. 432-439; 1974, pp. 412-415, 420-423; 1975, pp. 126-129, 136-139.

Table 5.2 Number of Family Court PINS petitions and number and percent of PINS youths placed in New York State juvenile corrections facilities, by type of placement and year, 1963-73

Year[a]	PINS petitions	Placement of PINS youths					
		Total	Percent of petitions	Training schools	Percent of placements	DFY facilities	Percent of placements
1963	6,404	564	9	551	98	13	2
1964	7,030	708	10	690	97	18	3
1965	7,172	669	9	658	98	11	2
1966	7,927	683	9	670	98	13	2
1967	9,161	699	8	682	98	17	2
1968	10,285	646	6	632	98	14	2
1969	10,884	672	6	633	94	39	6
1970	10,586	530	5	507	96	23	4
1971	9,727	347	4	284	82	63	18
1972	7,534	262	3	109	42	153	58
1973	8,271	309	4	96	31	213	69

[a]These data are for the judicial year July 1 through June 30. Thus, 1963 data are for the period July 1, 1963-June 30, 1964.

Source: Table constructed from data presented in New York State Judicial Conference, Report of the Adminsitrative Board of the Judicial Conference of the State of New York, 1965, pp. 328-335; 1966, pp. 328-335; 1967, pp. 310-317; 1968, pp. 400-407; 1969, pp. 294-301; 1970, pp. 342-349; 1971, pp. 386-393; 1972, pp. 396-403; 1973, pp. 432-439; 1974, pp. 412-415, 420-423; 1975, pp. 126-129, 136-139.

Table 5.3 Number of Family Court juvenile delinquency petitions and number and percent of adjudicated delinquents placed in New York State juvenile corrections facilities, by type of placement and year, 1963-73

Year[a]	Juvenile delinquency petitions	Placement of youths adjudicated delinquent						
		Total	Percent of petitions	Training schools	Percent of placements	DFY facilities	Percent of placements
1963	11,357	953	8	943	99	10	1
1964	12,414	1,240	10	1,218	98	22	2
1965	11,806	1,143	10	1,125	98	18	2
1966	12,340	1,025	8	1,007	98	18	2
1967	13,076	937	7	919	98	18	2
1968	14,267	928	7	913	98	15	2
1969	13,158	697	5	669	96	28	4
1970	13,734	644	5	618	96	26	4
1971	13,267	571	4	446	78	125	22
1972	12,980	569	4	372	65	197	35
1973	14,736	692	5	220	32	472	68

[a]These data are for the judicial year July 1 through June 30. Thus, 1963 data are for the period July 1, 1963-June 30, 1964.

Source: Table constructed from data presented in New York State Judicial Conference, Report of the Administrative Board of the Judicial Conference of the State of New York, 1965, pp. 248-255; 1966, pp. 328-335; 1967, pp. 310-317; 1968, pp. 400-407; 1969, pp. 294-301; 1970, pp. 342-349; 1971, 386-393; 1972, pp. 396-403; 1973, pp. 432-439; 1974, pp. 412-415, 420-423; 1975, pp. 126-129, 136-139.

Table 5.4 **Admissions, population, days of care, facility costs and per diem rate of New York State training schools, 1966–71**

Year	Admissions	End of year population	Days of care provided	Facility costs	Per diem[a]
1966	2,232	2,236	832,919	$17,296,228	$20.99
1967	2,019	2,084	776,092	18,780,451	24.20
1968	2,111	2,174	793,057	20,663,740	26.06
1969	2,154	2,288	803,401	24,889,672	30.98
1970	1,751	1,962	746,678	27,839,497	37.28
1971	1,334	1,489	564,839	29,786,003	52.73

[a]This refers to the rate used to calculate charge back costs to localities for youths sent to the training schools.

Source: New York State Division for Youth as cited in The Costs of Institutional Care for Delinquent Adolescents in New York State: Crisis and Legislative Remedies, A Report Prepared by the Assembly Ways and Means Committee, Albany, N.Y., 1973.

Figure 5.1 Influence patterns related to reduced training school populations, New York State, mid-1960-1975

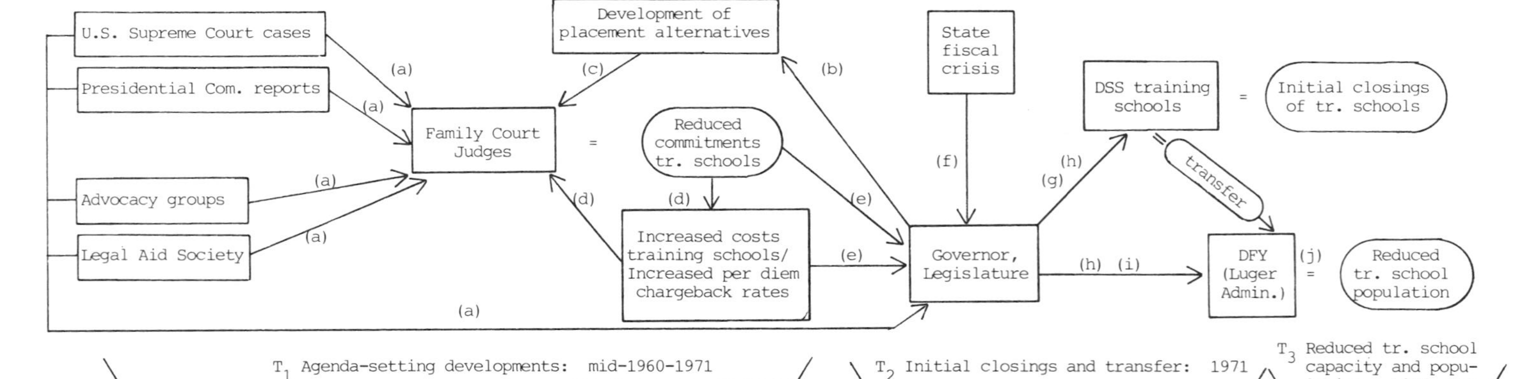

Policy Network

Link	Who (Initiator)	Influencing Whom (Target)	To Do What (Goals)	Tactics	Outcome
(b)	Governor, Legislature	DFY; Family Court judges	Develop experimental programs for court related youth	Provide resources for DFY to develop range of residential and nonresidential programs	Creates set placement alternatives to training schools
(g)	Governor	DSS	Reduce costs of training school system	Authority – order DSS to close two training schools	New Hampton and Wynantskill training schools closed
(h)	Governor	DFY and DSS	Transfer training schools from DSS to DFY	Authority – order DFY assume responsibility; Exchanges – allow DFY to draft legislation with provisions providing DFY control over facilities	Transfer training schools; DFY administration given control over training schools

Figure 5.1 (Continued)

Link	Who (Initiator)	Influencing Whom (Target)	To Do What (Goals)	Tactics	Outcome
(i)	Governor, Legislature	DFY	Reduce population of training schools	Authority/Mandate - instruct to "close and consolidate" facilities; reduce appropriations for training schools, increase for community based; transfer legislation gives DFY control over intake decision	Reduced training school capacity and population
(j)	DFY (Luger Administration)	DFY residential programs	Reduce population of training schools; increase community-based programs	Authority - enunciate agency policy, close several training schools, reduce population in training schools, develop community-based progams	Reduced training school capacity and population

Related Factors

Link	What	Influencing Whom	To Do What	How Influencing	Outcome
(a)	Supreme Court cases; Presidential Commission reports; Advocacy groups; Legal Aid Society	Family Court Judges; Governor, Legislature	Question traditional reliance on training schools	Criticism of traditional juvenile justice approach in general, and specific criticism of New York training schools	Reduced training school placements; support for deinstitutionalization policy
(c)	Development of placement alternatives	Family Court Judges	Place youths in alternate settings	With growth of DFY 1960-71 and development of local community based settings, Family Court judges given placement option other than training schools	Reduced training school placements
(d)	Reduced commitments to training schools	Training schools and localities	Increased costs of training schools/ Increased per diem chargeback rates	Fixed costs of large training schools in combination with lower population drives up per diem rate charged back to localities	Increased per diem creates further disincentive to send to training schools
(e)	Reduced commitments to, increased costs of tr. schools	Governor, Legislature	Cut costs of training schools	Training schools appear to be place to cut spending	Close several tr. schools, cut appropriations
(f)	State fiscal crisis	Governor, Legislature	Cut costs of state government	Governor and Legislature respond to fiscal crisis by ordering across the board spending cuts	Close several tr. schools, cut appropriations

professionals than did the training schools. Placing the training schools in DFY, the governor not only relieved DSS of its unwanted burden, but also gained political credit for placing the training schools within this "enlightened" administration. Respondents were in virtual agreement that the transfer decision was not so much based on substance as it was on the desire to remove a liability from DSS and gain some credit by putting the schools in DFY. As one official noted "the transfer did not have anything to do with what's best for kids."

Further Reductions in the Training School Population

Transferring twelve training schools housing 1,900 youths from a large state agency to a small experimental agency was an important change in and of itself, but what was most important was that this structural change opened the way for subsequent reform.

The training schools under DSS had developed as essentially independent facilities that looked to DSS administrators within the Bureau of Children's Institutional Services primarily to provide support services. The training schools' independence was sustained by the fact that each was formally supervised by a governing board of visitors who reported directly to the governor (bypassing DSS). The superintendent of each facility in turn controlled the Board of Visitors. DSS Central Office administrators reported that they were never clear what, if any, legal power they had over training school superintendents. In practice, DSS Central Office adopted a stance whereby they could "advise" but never tell the superintendents what to do.

The governor's office, having decided to transfer the training schools, approached DFY and told its administrators that they were to assume responsibility for the training schools and that it had five days to draft enabling legislation. DFY's response was to attempt to draft legislation that would give it some control over the training schools. DFY did this by including two key provisions in the legislation. The first gave the DFY director control over the appointment and removal of training school superintendents. The second gave DFY control over intake of youths. Previously, Family Court judges would place juveniles in a particular training school. Now placement would be to DFY with Central Office actually making the specific placement decision. These provisions were essential to providing the administrative structure necessary to gain any type of Central Office control over system-wide policy.

DFY Director Milton Luger was openly committed to smaller facilities and opposed to the large, congregate training school model. This

Figure 5.2 Influence patterns related to decision to transfer training schools, New York State, 1969–1971

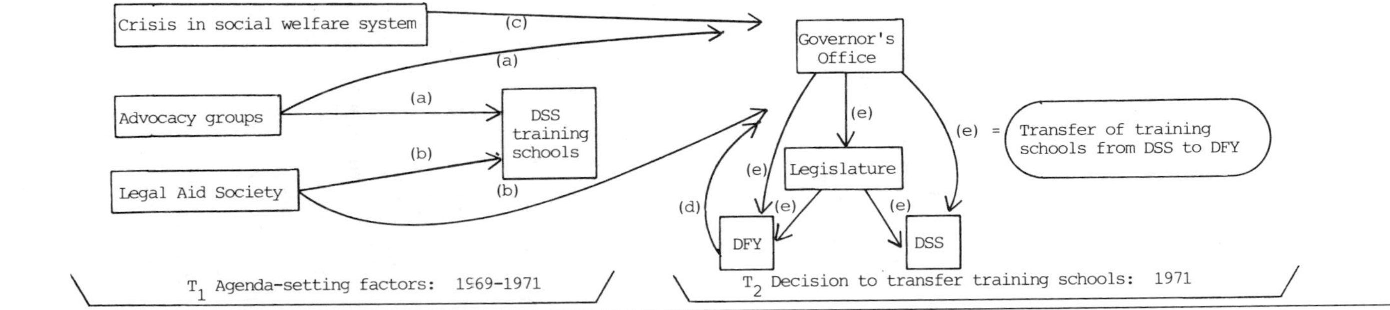

Policy Network

Link	Who (Initiator)	Influencing Whom (Target)	To Do What (Goals)	Tactics	Outcome
(a)	Advocacy groups	Direct – DSS training schools; Indirect – Governor's office	Decrease number of youths in training schools; improve conditions within	Investigations and criticism of system; provide information; enlist support of influentials; attend meetings	Apparent agenda-setting effect
(b)	Legal Aid Society	Direct – DSS training schools; Indirect – Governor's office	Improve conditions within training schools	Criticize system and interrupt traditional functioning of system through lawsuits	Apparent agenda-setting effect; ultimate restrictions on control practices
(e)	Governor	Legislature, DFY, DSS	Transfer responsibility for training schools from DSS to DFY	Authority – order transfer; enlist legislative support	Training schools transferred

Related Factors

Link	What	Influencing Whom	To Do What	How Influencing	Outcome
(c)	Crisis in social welfare system	Governor's office	Reorganize state's social welfare system	Crisis in social welfare system leads to major reorganization of DSS	Reorganization plan includes provision to transfer tr. schools
(d)	DFY	Governor's office	Place training schools under DFY jurisdiction	Perceived DFY success in running residential facilities creates available policy option for dealing with tr. school issue	Reorganization plan includes provision to transfer tr. schools

administrative commitment was coupled with the continued fiscal directive of the legislature to "close and consolidate" the large, expensive training schools. In 1972, this legislative pressure was clearly articulated as the Joint Legislative Fiscal Committee decreased appropriations to the training schools by $1.9 million while increasing appropriations to DFY community-based settings by $1 million. In its press release, the Joint Fiscal Committee stated:

> This reorganization of the training schools represents a positive step toward the elimination of large congregate institutions in the treatment of youth delinquency and will permit DFY to decentralize the cottage components at the training schools and gain the advantages inherent in small institutional rehabilitative environments ("Costs of Institutional Care," 1973:9).

The combination of Luger's commitment to small facilities and community-based settings and the fiscally driven support of the governor's office and the legislature led to the closing of several more training schools, reduced populations in the remaining schools, and increased community-based settings during 1971 and 1974. As indicated in Table 5.5, noncommunity-based populations (primarily training schools) were reduced somewhere in the vicinity of 1,000 during these years, while community-based populations increased from approximately 240 to 390. Furthermore, the proportion of DFY youths housed in community-based facilities increased from 10 percent to 26 percent.[6]

Analysis—The Luger Years

The 1960s and early 1970s thus were a period of significant change in New York State's juvenile corrections system. The changes were the product of a specific policy decision, the decision to transfer the training schools from DSS to DFY and the adoption of the more general deinstitutionalization policy. Figures 5.1 and 5.2 present the influence patterns involved in these policy developments. Figure 5.3 summarizes these factors according to the political economy framework. Recall that this framework emphasizes internal and external factors operating at the political and economic levels. Political factors are those shaping the conditions of the organization's existence and include factors such as goals, mandates, value systems, and power interests. Economic factors are those shaping basic service delivery and include factors such as service technologies, funding, and client flow.

Table 5.5 New York State Division for Youth year-end residential population, by year and facility classification, 1970-74

Year	Total residential population[a]	Noncommunity-based population[b]		Community-based population[c]	
		Number	Percent	Number	Percent
1970[d]	2,487	2,247	90	240	10
1971	2,025	1,713	85	312	15
1972	1,652	1,339	81	313	19
1973	1,371	998	73	373	27
1974	1,521	1,126	74	395	26

[a]Consists of the noncommunity-based and community-based populations.

[b]Includes training schools, special residential centers, and camps.

[c]Includes urban homes, youth development centers, and short-term adolescent resident treatment centers. Does not include foster care because annual data were not available.

[d]Includes DSS training schools and DFY facilities. Transfer of training schools to DFY occurred in 1971.

Source: Data provided by New York State Division for Youth, Statistics and Survey Unit.

Figure 5.3 indicates that a full range of political and economic factors, operating both externally and internally to the juvenile corrections system, were influential in shaping the policy directions of this period. At the external political level, questioning the traditional training school approach evident in the Presidential Commission Reports and the Supreme Court cases was manifested at the state level by investigations and lawsuits related to the training schools. This questioning was coupled with external economic changes (reduced commitments, state fiscal crisis) and led to the external political shift evidenced by the governor's and legislature's decisions to close several facilities, transfer the training schools, and appropriate funds for community-based programs. At the same time, two key internal political changes occurred. The transfer legislation brought about a power shift from training school superintendents to the DFY Central Office and the transfer placed this power in the hands of a director who sought to reduce training school populations and increase community-based options. The external actions of the governor and legislature also created an internal economic change be providing funds for the community-based programs. These findings provide strong support for the sequencing principle as the system changes clearly seem to be the products of both internal and external, political and economic factors.

Figure 5.3 Categorization of factors influencing New York's juvenile corrections system according to political economy model, 1968-1974

| | External | | Internal | |
	Political	Economic	Political	Economic
Deinstitutionalization Reduced training school populations and transfer training schools to DFY	Deinstitutionalization ideology--Presidential Commissions, Supreme Court, Youth advocacy groups Criticism of training schools, investigations, lawsuits Gubernatorial--Legislative support for alternatives to training schools Crisis social welfare system, reorganization DSS Legislative transfer of training schools to DFY	Increased local level community based options; development DFY Reduced commitments to training schools Increased costs of training schools State fiscal crisis Reduced appropriations for training schools Increased funding for alternatives	Transfer legislation gives DFY control over training schools Luger support for community based alternatives	Increased costs of training schools Diversification of technologies with development placement alternatives

The persuasiveness of the sequencing principle can perhaps best be illustrated by speculating on the effect of the lack of change of any one set of factors. For example, the external political factors (Commission Reports, Supreme Court cases, and criticism of the training schools), may not have had an impact if not coupled with the economic factors of increased costs and the state fiscal crisis. The fact that many states did not experience major reductions in training school populations during these years (Sarri and Vinter, 1976) may be indicative of this point. Similarly, the external political decision to transfer the training schools may not have resulted in the facility population changes if not accompanied by the internal political shifts (Central Office control and Luger support) and the funds for diversification of internal technology. The combination of factors seems to have led to change.

There is limited, although qualified, support for the crisis principle. As has been noted, the transfer of the training schools followed criticism of the training schools and DSS's administration of the schools. However, respondents pointed out that it was not a matter of widespread abuse and scandal as was the case in Massachusetts. Although the criticism and public scrutiny were considered new phenomena for the training schools, the situation was not perceived to be a crisis.

On the other hand, the state's fiscal situation was considered a major political crisis. The fiscal crisis and the related crisis in the state's social welfare system were considered the preeminent political issues of the times. Furthermore, both of these issues were considered integral in the deinstitutionalization and transfer decisions.

To infer unqualified support for the crisis principle based on these findings would probably be a matter of overinterpretation. Respondents did not view the criticism of the training schools as a crisis and the fiscal and social welfare crises were not focused on the juvenile corrections system. However, a more limited view of the crisis principle, one which relates state-level political crises to the political economy of juvenile corrections is supported. That is, to the extent that political crises impact on the internal and external political economy of the juvenile corrections system, they may be significant factors in change. The suggestion is that the importance of crises, whether specific to the juvenile corrections system or more general, is a product of the interrelationship of crises to the sequencing principle.

The key swing group principle is also supported. The political "swing" or "shift," however, was not the classical case where liberal and conservative interest coalitions vied for the support of key decisionmakers. Rather, the swing was in the form of key decisionmakers within the legislature (budget committee leaders) and the governor's office (staff responsible for reorganizing the social welfare system) moving from a *laissez-faire* position to the position of initiators of change. These political actors formed what Miller, Ohlin, and Coates (1977) term the Formal Decisionmaking Group in that their support was not so much ideologically driven as it was a functional response to political problems. Furthermore, these were actors with the political power to mandate the types of change that occurred.

As was the case with the crisis principle, the key swing group principle appears to be related to the sequencing principle. The shift of key legislators and the governor's staff represented a fundamental change in the external polity of the juvenile corrections system.

The fourth and fifth principles, related to interest coalition responses to changes in the system and the effects of extreme tactics are more fruitfully examined over time and will be considered in subsequent chapters.

Figure 5.4 summarizes the key changes in the relationships comprising the juvenile corrections arena. As noted in the methodology section, the retroactive nature of the study precluded measurement of all the variables describing these sets of relationships. However, changes among the relationships can be noted. In terms of the People Processing Relationship, the system moved from a predominant reliance on training schools to a more diversified system increasingly relying on community-based programs. A shift was also evidenced in the Relationship among Interest Groups in that key legislators and gubernatorial staff seized control of policy from what had traditionally been the domain of the training schools' superintendents. Later in the period, control over policy was placed within the office of the DFY director. The Liberal Interest Coalition had become increasingly active early in the period and had found its interests supported through the decline in training school populations and the expansion of community-based options. On the other hand, the Conservative Interest Coalition representing traditional custodial interests was considered to have been too fragmented and isolated to respond to the external political threats and thus saw its interest thwarted by the policy changes.

The changes among these key relationships became the context of juvenile corrections as a new DFY administration took office.

Figure 5.4 Summary of changes in key relationships of juvenile corrections arena, Luger years

Relationship	Beginning period (late 1960s)	Ending period (1971-1974)
People Processing Relationship	Placement in training schools predominant correctional technology. Alternative placements created with development DFY.	Traditional juvenile corrections technology diversified, decrease training school populations, increase community based programs.
Relationship among Interest Groups	Autonomous superintendents of training schools key formulators of juvenile corrections policy.	Formal Decisionmaking Group (governor and key legislators) move to support deinstitutionalization policy then delegate control to Luger Administration. Represents shift from traditional custodial interests to rehabilitation/community-based interests.
Conservative Interest Coalition	Custodial interests (training school superintendents) seen as too fragmented and isolated to respond to external political threats.	Custodial interests thwarted during period.
Liberal Interest Coalition	Youth advocacy groups increasingly involved in juvenile corrections (investigations, lawsuits).	Liberal interests ascendant-- closings of training schools, reduced training school populations, increased community-based populations.

Chapter Six

Divergent Trends:
The Edelman Years (1975–1979)

With the change from a republican to democratic governor in 1974, Peter Edelman replaced Luger as DFY director in 1975. This change did not signal the end of the move away from large institutions; rather, Edelman continued and even accelerated the move from institutions to community-based settings. Edelman, who came from the University of Massachusetts and was familiar with Jerome Miller's efforts to close the training schools in Massachusetts, entered with the "fundamental premise that young people are overinstitutionalized." While the Edelman Administration believed that for both substantive (larger population and more serious juvenile offending) and political (stronger conservative element in the legislature) reasons New York State would not be able to go as far in closing facilities as was the case in Massachusetts, reductions in the number of youths in training schools was a clear priority. Indeed, before Edelman officially arrived in New York State, he ratified a prior decision to close the Hudson training school for girls. Edelman's effort to reduce the number of noncommunity-based institutionalized juveniles involved two basic steps. The first was the total removal of PINS youths from the training schools. The second involved the development of additional community-based programs for both PINS and juvenile delinquents traditionally held in the training schools.

PINS Removal and Increased Community-Based Settings

The issue of PINS placement in the training schools had previously arisen in a 1973 court case, in which the New York Court of Appeals prohibited the placement of PINS in training schools that also housed juvenile delinquents.[1] DFY's response to this ruling was to prohibit the commingling of PINS and juvenile delinquents by dividing the training schools into facilities housing PINS and facilities housing juvenile delinquents. While the Luger Administration was committed to reductions in the training school populations, it still maintained that such placements were necessary in certain cases. Further, the question of whether to place a youngster in the training schools was to be based on the youth's needs, not on what was seen to be an artificial legal distinction between PINS and juvenile delinquents.

With Edelman's arrival in 1975, DFY's policy on placement of PINS changed. The reason for the shift in policy was largely attributable to the shift in personal philosophy following Edelman's succession of Luger as DFY director. Luger, an educator, was committed to the philosophy of basing placement decisions on the assessed needs of the youths. He opposed using legal labels such as *status offender* or *juvenile delinquent* as the criterion for making placement decisions (i.e., the decision to place in a training school, rural camp, or urban home). Furthermore, he argued that the use of such labels would result in racially segregated facilities because status offenders were predominantly white and juvenile delinquents predominantly Black.[2] Edelman, an attorney, felt that the failure to base placement decisions on legal criteria was irrational and unfair to less serious offenders. Thus, while both were committed to reducing the use of congregate institutions and expanding community options, they disagreed on the criteria employed for selecting youths for specific programs. Adopting legal criteria for placement decisions represented a fundamental change in DFY internal policy.

One of Edelman's first administrative efforts was to remove PINS youths from the training schools, which was codified by the legislature in 1976 with passage of a law prohibiting the placement of PINS in training schools.[3] The bill was part of DFY's legislative agenda and was supported by the governor's office, the Assembly's Child Care Committee and the Senate's Temporary Commission on Child Welfare. The legislation was sold on the basis that it merely codified existing DFY practice and that it was necessary to secure federal funds under the Juvenile Justice and Delinquency Prevention Act of 1974. The bill was passed with very little opposition. The results of Edelman's administrative policy and the subsequent legislation were dramatic. In 1973, at the time of the court decision on PINS placement, approximately 400 PINS youths were held in the training schools. By 1978, no PINS were in the training schools and only fifty-seven were in DFY noncommunity-based facilities. The set of factors involved in the PINS deinstitutionalization process are illustrated in Figure 6.1.

Figure 6.1 Influence patterns related to PINS deinstitutionalization from training schools, New York State, 1973-1976

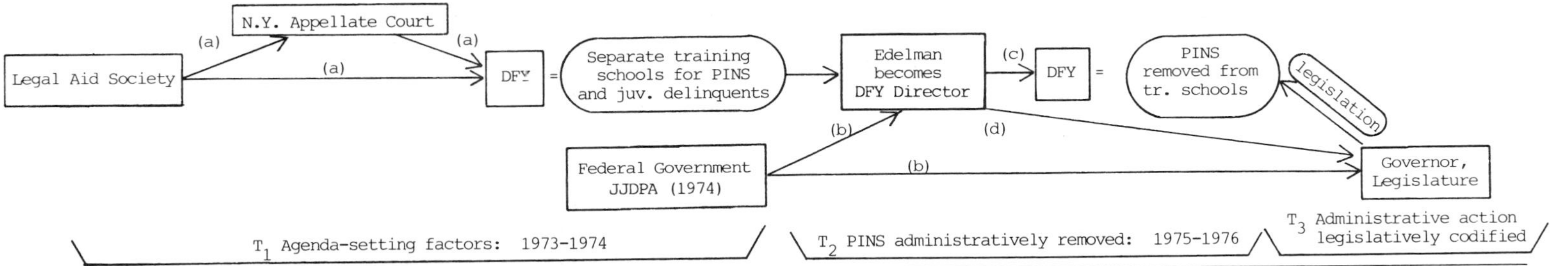

Link	Who (Initiator)	Influencing Whom (Target)	To Do What (Goals)	Tactics	Outcome
(a)	Legal Aid Society	DFY	Remove PINS from training schools	Criticize (through lawsuits) practice of housing PINS in tr. schools; interrupt routine way of handling PINS through court rulings; Exchanges – negotiate with DFY over placement policies	Initially prevent commingling of PINS and delinquents in training schools
(b)	Federal Government	DFY, Governor, Legislature	Remove PINS from training schools	JJDPA 1974 rewards compliance with Act, threatens loss of funds if no compliance; represents support of influentials for removal policy; Exchanges – reach Federal-State agreement on PINS policy	Creates impetus for removal and provides further rationale for removal arguments
(c)	Edelman	DFY	Remove PINS from training schools	Authority/Mandate – enunciates DFY policy removing PINS from training schools	Administrative removal of PINS from training schools
(d)	Edelman	Governor, Legislature	Codify prohibition of PINS in training schools	Authority/Mandate, Opportunity and Information – provide influential support, enlist support of Governor and key legislators, place on legislative agenda, show need to comply JJDPA; Momentum – administratively enact then seek codification	Passage of legislation prohibiting PINS placement

In addition to the PINS efforts, Edelman sought to further the goal of reduced institutionalization by closing several of the old training schools and increasing community-based placements. Formal goal statements included plans to decrease the training school population from approximately 600 to 240 beds and to expand total community-based options to a capacity for more than 2,000 youths.

The early years of the Edelman Administration were also the years of the New York City fiscal crisis that, in turn, created fiscal pressures on the state. The fiscal crisis became the main preoccupation of Governor Hugh Carey's Administration. One commentator noted, "no single event in the last half century has had a more dramatic impact on the State's executive budget system than the fiscal crisis that gripped New York City in the mid-1970s" (New York State Division of the Budget, 1981:161). Because of these fiscal pressures, DFY was asked to take budget cuts. Edelman responded by cutting appropriations for the training schools. In addition to his ratification of closing the Hudson facility, the Overbrook, Highland, and Warwick facilities were closed. At the same time, DFY was able to secure federal funds through the state's Division of Criminal Justice Services (LEAA funds) and the State Division of Budget (federal countercyclical funds). These federal dollars were used to fund a variety of alternative programs, the majority of which were community-based. Among these efforts were the expansion of group homes, youth development centers, and foster care and the development of new programs including day services and independent living programs. In addition to these federal funds, the move to increase community-based programs was enhanced by legislation passed in conjunction with the bill prohibiting PINS placement in training schools. These additional provisions gave DFY statutory authority to increase community-based programs, authority to contract with private nonprofit agencies for services to DFY youth, and provisions to make DFY youth placed in foster care eligible for federal reimbursement under the Aid to Families with Dependent Children (AFDC-FC) program (see Figure 6.2).

The result of these policy choices was that, by 1977 and 1978, training school populations were further reduced, the number of youths in noncommunity-based settings was reduced, and the number in community-based settings continued to increase (see Table 6.1). The peak year for these trends was 1977 when the proportion of DFY youths housed in community-based programs attained 46 percent. This compares with 10 percent in 1970 and 26 percent in 1974, the last year of the Luger Administration. Further, no PINS youths were in training schools and no institution housed in excess of 120 youths.

Figure 6.2 Influence patterns related to deinstitutionalization and increased community-based programs, New York State, 1975-1978

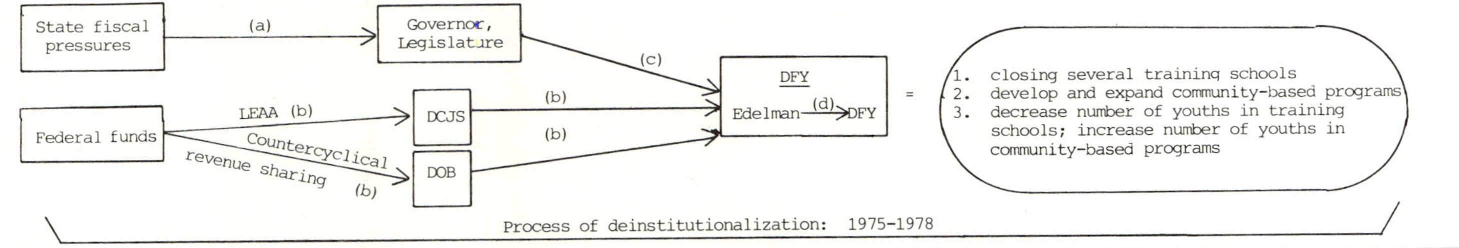

Process of deinstitutionalization: 1975-1978

Policy Network

Link	Who (Initiator)	Influencing Whom (Target)	To Do What (Goals)	Tactics	Outcome
(c)	Governor, Legislature	DFY	Reduce agency costs; provide alternative community-based programs	Authority - order budget cuts, provide legislative authority to develop community-based programs, to contract with private non-profit childcare agencies, to make DFY youth eligible for Federal AFDC funding	DFY takes budget cuts in training schools, increases community-based settings
(d)	Edelman	DFY	Decrease institutionalized population; increase community-based programs	Authority/Mandate - enunciate policy, enlist support of governor's office, and support of key funding agencies (DCJS and DOB)	Moves DFY youths from tr. schools to open and community-based programs

Related Factors

Link	What	Influencing Whom	To Do What	How Influencing	Outcome
(a)	State fiscal pressures	Governor, Legislature	Cut costs for state government	Governor and legislature asks DFY (and other state agencies) to cut costs	Edelman responds by closing several training schools
(b)	Federal funds	DFY	Create alternative programs	Resources - LEAA alternatives grant and countercyclical funds provide resources to develop community-based programs	DFY creates and expands alternative community-based programs

DCJS - New York State Division of Criminal Justice Services
DOB - New York State Division of Budget

Table 6.1 also indicates a slight change in this overall trend in 1978. The apparent reasons for this shift are the subject of subsequent sections.

Dealing with the Serious Juvenile Offender[4]

Sometime around 1974, interest in the issue of how to handle the serious juvenile offender arose. Over the course of the next four years, this question became a preeminent political issue in New York State.

Initial interest in the serious juvenile offender was stimulated by the investigations and findings of two legislative committees in 1974. The first of these was conducted by an Assembly Subcommittee on the Family Court, the second by the New York State Select Committee on Crime, which was chaired by a Republican Senator who also chaired the Senate Committee on Crime and Correction. The general theme of the reports issued by these Committees, which focused on gang violence and juvenile robbery respectively, was that violent juvenile crime had dramatically increased in New York City and that the Family Court was failing to adequately respond to the problem.

Legislative attention to juvenile crime continued in 1975. In addition to the continuing work of the Select Committee on Crime, the Senate-controlled Temporary State Commission on Child Welfare's Subcommittee on Juvenile Justice issued its first report, and the newly created Assembly Child Care Committee embarked on what was to be a sixteen-month investigation of juvenile crime and the juvenile justice system. The findings of these committees echoed many of those just described—an increase in juvenile crime and a Family Court system that failed to respond adequately to these juvenile lawbreakers. Additional criticism focused on the unfettered discretion of DFY. DFY was said to employ a "rapid release policy" and was criticized for having a large number of runaways. Consistent in the reports of these committees was the theme that the juvenile justice system in New York State was neither helping the youths nor protecting the community.

In addition to the legislative committee activity, the media began to focus on the topic of juvenile crime, and juvenile violence in particular. Respondents unanimously spoke of the importance of this heightened media attention in the subsequent legislative changes enacted from 1976 to 1978. The media attention, particularly among prominent New York City newspapers, was seen as key to keeping the juvenile violence issue alive and to expressing public pressure for a "toughened" system.

Table 6.1 New York State Division for Youth year-end residential population, by year and facility classification, 1974-78

Year	Total residential population[a]	Noncommunity-based population[b]		Community-based population[c]		Secure facility population[d]	
		Number	Percent	Number	Percent	Number	Percent
1974	1,521	1,126	74	395	26	–	–
1975	–	–	–	–	–	–	–
1976	1,428	879	62	549	38	112	8
1977	1,214	661	54	553	46	126	10
1978	1,294	761	59	533	41	154	12

[a]Consists of the noncommunity-based and community-based populations.

[b]For 1974 includes training schools, special residential centers, and camps. From 1976 to 1978 these programs were classified as Level I secure centers, Level II limited secure centers, Level III centers, centers, and camps. Note that the separately enumerated secure facilities are included in this category.

[c]Includes urban homes, youth development centers, and short-term adolescent resident treatment centers. Does not include foster care because annual data were not available.

[d]The secure centers are included in the category noncommunity-based programs. Prior to the designation of secure facilities as part of the Juvenile Justice Reform Act of 1976, the Goshen and Brookwood facilities, with a combined capacity of 135 to 160 beds, were considered DFY's secure care facilities.

Source: Data provided by New York State Division for Youth, Statistics and Survey Unit.

In response to the criticisms of the juvenile justice system, a number of bills were introduced during the 1975 legislative session, including several that provided for major reform of the traditional juvenile justice system. Among these reform bills, two distinct approaches arose that became the focus of a political battle waged over the next three years. The first approach was embodied in a bill sponsored by the Senate chair of the Select Committee on Crime and provided for waiver of juveniles accused of serious offenses into the adult criminal court. The Senate sponsor was joined in support of this bill by the Assembly Ways and Means Committee Chair, one of the Assembly's most powerful committees. The second approach, incorporated in a bill introduced by the Assembly Child Care Committee Chair, rejected waiver but provided measures to strengthen the Family Court. This second approach, supported by both the Assembly and Senate leadership, was passed. The bill was vetoed, however, by Governor Carey, who argued that he had just hired Peter Edelman as DFY director and, as such, Edelman should have a voice in such a significant policy change. Additionally, the governor announced that he was appointing a blue ribbon panel to study the problem of juvenile violence and to recommend policy changes for New York State's juvenile justice system.

Juvenile Justice Reform Act of 1976

The stage was thus set for policy debate in 1976. Conservative forces were advocating a waiver-up position. Many traditional liberals agreed that reform of the juvenile justice system was needed but did not want to go as far as a waiver-up system. The governor, on record as opposing waiver, awaited the findings of his blue ribbon panel.

The governor's panel, known as the Cahill Commission, comprised a number of prominent citizens from across the state. Within the panel, Peter Edelman took a key leadership role. Like the governor, Edelman opposed the waiver-up approach. He took the position that the juvenile justice system had problems and advocated an approach similar to that of the Assembly Child Care Committee. Edelman urged retention of Family Court jurisdiction but provision of procedures that would allow differential treatment of juveniles committing serious offenses. In taking this position, Edelman found himself between the traditional child advocacy groups who opposed any increase in sanctions for juveniles and the supporters of waiver to criminal court. This middle-of-the-road approach was sold to liberals as less punitive than a waiver-up approach (for which there was considerable legislative support) and to conservatives as a way of dealing with serious offenders that would also be politically feasible (in light of the governor's threatened veto of waiver bills). Eventually this approach prevailed and the panel issued its report with the recommendation that Family Court retain exclusive jurisdiction over all juveniles but be provided with placement options to increase sanctions for the serious juvenile offender.

Following release of the panel's recommendations, gubernatorial and DFY staff began drafting a governor's bill incorporating the panel's key themes. At the same time, supporters of the waiver-up approach had introduced bills providing for waiver. Once the governor's package was developed, the key parties entered negotiations. This involved the Senate and Assembly leadership, the Senate Committee on Crime and Correction Chair, the Assembly Child Care Committee Chair, as well as the governor's staff and DFY staff. Among these key actors, only the Senate Crime and Correction Committee Chair was opposed to the premise of retaining Family Court jurisdiction. The support of the Assembly and Senate leadership was key, particularly in light of expressions that the rank-and-file legislature preferred the "tougher" waiver-up proposals. While disagreements existed over specific provisions, these were resolved through negotiation, and an "agreed-upon" bill was presented to and passed overwhelmingly by the legislature (these factors are summarized in Figure 6.3).

The law, known as the Juvenile Justice Reform Act of 1976 (JJRA), retained Family Court jurisdiction over all juveniles but provided for differential procedures for dealing with juveniles accused of serious offenses.[5] For juveniles given a restrictive placement, the Act provided a three- or five-year sentence depending on the class of felony (as opposed to the traditional eighteen-month placement) and mandated that DFY keep the youth in secure confinement for a minimum of six or twelve months.

The JJRA represented a historic change in the New York State juvenile justice system. For the first time, the law made offense-based distinctions in procedure and sentencing. Judges were told to consider community protection in addition to the traditional focus on the child's needs. Finally, the law placed limits on DFY's release discretion and mandated that a portion of the placement be in a secure facility.

Juvenile Offender Law of 1978

The apparent consensus on the approach embodied in the JJRA lasted only eighteen months and, indeed, signs of discontent with retaining Family Court jurisdiction were immediately apparent. At the press conference announcing passage of the bill, the Republican Chair of the Senate Crime

Figure 6.3 Influence patterns related to passage of Juvenile Justice Reform Act of 1976, New York State, 1975-1976

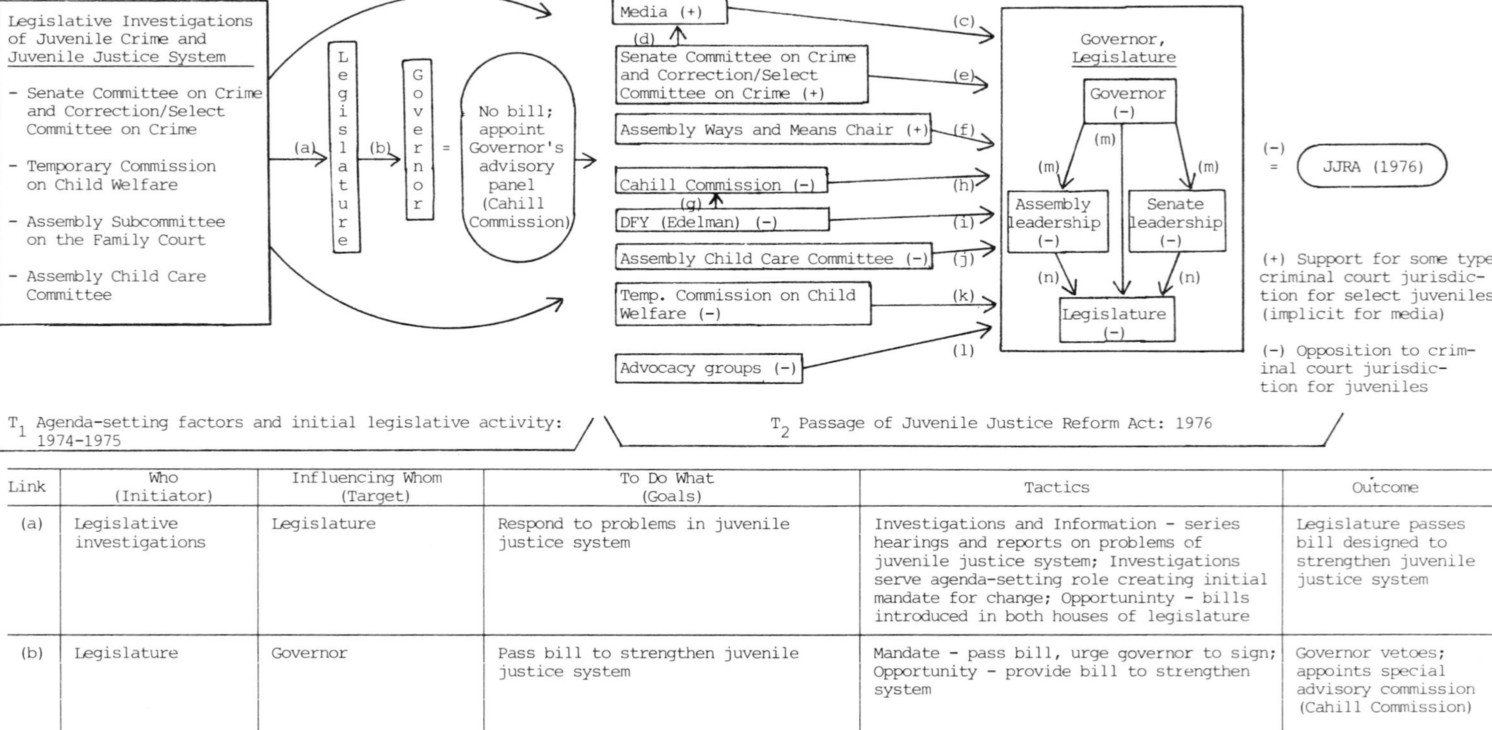

T$_1$ Agenda-setting factors and initial legislative activity: 1974-1975

T$_2$ Passage of Juvenile Justice Reform Act: 1976

Link	Who (Initiator)	Influencing Whom (Target)	To Do What (Goals)	Tactics	Outcome
(a)	Legislative investigations	Legislature	Respond to problems in juvenile justice system	Investigations and Information - series hearings and reports on problems of juvenile justice system; Investigations serve agenda-setting role creating initial mandate for change; Opportuninty - bills introduced in both houses of legislature	Legislature passes bill designed to strengthen juvenile justice system
(b)	Legislature	Governor	Pass bill to strengthen juvenile justice system	Mandate - pass bill, urge governor to sign; Opportunity - provide bill to strengthen system	Governor vetoes; appoints special advisory commission (Cahill Commission)

Figure 6.3 (Continued)

Link	Who (Initiator)	Influencing Whom (Target)	To Do What (Goals)	Tactics	Outcome
(c)	Media	Governor, Legislature	Respond to juvenile crime problem	Mandate - agenda-setting, focus on juvenile crime problem; Criticism - criticize juvenile justice system	Policymakers focus on juvenile crime issue
(d)	Senate Committee on Crime and Correction; Select Committee on Crime	Media	Publicize failing juvenile justice system	Information - provide media with information from committee hearings and investigations	Perceived increase in media attention; unclear whether attributable to committee
(e)	Senate Committee on Crime and Correction; Select Committee on Crime	Governor, Legislature	Pass bill providing waiver to criminal court	Investigations - hearings and reports on failing juvenile justice system; Criticism - criticize system; Opportunity - introduce bills; Mandate - enlist support of media; Information - through committee reports	Compromise bill - no waiver but strengthen Family Court
(f)	Assembly Ways and Means Chair	Governor, Legislature	Pass bill providing waiver to criminal court	Mandate - lend support to waiver bill; Opportunity - introduce waiver bills	Compromise bill - no waiver but strengthen Family Court
(g)	Edelman	Cahill Commission	Adopt position in favor of retaining Family Court jurisdiction but strengthen system	Takes leadership role within commission and offers proposals as compromise between no action and criminal court jurisdiction for select juveniles	Panel recommends retaining Family Court jurisdiction but strengthening response to serious juvenile offenders
(h)	Cahill Advisory Commission	Governor, Legislature	Retain Family Court jurisdiction but strengthen system	Mandate - proposals carry support of influentials, hold hearings, issue findings and recommendations; Information - provide information on system	JJRA largely incorporates panel's recommendations
(i)	DFY/Edelman	Governor, Legislature	Retain Family Court jurisdiction but strengthen system	Mandate - enlist support of influentials (Cahill Commission); Exchanges - reach agreements on specifics of bill through negotiations	JJRA

Figure 6.3 (Continued)

Link	Who (Initiator)	Influencing Whom (Target)	To Do What (Goals)	Tactics	Outcome
(j)	Assembly Child Care Committee	Governor, Legislature	Retain Family Court jurisdiction but strengthen system	Investigations and Information - hearings and reports on problems of juvenile justice system; Mandate - lend committee support to Cahill Commission proposals; Opportunity - introduce bills; Exchanges - reach agreements on specifics of bill through negotiations	JJRA
(k)	Temporary Commission on Child Welfare	Governor, Legislature	Retain Family Court jurisdiction but strengthen system	Investigations and Information - hearings and reports on problems of juvenile justice system; Mandate - lend committee support to Cahill Commission proposals; Exchanges - reach agreements over specifics of bill through negotiations	JJRA
(l)	Advocacy groups	Governor, Legislature	Oppose JJRA	Mandate - express opposition to JJRA through meetings, memoranda, etc.	Little effect, JJRA passed easily
(m)	Governor	Legislative leadership and legislative rank-and-file	Support JJRA, oppose bills providing waiver of juveniles to criminal court	Mandate - enlist support of influentials (Cahill Commission) as well as lend own support; restrict alternative choices by threat of veto; Opportunity - introduce bill; Exchanges - reach agreements over specifics of bills through negotiations	JJRA
(n)	Assembly and Senate leadership	Legislative rank-and-file	Support JJRA, oppose bills providing waiver of juveniles to criminal court	Mandate - lend support which restricts choices of rank-and-file; Exchanges - reach agreement over specifics of bill	JJRA

and Correction Committee, formally a cosponsor of the Act, announced that the Act did not go far enough to address the problem of serious juvenile crime and would not defuse the public clamor for tougher measures. The ranking Republican on the Assembly Child Care Committee called the legislation a "sham," acceptable only because of the governor's threatened veto of waiver-up provisions.

During 1977, several additional reports were issued critical of the juvenile justice system. The Senate Research Service issued a report that once again emphasized the theme that the juvenile justice system neither deterred nor rehabilitated. The Senate Committee on Crime and Correction and the Select Committee on Crime issued joint findings from public hearings that portrayed the juvenile justice system as overburdened by the large number of cases and unwilling to impose sufficiently harsh sentences. Although some amendments to the 1976 Act were passed, and despite the fact that the Senate Committee on Crime and Correction chair continued to introduce waiver-up bills, the 1977 and 1978 legislative sessions ended without significant changes in the juvenile justice system. However, the issue of juvenile crime proved resilient and emerged once again as a key issue during the summer of 1978.

Crucial to keeping juvenile crime a "hot" topic were the actions of the Senate Committee on Crime and Correction (and the corresponding Select Committee on Crime), which continued to hold hearings and issue reports and press releases critical of the Family Court and DFY. The committee also began to explore the idea of placing original jurisdiction of targeted offenses in adult criminal court and allowing for a reverse, or waiver-down, procedure. Additionally, the media continued to focus on the topic of juvenile crime, particularly on several sensational cases involving youths under DFY care. Respondents reported "unrelenting media coverage of juvenile crime" and that the media continued its "virulent campaign on juvenile violence" during 1978. Together, the action of the Senate Committee on Crime and Correction and the media attention ensured that the juvenile violence issue would not easily or quietly disappear.

Of particular importance in subsequent policy development was the fact that 1978 was an election year. As one respondent put it, "everyone saw themselves as vulnerable on the juvenile crime issue." This was particularly so for the Democrats who were accused of blocking the tough waiver proposals of the Senate Committee on Crime and Correction. Furthermore, the topic of crime became a key issue in the gubernatorial race. Perry Duryea, the Republican candidate for governor, portrayed Governor Carey as being soft on crime and made the governor's opposition to the death penalty a key campaign issue. Respondents associated with the Democratic Assembly indicated that the crime issue was seen as not only making Carey vulnerable but as putting some Democratic seats at risk. This concern, that the anticapital punishment and antijuvenile waiver stands were hurting the Democrats, was expressed to the governor by members of the Assembly.

These pressures appeared to erupt while the governor was on a campaign flight. The governor was handed a newspaper that headlined a story about a recently released DFY youth who had murdered two subway passengers. In response to the headline the governor stated, "there was a breakdown of the system, and it is really on the doorstep of the Division for Youth. The blame is squarely on the shoulders of the Department and, therefore, on the shoulders of the Governor" (*New York Times,* June 30, 1978:1). This was a particularly brutal and senseless murder that caused some of the staunchest opponents of juvenile waiver to question their stand. Upon learning that the fifteen-year-old repeat offender could only be held until his twenty-first birthday, the governor announced that he was going to submit legislation that would place this kind of youth in adult court and provide sentences that would ensure such a youth "never walks the streets again." Further, he stated, he would demand legislation that provides "nothing less than a total safeguard that keeps this kind of person out of society" (*New York Times,* June 30, 1978:12).

The governor's abrupt change in position, done without consultation of his key aides or of DFY Director Peter Edelman, moved Carey from the position of key opponent to that of key proponent of adult court jurisdiction for serious juvenile offenders. The governor's change in position also dissolved the coalition that had formed in support of the JJRA (compare changes in position indicated by + and − in Figures 6.3 and 6.4). The Senate leadership (Republican), which had opposed waiver-up provisions, now moved in line with the Senate rank-and-file and the Committee on Crime and Correction in favor of placing original jurisdiction of serious juvenile offenders in criminal court. Likewise, the Assembly leadership (Democratic) moved to support the governor. Attempts by the Assembly Codes Committee chair, the Assembly Child Care Committee chair, Edelman, and some of the governor's own staff to move to a less drastic stance, such as limited waiver-up, were fruitless because the political costs of the governor backing down from his campaign pronouncement were judged too high. As one key Assemblyman stated, "you can bury proposals in Committee, and you can fight the Senate, but you can't fight your own governor."

When key actors from the Senate, Assembly, governor's office, and DFY met to negotiate the specifics of the bill, it was clear that because the governor had already committed to the position favoring original criminal court jurisdiction for serious juvenile offenders there was little for those seeking a less drastic approach to bargain with. The conservatives knew the governor wanted to get credit for a strong bill and was not going to back down.

The law was drafted in a matter of a few days and was presented to the legislature as part of an omnibus crime control bill during an "extraordinary session" of the legislature. The bill, which became known as the Juvenile Offender Law, was distributed to the legislators on their way into session and voted upon in the same session. Because of the short time from drafting to passage, there was no time to examine the effects of the eighteen-month old JJRA, no chance to consider less drastic proposals, and no chance for advocacy groups to mobilize against the bill. As one member of the governor's staff said, "it was an absolutely insane atmosphere for making policy." What the legislators wanted to know was whether the law got tougher. Assured that the law did indeed get tougher, the bill was passed with overwhelming support (these factors are summarized in Figure 6.4).

The basic and fundamental provision of the Juvenile Offender Law is that it places original jurisdiction of thirteen-year-olds committing murder and fourteen- and fifteen-year-olds committing one of a list of the most serious offenses in the adult criminal courts.[6] While the district attorney, grand jury, or judge can waive a juvenile to Family Court, if convicted in adult court, the youth potentially faces among the most severe penalties for juveniles in the United States.[7] Furthermore, the law mandates that a youth convicted as a juvenile offender be confined in a secure DFY facility until release or transfer to the adult Department of Corrections at age twenty-one (although transfer may occur prior to age twenty-one). The provision requiring mandatory confinement in a secure facility is even more stringent than that for adult felons where the Department of Corrections has discretion to move prisoners among different levels of security. Finally, release decisions are placed with the Parole Board rather than DFY.

The passage of the Juvenile Offender Law represented a political defeat for Peter Edelman. As the architect of the JJRA, he had acted, with the governor's support, as the key formulator of juvenile justice policy. With the Juvenile Offender Law, the governor had adopted a policy to which Edelman was diametrically opposed. This shift in policy, coupled with well-publicized criticism of the Edelman administration following several heinous crimes committed by recently released or furloughed DFY youths (see *New York*

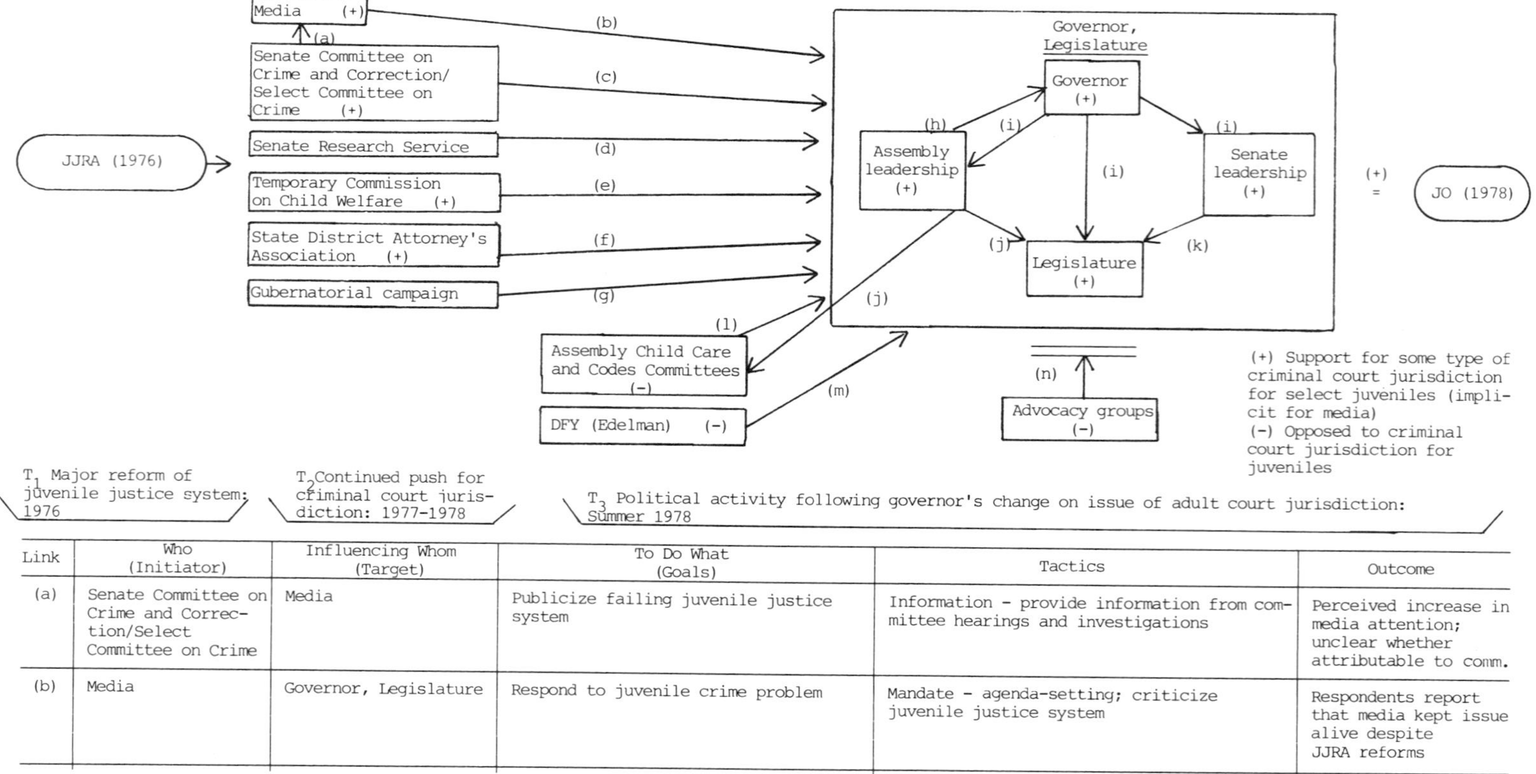

Figure 6.4 Influence patterns related to passage of Juvenile Offender Law of 1978, New York State, 1976–1978

T_1 Major reform of juvenile justice system: 1976

T_2 Continued push for criminal court jurisdiction: 1977–1978

T_3 Political activity following governor's change on issue of adult court jurisdiction: Summer 1978

Link	Who (Initiator)	Influencing Whom (Target)	To Do What (Goals)	Tactics	Outcome
(a)	Senate Committee on Crime and Correction/Select Committee on Crime	Media	Publicize failing juvenile justice system	Information – provide information from committee hearings and investigations	Perceived increase in media attention; unclear whether attributable to comm.
(b)	Media	Governor, Legislature	Respond to juvenile crime problem	Mandate – agenda-setting; criticize juvenile justice system	Respondents report that media kept issue alive despite JJRA reforms

Figure 6.4 (Continued)

Link	Who (Initiator)	Influencing Whom (Target)	To Do What (Goals)	Tactics	Outcome
(c)	Senate Committee on Crime and Correction/Select Committee on Crime	Governor, Legislature	Pass bill providing criminal court jurisdiction for certain juveniles	Mandate - enlist support of media; criticize juvenile justice system; Opportunity - introduce bills; Investigation and Information - through committee hearings and investigations; Exchanges - reach agreements on specifics of bill through negotiations	Kept issue alive; once governor changes position, criminal court jurisdiction enacted
(d)	Senate Research Service	Governor, Legislature	Unspecified	Investigation and report provides information on system; criticize system	Kept issue alive, adds to perception system not adequately dealing with juvenile crime
(e)	Senate Temporary Commission on Child Welfare	Governor, Legislature	Pass bill providing waiver to criminal court	Investigation and hearings provide information on system; criticize system; Exchanges - reach agreements on specifics of bill through negotiations	Kept issue alive; once governor changes position, criminal court jurisdiction enacted
(f)	State District Attorney's (DA) Association	Governor, Legislature	Pass bill providing criminal court jurisdiction for certain juveniles	Support of influential DAs through memos, personal contact	Once governor changes position, criminal court jurisdiction enacted
(h)	Assembly leadership	Governor	Deal with "soft on crime" issue	Express concern party will be hurt by capital punishment and juvenile crime stands	Governor changes position on criminal court jurisdiction for juveniles
(i)	Governor	Legislative leadership and legislative rank-and-file	Pass JO bill	Mandate - goes on record supporting criminal court jurisdiction for select juveniles; enlists support of legislative leadership; Exchanges - reach agreements on specifics of bill through negotiations	JO

Figure 6.4 (Continued)

Link	Who (Initiator)	Influencing Whom (Target)	To Do What (Goals)	Tactics	Outcome
(j)	Assembly leadership	Assembly Codes and Child Care Committees/ Assembly rank-and-file	Pass JO bill	Authority - "we will support governor"; Exchanges - reach agreements on specifics of bill through negotiations	JO
(k)	Senate leadership	Senate rank-and-file	Pass JO bill	Authority - "we will support criminal court jurisdiction bill"; Exchanges - reach agreements on specifics of bill through negotiations	JO
(l)	Assembly Codes and Child Care Comm.	Assembly leadership	Oppose JO bill	Mandate - urge leadership to oppose original jurisdiction in criminal court, offer to support limited waiver-up bill instead	No support - JO passed
(m)	DFY/Edelman	Governor, Legislature	Oppose JO bill	Mandate - urge leadership to oppose original jurisdiction in criminal court, offer to support limited waiver-up bill instead	No support - JO passed
(n)	Advocacy groups	Governor, Legislature	Oppose JO bill	No opportunity to voice opposition, enacted quickly and quietly	JO

Related Factors

Link	What	Influencing Whom	To Do What	How Influencing	Outcome
(g)	Gubernatorial campaign	Governor; Assembly leadership	Deal with crime problem	Mandate - fearful of "soft on crime" issue; need to provide tough provisions	Governor changes position on criminal court jurisdiction for juveniles

Times, July 22, 1978:1), led to Edelman's resignation in December, 1978, following the governor's reelection.

Analysis—Edelman Years

The Edelman years thus witnessed two distinct and divergent policy trends. The first trend was the deinstitutionalization movement, which involved removing all status offenders from the training schools, overall population reductions in noncommunity-based programs, and expansion of community-based programs. This policy trend, although heavily influenced by external factors, was largely the product of the internal initiative of the Edelman administration. The second trend involved the legislative responses to serious juvenile crime embodied in the 1976 and 1978 laws. Particularly in the case of the 1978 Juvenile Offender Law, this involved an externally imposed policy decision on DFY.

The effect of the deinstitutionalization trend is clearly reflected in the population data presented in Table 6.1. Whereas in the early 1970s only 10 percent of DFY youths were housed in community-based settings, by 1977 this figure had increased to 46 percent.

The impact of the policy emphasis on serious juvenile crime also appears to be reflected in the population data. These data indicate that 1978 witnessed a reversal in the trend toward increased reliance on community-based programs as the percent of youths in such programs dropped to 41 percent. Further, as shown in the following chapter, this reversal does not appear to be a mere anomaly but rather the beginning of a trend toward a renewed emphasis on noncommunity-based programs.

The reversal witnessed in the 1978 population data was not attributable to shifts in DFY internal policy but to external factors. The first of these was the impact of the JJRA. However, the direct impact of the law does not appear to have been a major factor as court data indicate that only 101 youths were placed with DFY under JJRA provisions during 1977 and 1978. The main factor appears to have been a shift in judicial sentencing practices among Family Court judges. Although the number of Family Court juvenile related petitions increased by 28 percent from 1973 to 1978, the number of youths placed in DFY increased by 74 percent. Placements increased from 1,032 in 1976, to 1,615 in 1977, to 1,742 in 1978, respectively. Furthermore, while juvenile delinquency petitions increased by 34 percent from 1973 to 1978, delinquency placements increased by 114 percent. These shifts in placement practices are shown in Table 6.2. These data also indicate that the proportion of youths placed who were adjudicated juvenile delinquents as opposed to status offenders, increased from approximately 70 percent between 1973 and 1975 to more than 80 percent between 1976 and 1978. Although available data are insufficient to determine if this shift was merely the product of labelling changes, DFY respondents noted that they believed they were now dealing with a proportionally more difficult group of youths.

The population shift reflected in the increase in youths in noncommunity-based facilities, from 661 in 1977 to 761 in 1978, was thus primarily a product of the increase in the number of youths placed with DFY by the Family Courts, and secondarily an increase of youths in secure care under the provisions of JJRA.

Theoretical Principles

Figure 6.5 illustrates that the PINS deinstitutionalization effort and the further development of community-based alternatives were the products of a range of internal and external, political and economic factors. At the external political level traditional DFY policy on the housing of status offenders had been criticized by child advocacy groups and the subject of several lawsuits. The JJDPA represented a change at the external political and economic levels in that the Act enunciated federal policy advocating removal of status offenders from training schools and provided federal funds for the development of community-based programs. An external economic factor, the state fiscal pressures caused by the New York City fiscal crisis, created an external political shift as the governor and legislature ordered state agencies to make budget cuts. Further, the fiscal pressure created support among the governor and legislature for Edelman's PINS deinstitutionalization legislation which included provisions authorizing DFY to expand community-based programs, to contract with private voluntary agencies for care for DFY youths, and to make DFY youths in foster care eligible for federal funding.

At the internal political level, the change in administrators from Milton Luger to Peter Edelman resulted in a shift in DFY policy in relation to the institutionalization of status offenders. An early goal of the Edelman Administration was to remove all status offenders from the training schools. In a related policy choice, the external fiscal constraints were responded to by closing several training schools. At the internal economic level, federal funds were used to diversify DFY technologies by expanding community-based alternatives.

Table 6.2 Number and percent of Family Court juvenile petitions and number and percent of juveniles placed in New York State juvenile corrections facilities, by adjudication status and year, 1973-78

	Petitions			Placements							
Year	Total	Percent PINS	Percent delinquency	Total	Percent of total petitions	PINS youths	Percent of PINS petitions	Percent of place-ments	Adjudi-cated delin-quent	Percent of delin-quency petitions	Percent of place-ments
1973[a]	23,007	36	64	1,001	4	309	4	31	692	4	69
1974[b]	13,690	33	67	543	4	148	3	27	395	4	73
1975	26,218	33	67	1,044	4	323	4	31	721	4	69
1976	25,778	29	71	1,032	4	170	2	16	862	5	84
1977	27,507	33	67	1,615	6	307	3	19	1,308	7	81
1978	29,335	33	67	1,742	6	263	3	15	1,479	7	85

[a]The 1973 data are for the judicial year July 1, 1973 through June 30, 1974. The 1975-78 data are for the calendar year. [b]The 1974 data are for the six month period July 1, 1974 through December 31, 1974.

Source: Table constructed from data presented in New York State Judicial Conference, Report of the Administrative Board of the Judicial Conference of the State of New York, 1975, pp. 126-129, 136-139; 1975b, pp. 104-107, 114-117; 1976, pp. 148-151, 158-161; 1977, pp. 156-159, 166-169; 1978; 1979, pp. 85, 86, 90, 91.

Figure 6.5 Categorization of factors influencing New York State's juvenile corrections system according to political economy model, 1975-1978

	External		Internal	
	Political	Economic	Political	Economic
PINS deinstitutionalization and development of community-based alternatives	Criticism PINS policy, lawsuits JJDPA 1974 Governor--legislature order budget cuts; legislation authorizes development community-based programs, contracting with private agencies, DFY youths eligible AFDC funding	Federal funding of alternatives (JJDPA) State fiscal pressures	Edelman adopts goal PINS deinstitutionalization and continued expansion community-based programs; takes budget cuts in institutional programs	Use of federal funds to diversify technologies with development placement alternatives
Dealing with serious juvenile crime	JJRA 1976 High-level legislative activity--investigations, bills introduced Media attention Governor's commission JO 1978 Media attention Gubernatorial campaign Governor changes position on criminal court jurisdiction for juveniles	Increased Family Court placements (1977, 1978)	Edelman seeks offense based differentiation of placement alternatives	JJRA places reductions on DFY release discretion

The findings of the importance of these wide-ranging but complementary political and economic factors operating internally and externally to DFY provides strong support for the sequencing principle.

In the case of the second major policy trend, the legislative response to serious juvenile crime, the actual passage of the JJRA was primarily the product of external political factors. These included legislative investigations, media attention, and the governor's Commission on Juvenile Violence. The shape of the legislation was heavily influenced by the leadership role of Peter Edelman (with the support of the governor and key legislative leaders). In order to assess the relevance of the sequencing principle, one must consider the impact of the JJRA on the juvenile corrections system. As noted, 1978 witnessed a population shift in that the proportion of DFY youths in noncommunity-based settings increased. This was considered to have been a product of the JJRA (an external political shift) that affected DFY internal economy by restricting placement options. This was also a product of external economic shifts in the increase in placements from Family Court. Thus, one can identify internal and external, political and economic shifts (with the exception of internal polity) that seem to account for the 1978 population shifts. However, the actual impact of these factors is difficult to assess because of the passage of the Juvenile Offender Law approximately eighteen months after the JJRA went into effect. In order to assess more adequately the impact of these legislative changes on DFY and to assess better the applicability of the sequencing principle, one must examine the post-1978 period. Thus, assessing the sequencing principle in relation to these legislative changes and their impact on DFY is discussed in the next chapter.

The crisis principle receives support in relation to the context in which the Juvenile Offender Law of 1978 was drafted and passed. The years from 1975 to 1978 saw juvenile crime, particularly violent crime, become one of the key political issues in the state. A number of legislative committees seized upon the issue and it became a central issue in the 1978 gubernatorial campaign. As previously noted, the governor's change in position on the adult court jurisdiction issue came during a campaign flight when handed a newspaper headline about a particularly heinous crime committed by a recently released DFY youth. The crisis atmosphere is also suggested by the findings of heightened coverage in the *New York Times* (see next section) and by the process in which the law was enacted. Respondents described the drafting process as "an insane atmosphere for making policy." Key professionals, such as the DFY director were, in effect, excluded from the legislative process. In the case of Peter Edelman, this was particularly ironic because in 1975 the governor had vetoed legislation on the basis that Edelman had not been involved. In terms of legislative debate, legislators were described as being unconcerned with anything but the question of whether this bill "got tough." In short, the passage of the Juvenile Offender Law was seen as the product of crisis politics.

On the other hand, the JJRA did not seem to be the product of a crisis. While serious juvenile crime was a key political issue in 1976, the political response was more akin to a rational decisionmaking process as the issue was studied, alternatives were debated, and the final product represented a pluralistic compromise.

The PINS deinstitutionalization effort also does not appear to be the product of a crisis. Edelman administratively removed PINS youths from the training schools and the legislature formally codified the decision with little controversy or opposition.

Interestingly, state budget pressures caused by the New York City fiscal crisis were an important factor in Edelman's efforts to continue the move away from institutions and toward community-based programs. As in the 1971 fiscal crisis, budget cuts were used to promote the deinstitutionalization policy goal. As noted in Chapter Five, the theoretical importance of this type of crisis may best be understood in relation to the sequencing principle. The fiscal crisis is an external economic factor that may affect external political support (e.g., the governor's and legislature's support for closing institutions) for internal policy choices. The ultimate product is a change in internal technology, i.e., decreasing reliance on institutions. These findings indicate that although crises may be important factors in system change, they do not appear to be a necessary cause of change.

Analysis of the developments during the Edelman years provides support for the third principle, the importance of key swing groups. In the early 1970s, pressure for removing PINS from the training schools was blocked by Milton Luger. Luger opposed making placement decisions on the basis of legal labels. Further, he argued that the result of such a policy would be racially segregated facilities because youths adjudicated delinquent were disproportionately Black. When Edelman, who favored removal of PINS, replaced Luger, status offenders were administratively removed from the training schools. Edelman's appointment swung the balance of forces to the position favoring PINS deinstitutionalization.

The key swing group principle is also supported when analyzing the shift from the approach embodied in the JJRA with that of the Juvenile Offender Law of 1978. In both instances, liberal and conservative forces were opposed on the issue of retaining exclusive Family Court jurisdiction for juveniles. Governor Carey's promised veto of any bill that would place juveniles in adult court was considered a key to the passage of the JJRA. The governor's abrupt change of position in 1978 was a clear example of a key swing actor. His change in position dissolved the Liberal Interest Coalition and precluded any effective opposition to the passage of what became the Juvenile Offender Law.

Miller, Ohlin, and Coates's (1977) fourth principle holds that the Conservative and Liberal Interest Coalitions will respond to changes in the juvenile corrections system. Three predictions can be made from this principle. The coalition whose interests are not reflected in policy and program is likely to attempt to discredit the current system. The coalition whose interests are reflected in current policy and program ". . . is likely to slack off and simply do nothing, even to the point of letting down its defenses altogether" (1977:170). The coalition whose interests are reflected in current policy and program is also likely to respond with extreme tactics when it finds its control over policy is threatened. Extreme tactics are defined as the attempt to assert sole dominance over policy and to reject the Formal Decisionmaking Group's role in policymaking.

The first point is supported. As noted at the end of Chapter Five, custodial interests had been thwarted during the Luger years. The appointment of Edelman, who advocated the deinstitutionalization/community-based ideology, reinforced this policy direction. Custodial interest groups responded by becoming increasingly active and questioning the legitimacy of the DFY administration. Dormant interests within the legislature responded with a series of investigations of serious juvenile crime and the juvenile justice system. The Family Court and DFY were criticized as too soft and as failing to protect the community. These groups also seized upon the findings of social science research that questioned the rehabilitative model. Further, respondents noted that traditional custodial personnel from the training schools leaked information on escapes and crimes committed by DFY youths to the conservative legislative groups conducting investigations.

Thus, it does appear that the "out-group" of this period, the Conservative Interest Coalition, did become increasingly active and did question the legitimacy of current juvenile corrections policy. One problem in interpreting this, however, is separating it from nationwide developments evident in the increasing focus on serious juvenile crime. This issue is best addressed by considering the applicability of the principle over the entire timeframe, as in Chapter Eight.

The second point is that the group controlling policy tends to "slack-off" from political involvement. This does not appear to have occurred during the Edelman years. Indeed, most felt that Edelman increased DFY's role in state-level decisionmaking. Edelman personally played a leadership role in the PINS deinstitutionalization effort and in building the coalition in support of the JJRA. Edelman's administration also played a very active role in locating federal funds used for the development of the community-based program. Edelman also worked to maintain the coalition among the governor's office and party and committee leaders opposed to criminal court jurisdiction. These efforts were successful through the 1977 and 1978 regular legislative sessions but, as has been noted, the coalition fell apart with the governor's change in position. Thus, there does not appear to be support for the proposition that the Liberal Interest Coalition, having gained control of policy during the Luger and Edelman Administrations, let down its defenses. Finally, no evidence is found that the Edelman Administration reacted to the threatened loss of control over policy with extreme tactics.

The fifth principle focuses on the short- and long-run effects of extreme tactics. As previously noted, extreme tactics involve the attempt of an interest coalition to assume sole power over a particular issue or issue area. The usurpation of power consequently repudiates the power of the Formal Decisionmaking Group. While such tactics may promote short-term change they carry long-term negative consequences. The repudiation of the Formal Decisionmaking Group tends to lead to a realignment between the Formal Decisionmaking Group and the opposition interest coalition.

One distinction between the Massachusetts and New York State systems in terms of the deinstitutionalization effort is that the change in Massachusetts was an abrupt and wholesale shift, while in New York State the change involved a more gradual trend. Related to the distinction, whereas in Massachusetts Jerome Miller was found to have employed extreme tactics (closing the training schools while the legislature was out of session, public repudiation of a state legislator who was investigating the juvenile corrections system), in New York State the key change agents, Luger and Edelman, proceeded more gradually. Both directors, and particularly Edelman, actively worked to enlist the support of key decisionmakers within the governor's office and the legislature. One issue where disagreement arose between Edelman and elements within the legislature was the issue of how to deal with serious juvenile crime. This issue was resolved through compromise and negotiation and the JJRA emerged as an "agreed-upon" bill. Thus, in both the deinstitutionalization effort and the initial response to the question of serious juvenile crime, the change agents initiated their programs without the use of extreme tactics.

The tactics employed by the Conservative Interest Coalition following the passage of the JJRA may be examples of extreme tactics. Although formally sponsors of the Act, several key legislators quickly denounced the law as a "sham" that did not go far enough in protecting the public. These legislators rejected the compromise legislation and continued to criticize DFY and the Family Court, conduct investigations, and introduce bills to place juveniles in criminal court. Eventually, of course, the Juvenile Offender Law embodied this type of approach. Thus, if these tactics were considered extreme, they were also effective. Further, this was not merely a short-term change but rather a long-term change. It remains to be seen whether longer range effects will result. From the theory, a backlash against the Conservative Interest Coalition in the post-Juvenile Offender Law years is predicted.

Assessing this theoretical principle is difficult because of the absence of extreme tactics. While fundamental change occurred in the deinstitutionalization area, these changes were more gradual and more the result of coalition building than was the case in Massachusetts. To a large extent, this principle remains untested in the New York State case. However, at least two points are suggested. Extreme tactics do not appear to be a necessary ingredient in significant policy change. Second, whether groups utilizing these tactics are dismissed from consideration in further policy issues is not clear.

The Role of the Media

As noted throughout this chapter, a number of factors were considered by respondents to have influenced the passage of the JJRA and the Juvenile Offender Law of 1978. One factor, the role of the media, was interesting due to the unanimity with which policy participants mentioned it. Briefly, newspapers, particularly the large New York City papers, were seen as playing a key role in the passage of these legislative acts by their elevated and prolonged attention on the problem of juvenile crime during the mid-1970s. Respondents spoke of "unrelenting media coverage of juvenile crime" and accused the press of engaging in a "virulent campaign on juvenile violence." The idea of the media influencing crime oriented legislation was suggested in a number of studies reviewed in Chapter Two. However, with the exception of Berk, Brackman, and Lesser's (1977) study of changes in the California penal code, most of the findings are based on anecdotal observations. The following sections, based on a content analysis of the *New York Times*, attempts to explore further this possible relationship between the media and juvenile justice policy.

METHODOLOGY AND DATA

The media data come from a content analysis of articles about juvenile crime and juvenile justice culled from the *New York Times Annual Index* from 1968 to 1984. Initially, consideration was given to an analysis of several New York City and upstate newspapers. However, in the interviews, the perceived media effect clearly was isolated to the impact of the large New York City newspapers, primarily the *New York Times,* the *Daily News,* and the *New York Post.* The choice of the *New York Times* was dictated by two facts, one methodological the other theoretical. The first is simply the availability of the *Annual Index.* The second is that Berk, Brackman, and Lesser's (1977) findings suggest that a prominent newspaper such as the *New York Times* might be particularly influential with elites such as state-level politicians.

The intent in the content analysis was to include all articles dealing with (1) New York State juvenile crime incidents; (2) juvenile crime as a general topic; or (3) some aspect of the juvenile justice system. One area of possible ambiguity arose in relation to articles describing specific crime incidents in which the age of the perpetrators was unclear. To be included, the article had to mention that at least one of the suspects was younger than age sixteen (New York State's traditional age of criminal responsibility), or have described the perpetrators as youths, juveniles, kids, teen gang members, etc. Only New York State crime incidents were included; however, stories on juvenile justice developments with a nationwide impact were included (e.g., Supreme Court decisions).[8]

The selection of juvenile crime/juvenile justice articles provided the first measure of importance for the analysis—the frequency of such articles over the seventeen-year period. Once articles were chosen, several different variables, selected primarily on the basis of policymaker comments, were coded.[9]

ISSUES RELATED TO MEDIA COVERAGE

As mentioned, respondents were nearly unanimous in stressing the role of New York City newspapers in the passage of this legislation. The newspapers, by increasing the amount of attention on juvenile crime, highlighting sensational juvenile crimes, and emphasizing the failings of the juvenile justice system, were considered key in arousing public interest in the juvenile crime issue and pressuring elected officials to respond to the juvenile crime problem.

The *New York Times* data are most useful in examining the proposition that heightened media attention was a factor in the legislative changes. A key question is whether press coverage actually increased during the mid-1970s. On the basis of interviews with key policymakers, one would expect a dramatic increase in the number of juvenile crime articles during the mid-1970s. However, an alternative hypothesis is that the policymakers' perception of increased media attention was due to their heightened awareness of media coverage during a time of personal involvement in the juvenile crime issue. According to this hypothesis, the perceived increase is an artifact of heightened awareness as opposed to any real increase in reporting.

A second question is whether the increased media attention preceded passage of the JJRA. While such a finding cannot prove causality, the absence of such a finding would raise serious doubts as to the causal role of the media.

The next set of questions involve the nature or characteristics of the articles. Several respondents reported that a precursor to the increased media focus on juvenile crime was a reported upsurge in teen gang activity in the early 1970s. If respondents are correct, one should see an increase in articles reporting gang involvement either preceding or accompanying a general increase in juvenile crime articles. Respondents also noted that during the mid-1970s, the media portrayed juvenile crime as a constantly rising phenomenon, called for the enactment of policies to crackdown on juvenile crime, and criticized the system as too lenient and incapable of controlling the problem. Thus, several issues to be considered are whether there were increased reports of rising juvenile crime, increased policy recommendations and criticisms, and whether the relative distribution of crime control versus youth rights orientations changed over the course of this time period.

FINDINGS ON MEDIA COVERAGE

The first research question relates to the level of reporting of juvenile crime and juvenile justice over time. Table 6.3 clearly demonstrates a dramatically elevated level of reporting during the years 1972 to 1978. The number of juvenile crime related articles rose from levels of forty to seventy per year during the 1968 to 1971 period, to 107 to 155 during the 1972 to 1978 period. Since 1978, the number of articles declined to approximately the same level as the 1968 to 1971 period. These data clearly indicate that in relation to the *New York Times,* policymakers were indeed reporting an actual increase in the amount of newspaper coverage. These impressions were not based solely on respondents' heightened awareness of the issue.

Table 6.3 Number of New York Times articles on juvenile crime and juvenile justice and selected characteristics of articles, by year, 1968-84

| | | | Characteristics of article | | | | | |
| | | | Describing juvenile crime incident | | Mentions youth gang involvement | | Mentions increasing juvenile crime | |
Year	Articles	Percent distribution of articles	Number	Percent of total articles	Number	Percent of total articles	Number	Percent of total articles
1968	39	3	25	64	3	8	1	3
1969	48	3	21	44	6	12	2	4
1970	45	3	31	69	5	11	1	2
1971	68	5	37	54	12	18	4	6
1972	107	7	60	56	38	36	7	6
1973	155	11	100	64	37	24	6	4
1974	130	9	92	71	27	21	9	7
1975	122	8	59	48	8	7	8	7
1976	132	9	63	48	21	16	2	2
1977	126	9	51	40	11	9	4	3
1978	114	8	56	49	6	5	0	0
1979	87	6	51	59	4	5	0	0
1980	60	4	45	75	5	8	1	2
1981	63	4	31	49	1	2	1	2
1982	69	5	40	58	1	1	1	1
1983	52	4	38	73	8	15	0	0
1984	37	2	23	63	0	0	1	3
Total	1,454	100	823	57	193	13	48	3

A second issue is whether the increased media attention preceded the 1976 and 1978 legislative acts. Table 6.3 demonstrates that media attention increased in 1971 and 1972 and peaked in 1973. Media coverage remained at high levels, more than 100 articles per year, until 1979.[10] Thus, the media as causal factor thesis remains plausible on the basis of the time precedence criterion.

The next set of issues relate to characteristics of the articles. Table 6.3 indicates that the number of articles reporting specific juvenile crime incidents roughly paralleled changes in the total number of articles. One finding is that the gap between total articles and reports of specific crime incidents was widest during the 1975 to 1978 period. This suggests an increased media focus on juvenile crime in general (as opposed to specific incidents) and the juvenile justice system during this period. Table 6.3 also shows an increase in articles mentioning youth gangs during 1972 to 1974. This is consistent with policymaker statements of a media reported upsurge in youth gang activity in the early 1970s. The 1972 to 1975 period also witnessed an increase in news reports of rising juvenile crime, although the small numbers raise questions as to the significance of this variable.

Table 6.4 presents data relating to articles expressing policy recommendations for the juvenile justice system. The same general pattern emerges with the number of such articles peaking during the 1973 to 1978 period. In terms of the type of recommendations, Table 6.4 indicates that the number of crime control recommendations, for example, "Senator urges tougher sentences for youths," increased during the 1975 to 1978 period. On the other hand, youth rights recommendations, for example, "citizens groups urges juveniles be diverted from justice system," remained comparatively stable during the seventeen-year period.

In terms of articles expressing criticism of the system, Table 6.5 indicates a similar pattern with the number of such articles peaking during the years from 1972 to 1976. Crime control criticisms, for example, "police officials claim Family Court too lenient," which were rare throughout the entire period (N=29), were virtually nonexistent from 1968 to 1971 and from 1979 to 1984. Youth rights criticisms, e.g., "Legal Aid Society criticizes juvenile corrections officials for excessive use of solitary confinement," were more constant throughout the overall timeframe reaching peaks in 1973 and 1975.

These data indicate that the *New York Times's* coverage of juvenile crime and juvenile justice changed both in magnitude and character during the period from 1968 to 1984. Table 6.6 vividly demonstrates these changes, presenting these data with the variable year trichotomized into three periods, 1968 to

Table 6.4 Number of New York Times articles on juvenile crime and juvenile justice and number of articles expressing policy recommendations, by type of recommendation and year, 1968-84

| | | Total | | | Articles expressing policy recommendations | | | | | |
| | | | | | Crime control recommendations | | | Youth rights recommendations | | |
Year	Articles	Number	Percent of total articles	Percent distribution[a]	Number[b]	Percent of total articles	Percent of total recommendations	Number[b]	Percent of total articles	Percent of total recommendations
1968	39	1	3	(c)	0	0	0	1	2	100
1969	48	6	12	3	2	4	33	2	4	33
1970	45	6	13	3	1	2	17	2	4	33
1971	68	9	13	4	0	0	0	5	7	56
1972	107	12	11	6	1	1	8	6	6	50
1973	155	21	14	11	0	0	0	14	9	67
1974	130	13	10	7	5	4	38	3	2	23
1975	122	23	19	12	10	8	44	6	5	26
1976	132	30	23	15	13	10	43	7	5	23
1977	126	22	18	11	11	9	50	4	3	18
1978	114	22	19	11	10	9	46	2	2	9
1979	87	10	12	5	2	2	20	5	6	50
1980	60	6	10	3	1	2	17	1	2	17
1981	63	5	8	2	2	3	40	3	5	60
1982	69	8	12	4	0	0	0	2	3	25
1983	52	1	2	(c)	0	0	0	0	0	0
1984	37	3	8	2	0	0	0	3	8	100
Total	1,454	198	14	100	58	4	29	66	4	33

[a] Percents may not add to 100 due to rounding.
[b] Crime control recommendations and youth rights recommendations do not sum to the total number of articles expressing policy recommendations because a number of articles were classified as either mixed, i.e., expressing both perspectives, or ambiguous.
[c] Less than one percent.

Table 6.5 **Number of New York Times articles on juvenile crime and juvenile justice and number of articles expressing criticisms of the juvenile justice system, by type of criticism and year, 1968–84**

| | | | | | Articles expressing criticism of juvenile justice system | | | | | |
| | | Total | | | Crime control criticisms | | | Youth rights criticisms | | |
Year	Articles	Number	Percent of total articles	Percent distribution[a]	Number[b]	Percent of total articles	Percent of total criticisms	Number[b]	Percent of total articles	Percent of total criticisms
1968	39	2	5	1	0	0	0	2	5	100
1969	48	10	21	6	0	0	0	4	8	40
1970	45	3	7	2	0	0	0	3	7	100
1971	68	8	12	5	1	1	12	6	9	75
1972	107	16	15	10	4	4	25	8	7	50
1973	155	23	15	14	2	1	9	17	11	74
1974	130	12	9	7	7	5	58	2	2	17
1975	122	18	15	11	2	2	11	11	9	61
1976	132	16	12	10	4	3	25	6	4	38
1977	126	12	10	7	3	2	25	4	3	33
1978	114	10	9	6	2	2	20	2	2	20
1979	87	4	5	2	0	0	0	4	4	100
1980	60	9	15	6	2	3	22	2	3	22
1981	63	5	8	3	1	2	20	3	5	60
1982	69	6	9	4	1	1	17	4	6	67
1983	52	5	10	3	0	0	0	1	1	20
1984	37	4	11	2	0	0	0	3	2	75
Total	1,454	163	11	100	29	2	18	82	6	50

[a]Percents may not add to 100 due to rounding.
[b]Crime control criticisms and youth rights criticisms do not sum to the total number of articles expressing criticisms because a number of articles were classified as either mixed, i.e., expressing both perspectives, or ambiguous.

1971, 1972 to 1978, 1979 to 1984; policy recommendations or criticisms; crime control recommendations or criticisms; and youth rights recommendations or criticisms are collapsed into single variables.[11] This table indicates that the *New York Times's* coverage of juvenile crime and juvenile justice fell into three distinct periods. During the 1968 to 1971 and 1979 to 1984 periods, coverage was approximately fifty to sixty articles per year, with about ten articles per year expressing policy recommendations or criticisms. Virtually no articles expressing crime control recommendations or criticisms were run and about five articles per year were run expressing youth rights recommendations or criticisms. The third period, from 1972 to 1978, was quite different from either of these two periods. During the 1972 to 1978 period, the number of articles more than doubled to 126 per year. Furthermore, the number of articles expressing policy recommendations or criticisms tripled to thirty per year. The number of crime control and youth rights recommendations and criticisms both increased during these years and were expressed in approximately the same number of articles per year.

These data clearly support the impressionistic observations of New York State juvenile justice policymakers. Between 1972 and 1978, the *New York Times* appears to have seized upon juvenile crime and juvenile justice as a key issue and shifted its reporting practices to reflect this importance. The fact that the periods preceding and following the 1972 to 1978 period are relatively similar seems to indicate that these data do not merely reflect a trend in reporting but rather a discrete period in which this issue was accorded prominence.

DISCUSSION OF MEDIA'S ROLE

One of the early developments considered to have been important in the ultimate policy developments embodied in the JJRA and the Juvenile Offender Law of 1978 were the investigations of several legislative committees beginning in 1974. This newfound legislative interest was perceived by policymakers to be in response to a media reported upsurge in gang related youth crime. Continued media attention, coupled with the investigations of the Senate Committee on Crime and Correction, Select Committee on Crime, and the Assembly Subcommittee on the Family Court, led to further political activity as the Senate Temporary Commission on Child Welfare, the Assembly Child Care Committee, and the governor's blue ribbon panel on juvenile violence were created and began to study and offer policy proposals on the issue of serious juvenile crime. The culmination of this activity was the passage of the JJRA.

Table 6.6 **Number and rate of <u>New York Times</u> articles on juvenile crime and juvenile justice and number and rate expressing policy recommendations or criticisms of system, by type of recommendation or criticism and time period, 1968-84**

Time period	Articles	Rate per year	Articles expressing recommendations or criticisms		Articles expressing crime control recommendations or criticisms		Articles expressing youth rights recommendations or criticisms	
			Number	Rate per year	Number[a]	Rate per year	Number[a]	Rate per year
1968-1971	200	50	41	10	4	1	22	6
1972-1978	886	126	212	30	71	10	77	11
1979-1984	368	61	57	10	8	1	28	5
Total	1,454	86	310	18	83	5	127	7

[a]Crime control recommendations and criticisms and youth rights recommendations and criticisms do not sum to the total number of articles expressing recommendations or criticisms because a number of articles were classified as either mixed, i.e., expressing both perspectives, or ambiguous.

While policymakers believed the media were important in the development and passage of the 1976 law, many believed the real impact was in relation to the 1978 Juvenile Offender Law. What surprised a number of respondents was that passage of the 1976 law did not dissipate pressure to further toughen state statutes. Because the 1976 law was based on the recommendations of the governor's blue ribbon panel and supported by the governor, leaders of both houses of the legislature, the director of the state's juvenile corrections agency, and leaders of most of the relevant legislative committees, most respondents felt the law would put the juvenile crime issue to rest. However, policymakers noted that rather than the media shifting its focus to other issues, as expected by policymakers based on experience in other issue areas, the media continued what was termed a "relentless" and "virulent" campaign against juvenile crime. While the data indicate a slight decline from the peak year of 1973, the level remained very high compared to the 1968 to 1971 and 1979 to 1984 periods (see note 10). The continued media attention, combined with the activity of the law-and-order faction within the Senate and gubernatorial election year politics of 1978 were seen as key to keeping the juvenile crime issue on the political agenda and ultimately pressuring the governor to endorse legislation placing juveniles in adult criminal court (something the governor had vowed not to do). Only after passage of the 1978 law did the media return to earlier levels of reporting on juvenile crime and juvenile justice.

In creating pressure for policy change, the media appears to have acted in what political scientists term an agenda-setting role (Cobb and Elder, 1983). That is, the *New York Times*, and according to policymakers the other major New York City newspapers, placed the issue of juvenile crime on the formal policy agenda. Media coverage focused attention on the typically anonymous juvenile justice system and created pressure for change.

One key feature of agenda setting is the process of issue expansion (Cobb and Elder, 1983). This refers to the process whereby an issue moves beyond the control of the limited number of decisionmakers typically responsible for a particular issue area, to the agenda of the entire political decisionmaking body. The movement of the issue beyond the more limited group of policymakers, typically referred to as a policy subsystem, is usually necessary for anything other than incremental decisionmaking. When an issue moves beyond the subsystem to the more formal political system, the potential for fundamental change arises. In New York State, the media appears to have played a key role in this issue expansion process. Early media attention on youth gangs led to initial legislative investigations. Continued media coverage and these early investigations led to further political investigation and moved the issue beyond the control of the policy subsystem (administrators of the state's juvenile corrections system, legislative and gubernatorial staff) and placed it on the agenda of the more generalized political system. Once the issue moved from the policy subsystem to the larger political system, the opportunity for fundamental as opposed to incremental change was created. The radical departure from traditional juvenile justice policy embodied in the Juvenile Offender Law was the result.

Summary

The Edelman years thus witnessed several distinct and divergent policy trends. Status offenders were removed from the training schools and a general shift toward increased reliance on community-based programming occurred. Additionally, the issue of serious juvenile crime became a key political issue resulting in two pieces of legislation that fundamentally altered New York State's traditional approach to juvenile justice. In viewing these divergent policy trends it is interesting that, although supported by different interests, they share one trait in common. They both represent attempts to discriminate placement decisions, i.e., correctional technology, on the basis of legal distinctions (PINS youths, juvenile delinquents, serious juvenile offenders). This, of course, represents a fundamental shift from traditional juvenile processing based on assessed youth needs.

As a final point, Figure 6.6 summarizes the changes among the key set of relationships. While these points have been addressed, this figure indicates that a shift in control over policy occurred from the Edelman Administration to the Formal Decisionmaking Group. Further, conservative or custodial interests found expression in the 1978 legislation promulgated by the Formal Decisionmaking Group. The impact of these changes is the subject of the following chapter.

Figure 6.6 Summary of changes in key relationships of juvenile corrections arena, Edelman years

Relationship	Beginning period (1975-76)	Ending period (1978)
People Processing Relationship	Status offenders removed from training schools. Continued development of community-based alternatives and decline in number and proportion of youths in noncommunity-based settings.	Expansion community-based programs halted. Slight increase of youths in non-community settings. Planned expansion of secure facility component.
Relationship among Interest groups	Edelman key formulator of juvenile corrections policy.	Formal Decisionmaking Group assumes control over policy in relation to issue of serious juvenile crime. Represents defeat for Edelman and renewed emphasis on use of institutions for juvenile offenders.
Conservative Interest Coalition	Custodial interests increasingly active. Discontent with policy direction receives outlet in legislative investigations.	Custodial interests ascendant in passage of Juvenile Offender Law.
Liberal Interest Coalition	Liberal interests expressed in policy direction of expanded community-based program, removal status offenders from training schools, and decline non-community-based population.	Liberal interests lose control over policy in relation to issue of serious juvenile crime.

Building the Secure Component and Consolidating the System: The Hall and Dunston Years (1979–1984)

The Juvenile Offender Law had a clear impact on the juvenile corrections system in New York State. While the population of secure centers had slightly increased in 1977 and 1978, following passage of the Juvenile Justice Reform Act of 1976, the years from 1978 to 1982 saw a substantial increase in the population of the secure centers. In addition to, and as a partial consequence of, the growth in the secure centers, an overall increase in the total residential population and the noncommunity-based population was evidenced. At the same time, a decline in the proportion of youths placed in community-based settings was seen. Table 7.1 illustrates these trends. In 1977, the proportion of youths in community-based settings peaked at 46 percent. By 1984, this figure had dropped to 28 percent. Further, the proportion of youths in the secure center component of the noncommunity-based population had increased from 10 percent in 1977 to 27 percent in 1984.

The rise in the secure facility population was largely attributable to the placement of Juvenile Offenders with DFY.[1] The unique feature of the Juvenile Offender Law, and that which differentiated this law from the JJRA in terms of impact on DFY, was that whereas the 1976 law mandated secure confinement for six- to twelve-month periods, the Juvenile Offender Law mandated such placements for the duration of the youth's stay with DFY. DFY was given no discretion or ability to move Juvenile Offenders to any of its nonsecure facilities. Hence, the growth in DFY's secure center population was the product of an externally imposed statutory provision coupled with external decisions related to the actual court processing of these youths. Table 7.2 presents data on the number of youths sentenced as Juvenile Offenders

Table 7.1 New York State Division for Youth year-end residential population, by year and facility classification, 1976-84

Year	Total residential population[a]	Noncommunity-based population[b]		Community-based population[c]		Secure facility population[d]	
		Number	Percent	Number	Percent	Number	Percent
1976	1,428	879	62	549	38	112	8
1977	1,214	661	54	553	46	126	10
1978	1,294	761	59	533	41	154	12
1979	1,336	825	62	511	38	162	12
1980	1,374	911	66	463	34	204	15
1981	1,478	1,033	70	445	30	341	23
1982	1,803	1,332	74	471	26	545	30
1983	1,745	1,277	73	468	27	490	28
1984	1,702	1,219	72	483	28	468	27

[a]Consists of the noncommunity-based and community-based populations.
[b]Includes programs classified as Level I secure centers, Level II limited secure centers, Level III centers, centers, and camps. Note that the separately enumerated secure facilities are included in this category.
[c]Includes urban homes, youth development centers, and short-term adolescent resident treatment centers. Does not include foster care because annual data were not available.
[d]The secure centers are included in the category noncommunity-based programs.

Source: Data provided by New York State Division for Youth, Statistics and Survey Unit.

who were placed with DFY. These data indicate that the number of such youths increased from 1978 to 1982. The number decreased in 1983 and 1984 as the number of youths arrested under Juvenile Offender charges decreased.

Table 7.2 Number of Juvenile Offender arrests and number and percent sentenced to Division for Youth care, 1978-84

Year	Arrests	Sentenced to DFY	
		Number	Percent
1978[a]	581	2	0.3
1979	1,583	84	5
1980	1,485	164	11
1981	1,613	231	14
1982	1,421	311	22
1983	1,263	274	22
1984	1,266	192	15

[a]Sept. 1, 1978 to Dec. 31, 1978.

Source: New York State Division of Criminal Justice Services, Juvenile Offenders in New York State: 1983 Report, p. 6; and data provided by New York State Division of Criminal Justice Services and New York State Division for Youth, Statistics and Survey Unit.

In addition to the increase in youths processed under the Juvenile Offender Law, an increase was found in the rate of placement of juvenile delinquents from the Family Courts. As Table 7.3 indicates, although the number of Family Court delinquency and status offense petitions was relatively constant from 1975 to 1982, the number of youths placed in DFY substantially increased during these years. In 1975 and 1976, slightly more than 1,000 youths were placed in DFY. This represented 4 percent of the Family Court petitions. In 1977 and 1978, more than 1,600 youths were placed representing 6 percent of all petitions. The following years, 1979 and 1980, saw a decline to 1,230 (4 percent) and 1,404 (5 percent) youths placed. Placements then increased in 1981 and 1982 to 1,632 and 1,897 representing 6 percent and 7 percent of petitions, respectively. Finally, in 1983 and 1984, the number of petitions and placements declined, although the rate of placement remained at 6 percent and 7 percent, respectively.

Table 7.3 Number and percent of Family Court juvenile petitions and number and percent of juveniles placed in New York State juvenile corrections facilities, by adjudication status and year, 1975–84

	Petitions			Placements							
Year	Total	Percent PINS	Percent delinquency	Total	Percent of total petitions	PINS youths	Percent of PINS petitions	Percent of place-ments	Adjudi-cated delin-quent	Percent of delin-quency petitions	Percent of place-ments
1975	26,218	33	67	1,044	4	323	4	31	721	4	69
1976	25,778	29	71	1,032	4	170	2	16	862	5	84
1977	27,507	33	67	1,615	6	307	3	19	1,308	7	81
1978	29,335	33	67	1,742	6	263	3	15	1,479	7	85
1979	27,898	36	64	1,230	4	217	2	18	1,013	6	82
1980	26,717	35	65	1,404	5	183	2	13	1,221	7	87
1981	26,591	37	63	1,632	6	201	2	12	1,431	9	88
1982	26,007	38	62	1,897	7	143	1	8	1,754	11	92
1983	24,756	40	60	1,489	6	110	1	7	1,379	9	93
1984	18,121	44	56	1,296	7	100	1	8	1,196	12	92

Source: Table constructed from data presented in New York State Judicial Conference, Report of the Administrative Board of the Judicial Conference of the State of New York, 1976, pp. 148-151, 158-161; 1977, pp. 156-159, 166-169; 1978; 1979, pp. 85, 86, 90, 91; 1980, pp. 83, 84, 88, 89; 1981, pp. 94, 95, 99, 100; 1982, pp. 97, 98, 102, 103; 1983, pp. 160-163, 167-170; 1984, pp. A-32-A-35, A-44-A-47; 1985, Tables A-22, A-23, A-30, A-31.

Table 7.3 also indicates a change in the legal status of youths placed with DFY. The number of PINS youths placed with DFY has steadily declined from approximately 300 in the mid-1970s to 100 in 1984. The percentage of PINS petitions resulting in a DFY placement has declined from 3 percent to 1 percent during these years. The increase in overall placements to DFY is the result of an increase in the number and percent of juvenile delinquents placed. The number of delinquents placed has increased from 721 and 862 in 1975 and 1976 to more than 1,000 in all subsequent years. The percentage of delinquency petitions resulting in placement has increased from 4 and 5 percent in 1975 and 1976 to between 9 percent and 12 percent from 1981 to 1984. As a result of these Family Court practices the proportion of youths placed with DFY who are classified as juvenile delinquents as opposed to status offenders, has significantly increased. More than 90 percent of youths placed by the Family Courts with DFY between 1982 and 1984 were juvenile delinquents. This compares with 55 percent and 69 percent in 1970 and 1975, respectively.[2] Further, this percent is even higher if one includes youths processed in criminal court as Juvenile Offenders.

The years from 1978 to 1982 thus saw an increase in the rate of placement of youths with DFY. This increase was the product of the criminal courts processing of youths under the Juvenile Offender Law and the increased number and percent of juvenile delinquents placed by the Family Courts. These increases more than offset the decline in the number and percent of status offenders placed with DFY. Not until 1983 and 1984 was a decline in these placement trends evidenced.

Hall Years (1979–1982)

For DFY, the years following passage of the Juvenile Offender Law involved a concerted effort to respond to these externally imposed program inputs. The task of responding to these forces fell to Frank Hall, who replaced Peter Edelman as DFY director in February 1979. Hall, who had previously been Commissioner of the Massachusetts Adult Corrections system, came to New York State with the clear mandate to build the secure component necessary to respond to these external demands.

Building the Secure Component

Following passage of the Juvenile Offender Law, the governor's office and the legislature seemed to retreat from the issue of serious juvenile crime.

The apparent feeling was that the political decisionmakers had spoken, now it was time for implementation. To a large extent the governor and legislature took a laissez-faire approach and let the Hall Administration and the Division of the Budget (DOB) work out the details of building the secure component of the juvenile corrections system.

The Hall Administration's overriding goal for meeting this mandate was to build a secure facility component that retained a "juvenile justice orientation," while maintaining the rest of the DFY program (nonsecure residential program, community-based programs, and local assistance delinquency prevention programs). The informal definition of a *juvenile justice orientation* for the secure facilities was based on factors such as small size (100 beds or fewer), single rooms, heavy staffing, and provision of educational and vocational programs. One implication of building the secure component according to this model, as opposed to one or two large, congregate, prison-like facilities, was that the development and maintenance of the secure facilities was very expensive.[3] This created potential conflict with the goal of maintaining the rest of the DFY program.

The Hall Administration's approach to these goals was to enlist the support of the governor and key legislators for the overall shape of the secure system. With this general support, DFY then entered an extended period of negotiation with DOB in the effort to secure adequate fiscal support for the building and maintenance of the secure system. These years involved what was described as a "constant struggle" to locate funds and facility sites.

In relation to the secure facilities, the main external force on DFY was the actual processing of youths under the Juvenile Offender Law. From 1979 to 1982, juveniles were being processed faster than DFY could open secure beds. This created a situation in which youths sentenced as Juvenile Offenders were being held in local detention centers, principally the Spofford Juvenile Detention Center in New York City, for long periods of time before transfer to DFY secure facilities. The delay was so long, in some cases, that several youths were paroled directly from Spofford. This delay in DFY's acceptance of sentenced Juvenile Offenders caused a backlog in detention cases and an overcrowding problem at Spofford, which created a conflict situation for DFY. On the one hand, DFY could only accept sentenced Juvenile Offenders by tolerating overcrowding in its own secure facilities. On the other hand, DFY had to ignore enforcing its standards of certification for detention facilities by overlooking the overcrowding at Spofford.

New York City Department of Juvenile Justice administrators were pressuring DFY to accept these detained youths and eventually cooperated with the New York City Legal Aid Society in a suit against DFY. This was one of two suits brought by the Legal Aid Society against DFY in relation to detention practices.[4] Both of these suits sought to force DFY to accept sentenced juveniles in timely fashion. One dealt with Juvenile Offenders, the other with juvenile delinquents. In both cases, the lower courts ruled that DFY must accept sentenced juveniles within certain time limits. For juvenile delinquents, an interim stipulation was entered in 1980 that required DFY to accept adjudicated youths detained in Spofford within fifteen days. For Juvenile Offenders, the New York County Supreme Court ruled in 1981 that DFY must accept such youths within ten days of sentence. Because DFY did not have sufficient secure beds to meet this requirement it appealed the decision in an attempt to "buy time" until adequate bedspace could be created.

In addition to these pressures to accept sentenced youths, DFY also faced community opposition to the opening of several planned secure facilities. One proposed facility involved the conversion of an unused former state psychiatric center, the Pilgrim Psychiatric Center in Suffolk County. In 1979, DFY began renovating the Center; it hired staff and was ready to move youths in when the governor ordered the planned opening stopped. The governor's decision was prompted by a strong lobbying effort conducted by local community groups (including lawsuits), local elected officials, and area legislators. The decision was described as having literally taken the facility keys out of Hall's hands. The planned eighty-bed facility would have had a significant impact on the backlog of sentenced juveniles in the Spofford Detention Center.

Opposition also arose to the conversion of a second former psychiatric hospital, the Harlem Valley State Hospital. Despite lawsuits by local community groups, renovations were completed and the facility was opened in 1981. In comparing the success in opening the Harlem Valley facility as opposed to the Pilgrim facility, respondents believed that a key was that the Pilgrim opening was scheduled just prior to the 1980 election involving several local Democratic assemblymen. The impending election was seen as making the legislators, and consequently the governor, particularly responsive to local concerns.

A third facility, the Masten Park secure center was opened in Buffalo on the grounds of a facility that had previously been used as a drug abuse program. The planned opening of this facility also aroused local opposition, but DFY was able to enlist support by agreeing to limit the number of youths housed in the facility and to limit the number of New York City youths housed in the facility.

Three other secure centers opened by the Hall Administration did not generate the same degree of local opposition. One facility, the Oneida secure center, was opened by using two floors of the New York Central Hospital for the Criminally Insane on the grounds of the Marcy Psychiatric Center. The remaining two facilities, the Chodikee and MacCormick secure centers, were opened on the grounds of a former training school and a former DFY forestry camp. Apparently the presence of these new secure centers were not perceived as sufficiently "new" threats to justify strong community opposition.

Thus, by 1982 DFY had opened five new secure centers. These new facilities, combined with the expansion of existing secure centers, provided adequate capacity for DFY to comply with the 1982 ruling by the Court of Appeals that DFY accept Juvenile Offenders within ten days of sentencing. DFY's ability to accept Juvenile Offenders shortly after sentencing also eased the overcrowding crisis in the Spofford detention center.

Figure 7.1 illustrates the influence patterns related to the development of the secure facilities. While DFY was being pressured to accept sentenced youths, it was also being pressured to control costs. Furthermore, efforts to open new facilities were met with community opposition. The result was that the building of the secure centers lagged behind demand, but the facilities were eventually opened. Additionally, the facilities conformed to the model outlined by the Hall Administration: small in size and characterized by high staff-inmate ratios.

Impact on Other DFY Programs

As mentioned earlier, the Hall Administration's corollary goal to building the secure component was to maintain the rest of the DFY program. There was a fear that the focus on secure facilities would result in emasculation of community-based programs and the local assistance delinquency prevention funds.

As Table 7.1 shows, by 1982, the number of youths in community-based settings dropped from the peak levels of 1976 through 1978. More dramatic than the decline in actual numbers was the decline in the proportion of DFY youths held in community-based settings from 46 percent in 1977 to 26 percent in 1982. This trend was also noted in Chapter Four in relation to the slight decline of the proportion of budget allocations to community-based settings from 1979 to 1983. Additionally, cuts were made in the number of foster care beds from approximately 370 in 1978 to approximately 270 in 1982.

Several factors appear to affect the decline in the community-based population. First, in order to accommodate the building of the secure centers, some reallocation of resources from community-based programs to noncommunity-based programs was necessary. Second, a decline in the placement of status offenders with DFY and an increase in admissions of juvenile delinquents and Juvenile Offenders was evidenced from 1979 to 1982. Whether these reflect actual changes in youth behavior, diversion of status offenders, or changes in labelling at the police and court stages is unclear. What is clear is that the proportion of status offenders in DFY residential care declined and DFY increasingly utilized noncommunity-based facilities as the most appropriate placement.

A third factor was DFY's increasing reliance on private, voluntary agency group foster care as an appropriate community-based placement. During the Edelman years, DFY had sought to increase placements in private voluntary programs as part of the overall emphasis on increasing community-based placements. To facilitate these placements, Edelman, working with key legislators, included provisions in the 1976 PINS legislation that made youth committed to DFY but placed in private voluntary agencies eligible for federal funding under the AFDC-FC program. In addition to this statutory change, Edelman established a joint committee comprised of DFY leadership and the administrators of the private voluntary agencies in order to encourage such placements. Between 1978 and 1982, the number of annual DFY placements in voluntary agencies rose from around 150 to just less than 500. These figures, however, must be interpreted cautiously, because they include both Family Court placements with voluntary agencies and actual DFY discretionary placements with voluntary agencies.[5] Only the latter cases, estimated as comprising 50 percent of the voluntary agency placements, can be considered as DFY attempts to provide community-based services in lieu of cutbacks in its own community-based programs.

In terms of local assistance funds for delinquency prevention programs, while the proportion of the DFY total budget devoted to local assistance dropped from 45 percent in fiscal year 1978–79 to 38 percent in 1982–83, an overall 20 percent increase was seen in local assistance allocations during these years. Further, several new local assistance programs were statutorily created in 1978,[6] in part, as a concession to opponents of the Juvenile Offender Law (particularly the Black and Hispanic caucus of the legislature). Respondents noted that any threat to local assistance funds posed by the funding drain associated with the development of the secure facilities was thwarted by the support of the Hall Administration and the general political

Figure 7.1 Influence patterns related to development of secure facility component of juvenile corrections system, New York State, 1979-1982

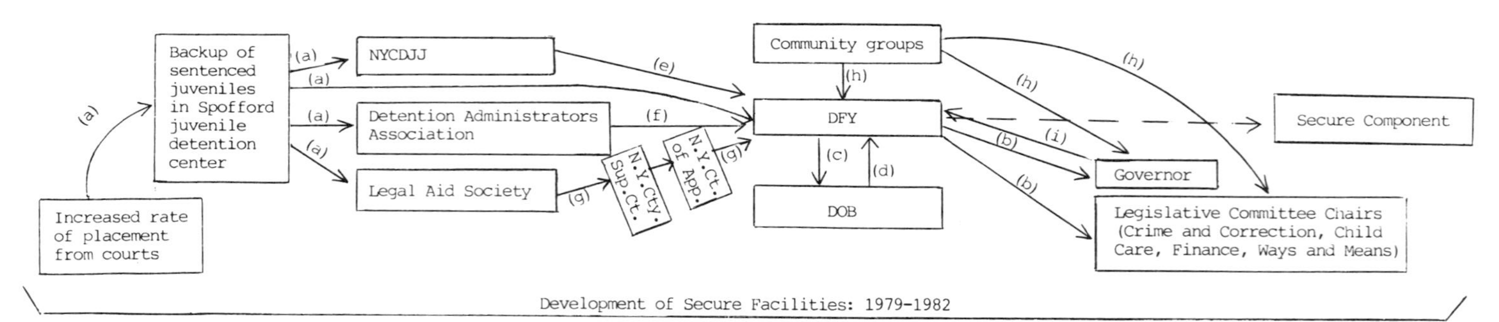

Development of Secure Facilities: 1979-1982

Policy Network

Link	Who (Initiator)	Influencing Whom (Target)	To Do What (Goals)	Tactics	Outcome
(b)	DFY/Hall	Governor, Key Legislative Committee Chairs	Support Hall goal of relatively small (100 or fewer), heavily staffed, etc., secure centers	Enlist support through meetings, document need	Unclear – assessments range from "quiet support" to "hands off" to "no help"
(c)	DFY/Hall	DOB	Support budget requests, allocate capital and operating funds	Meetings, negotiations, document need, budget shifts	Unclear – many see DOB as obstacle to building secure component
(d)	DOB	DFY	Hold down costs of development of secure facility component	Authority – review DFY budget requests, recommendations to Governor on budgetary requests, negotiations over budget levels and shifting of funds	Unclear – many see DOB as obstacle to building secure component

Figure 7.1   (Continued)

Policy Network

Link	Who (Initiator)	Influencing Whom (Target)	To Do What (Goals)	Tactics	Outcome
(e)	NYCDJJ	DFY	Accept sentenced JOs and JDs held in detention centers in "timely fashion"	Initially meetings, negotiations, enlist support of mayor; eventually cooperate with Legal Aid in lawsuit	Eventual agreement based on court decisions to accept youths within 10-14 days of sentence
(f)	Detention Adminis-trators Association	DFY	Accept sentenced JOs and JDs held in detention centers in "timely fashion"	Initially meetings, negotiations; eventually cooperate with Legal Aid in lawsuit	Eventual agreement based on court decisions to accept youths within 10-14 days of sentence
(g)	Legal Aid Society	DFY	Accept sentenced JOs and JDs held in detention centers in "timely fashion"	Brought two lawsuits seeking court order forcing DFY to accept youths held in detention	DFY appealed early rulings but eventu-ally complied with Appellate Court ruling
(h)	Community groups, local politicians	Governor, Legislature	Not to open secure facilities in their community (Pilgrim Psychiatric Center and Harlem Valley facilities)	Mandates - letter writing, phone campaigns to elected officials, lawsuits	Pilgrim Psychiatric Center dropped as site day before opening; Harlem Valley opened
(i)	Governor	DFY	Drop plan to open Pilgrim Psychiatric Center	Authority - orders no opening	Pilgrim Psychiatric Center dropped as site day before opening

Figure 7.1   (Continued)

Related Factors

Link	What	Influencing Whom	To Do What	How Influencing	Outcome
(a)	Increased rate of placement from courts (criminal and Family Court); backup of sentenced juveniles held in detention (principally Spofford) awaiting transfer to DFY facilities	NYCDJJ; Detention Administration Association; Legal Aid Society; DFY	Develop adequate bedspace in DFY facilities	Youths being held for long post-sentence periods in overcrowded detention center	Short-term crisis in detention center, eventually adequate secure center bedspace created. Long-term outcome – five new secure facilities opened with adequate capacity to accept youths within court-mandated periods

DOB – New York State Division of Budget
NYCDJJ – New York City Department of Juvenile Justice

support for these programs. The general political support is attributed to the fact that the local disbursement of these funds creates a strong constituency for the programs.

Efforts to Repeal or Modify the Juvenile Offender Law

While the period following passage of the Juvenile Offender Law has been characterized as a time in which the legislature and governor adopted a *laissez-faire* approach to juvenile corrections and the issue of serious juvenile crime, this is not to say no political activity occurred in the juvenile justice area during these years. Indeed, political issues arose both in relation to the Juvenile Offender Law and in respect to other aspects of the juvenile justice system.

In the years immediately following passage of the Juvenile Offender Law, a number of advocacy groups mobilized in an attempt to repeal the law and have it replaced with a waiver-up system from Family Court to criminal court. Several groups conducted or sponsored studies and issued reports on the initial implementation of the law. The reports were uniformly critical and argued that the law produced inequitable treatment of youths and increased inefficiency and delay. Several groups distributed the reports to members of the legislature and urged repeal of the law. These calls for repeal were met with deaf ears in the legislature and governor's office. The fact that the Juvenile Offender Law was a "three-house" bill, i.e., supported by the governor and both houses of the legislature, made repeal a difficult argument to sell. Although some members of the Assembly expressed personal dissatisfaction with the law, repeal was seen as politically impossible and no one was willing to lead an effort for repeal. One of the Assembly opponents of the Juvenile Offender legislation summarized the perceived futility of repeal efforts by commenting that with conservative crime legislation, "the legislative door only goes one way." In light of the adamant political opposition to repeal, most of the advocacy groups focused on other issues during the early 1980s. These groups saw the repeal effort as futile and did not wish to use up their efforts, or "bargaining chips," on a losing proposition.

While efforts at repeal failed, DFY attempted to modify the restrictions on placement discretion contained in the Juvenile Offender Law. The Hall Administration included bills as part of its legislative package that would allow DFY to transfer Juvenile Offenders to nonsecure facilities. DFY argued that such transfer discretion was both program and fiscally desirable and would provide DFY with the same discretion as exists in the adult Department of Corrections. DFY was able to secure DOB's support but was unable to win either legislative or gubernatorial support. Senate leaders considered the bill an attempt to "emasculate" the law and no one within the Assembly or governor's office actively supported the bill.

While direct lobbying efforts were unable to win political support for any modification of the Juvenile Offender Law, several amending provisions were passed as the result of litigation. In 1979, the year following passage of the Juvenile Offender Law, the legislature passed a number of what were described as "noncontroversial, technical" amendments to the law,[7] designed to clarify procedural issues overlooked in the 1978 bill. One of these provisions provided judges the option of granting Youthful Offender status to youths convicted as Juvenile Offenders. The Youthful Offender provision had traditionally been available as a sentencing option for youths between ages sixteen and nineteen. In such cases, granting Youthful Offender status replaces the criminal conviction with sentences ranging from probation to an indeterminate four-year prison term. By denying Youthful Offender status in the Juvenile Offender Law, lawmakers had created a situation where thirteen-to fifteen-year-olds in criminal court were denied this mitigating sentencing option available to their sixteen-to nineteen-year-old counterparts. As early as April 1979, the Supreme Court of Queens County had found the denial of Youthful Offender status to thirteen- to fifteen-years-olds in criminal court a violation of the equal protection and due process clauses of the constitution.[8] Recognizing these constitutional issues, the legislature included a provision making Juvenile Offenders eligible for Youthful Offender status in the 1979 amendments. This was a significant provision because it provided a more lenient sentencing option than provided for in the Juvenile Offender Law. Indeed, probation now became an option for Juvenile Offenders deemed eligible for Youthful Offender status.[9]

One further modification of the Juvenile Offender Law was also initiated by court action. In 1982, two court cases were brought in the Orange County Supreme Court that sought to allow Juvenile Offenders to participate in temporary release programs.[10] DFY, in cooperation with the Department of Correctional Services (DOCS) and the Division of Parole (DOP), entered into a stipulation agreement in April 1982 whereby DFY agreed to operate a temporary release program for Juvenile Offenders. The program was opened through the conversion of a twenty-bed Youth Development Center in New York City. Subsequent legislation passed in 1983 granted DFY the authority to operate the temporary release program governed by the provisions applicable to inmates of the adult correctional system.[11] Although more limited than the sought-for provisions allowing DFY to transfer Juvenile Offenders to less secure facilities, the temporary release program did provide some previously unavailable flexibility for easing youths' transition from secure centers to community living.

Figure 7.2 illustrates the influence patterns related to the provision of Youthful Offender status, the opening of the temporary release program, and the unsuccessful attempt to secure provisions allowing DFY to transfer sentenced Juvenile Offenders to nonsecure facilities. One distinction between these efforts is that the provision of Youthful Offender status and the temporary release program were the products of court intervention. The effort to secure transfer provisions did not involve a court ruling or pending litigation. Policymakers apparently were only willing to modify the law when forced to do so by the courts.

Political Interest in Other Juvenile Justice Issues

As previously noted, following the passage of the Juvenile Offender Law the legislature and governor's office seemed to adopt a *laissez-faire* approach to juvenile corrections in New York State. The Juvenile Offender Law represented the culmination of several years of debate and clearly demarcated the desired shape or direction of the juvenile justice system, and in terms of this study, the juvenile corrections system. This, however, does not mean that all political interest in juvenile justice disappeared. Rather, with policy firmly established in relation to the problem of serious juvenile crime, attention turned to other issues.[12]

Perhaps the most important issue in relation to the juvenile corrections system, in terms of potential impact, was the question of PINS diversion. This issue was brought to the fore by a number of advocacy groups which urged adoption of various forms of PINS diversion bills. These groups urged either removal of PINS cases from the Family Court or sharp restrictions on such jurisdiction. These proposals were objected to by groups arguing that such bills deny, perhaps unconstitutionally, access to the Family Court and that they provide no assurance of adequate service delivery to youths falling in the status offender category. The resolution of this issue could have ramifications for the juvenile corrections system in the potential for further decreasing the already reduced number of status offenders with DFY. The issue was not resolved and debate continued through the Dunston Administration.

Dunston Years (1983–1984)

With the election of Governor Mario Cuomo in 1982, Leonard Dunston replaced Frank Hall as DFY director. Perhaps the most significant factor

Figure 7.2 Influence patterns related to attempts to modify Juvenile Offender Law, New York State, 1979-1984

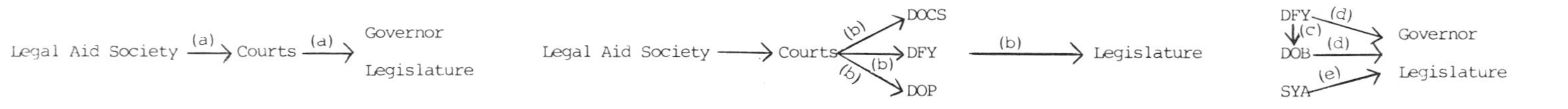

Youthful Offender Status : 1979 — Temporary Release : 1982, 1983 — Transfer Provisions: 1979-1982

Policy Network

Link	Who (Initiator)	Influencing Whom (Target)	To Do What (Goals)	Tactics	Outcome
(a)	Legal Aid Society	Formal Decisionmaking Group - Governor, Legislature	Grant Youthful Offender (YO) status to Juvenile Offenders	Challenged denial of YO status as violation of equal protection and due process clauses of constitution - court held was violation of constitution	Yes - following court decision, legislation amends law to grant YO status
(b)	Legal Aid Socity	Administration of DFY, DOCS, and DOP; Governor; and Legislature	Provide temporary release for Juvenile Offenders	Challenged lack of temporary release program in court, action named Administrators of DFY, DOCS and DOP - these three agencies then entered into a stipulation to operate program	Yes - conversion of 20-bed DFY program into temporary release program
(c)	DFY	DOB	Support provision to allow transfer of Juvenile Offenders to nonsecure facilities	Meetings - document need and programmatic and fiscal benefits	Yes - DOB provides supporting memoranda
(d)	DFY, DOB	Formal Decisionmaking Group - Governor, Legislature	Support provision to allow transfer of Juvenile Offenders to nonsecure facilities	Introduce bill as part of DFY legislative package, meetings to show need and programmatic and fiscal benefits; DOB provides supporting memoranda	No - no support among Formal Decisiomakers
(e)	Statewide Youth Advocacy	Formal Decisionmaking Group - Governor, Legislature	Support provision to allow transfer of Juvenile Offenders to nonsecure facilities	Mandates - voice support for DFY bill	No - no support among Formal Decisionmakers

DOCS - New York State Department of Correctional Services
DOP - New York State Division of Parole
SYA - Statewide Youth Advocacy

affecting DFY during these years was the decline in the number of sentenced Juvenile Offenders and juvenile delinquents sent to DFY.

Decline in the Juvenile Offender Population

Following a rise in late 1981 through mid-1982 in both the monthly arrest rate for offenses under the Juvenile Offender Law and the number of Juvenile Offenders placed with DFY, a decline occurred in both the arrest rate and number of youths placed. Additionally, increasing numbers of Juvenile Offenders were receiving the shortest available maximum sentence (for those sent to DFY) of one year. In 1979, less that 2 percent received the one-year maximum sentence. By the second half of 1983, more than 20 percent received this sentence (Division for Youth, "Population Growth," 1984). In response to these changes, the secure facility population declined since 1982 (see Table 7.1). Whereas in 1982, there were 545 youths in secure centers, by the end of 1984, there were 468 youths in secure centers. This decline was unexpected by DFY, which in its 1983–84 budget request sought funding for 815 secure beds. As with the increase in the secure center and noncommunity-based population from 1978 to 1982, the decline does not seem attributable to any change in DFY policy, but rather to the external factors determining the rate of input and the prescribed sentences of youths placed with DFY. While existing data do not definitively document the causes of this change in input, factors such as demographic shifts, changes in youth offending rates, and changes in arrest, prosecution, and sentencing practices may be contributing.

In addition, as indicated in Table 7.3, 1983 and 1984 witnessed a decline in Family Court petitions and the number of PINS and juvenile delinquents placed with DFY. The number of Family Court placements with DFY dropped from its peak level of 1,897 in 1982, to 1,489 in 1983, to 1,296 in 1984. Despite this decline in placements, the noncommunity-based population remained fairly stable (other than the decline in the secure facilities). Community-based populations also remained stable, although the population in DFY foster care continued to decline.

At the same time, the number of DFY youths placed in private, voluntary agencies increased. The average daily population of DFY youths in private facilities increased from 502 in 1982 to 821 in early 1984 (see note 5). Figure 7.3 indicates some of the factors leading to this increase. As previously noted, the 1976 PINS legislation contained provisions that made these placements an available option. However, it was the combined effect of two subsequent pieces of legislation that had the most impact. The bed pressures resulting from the Juvenile Offender Law forced DFY to reallocate some of its community-based resources to noncommunity-based programs. Consequently, DFY began to view private, voluntary facilities as a potential placement option for youths who may have previously been placed in a DFY community-based facility. The second piece of legislation was the Child Welfare Reform Act of 1979. This Act did not directly impact on DFY but did affect the private facilities. The Act included the formal goal statement that local DSS units should attempt to keep youths within their homes and place youths in the least restrictive setting. In addition, the Act created fiscal incentives for local districts to decrease institutional placements. Respondents indicated that as a result of the Act and demographic changes, the number of youths placed by DSS in private facilities declined. Although data on the number of youths placed in these facilities are unavailable, a 36 percent reduction in the capacity of these facilities occurred from 1977–78 to 1982–83 (Department of Social Services, "Changing Characteristics," 1984). Because of the decline in demand from local DSS units, the private, voluntary facilities have been more willing to accept DFY youths. Although neither the Juvenile Offender Law nor the Child Welfare Reform Act were intended to increase placements of DFY youths in private facilities, in effect, they forced DFY to look to the private facilities and forced the private facilities to accept increasing numbers of DFY youths. The net result was the above-mentioned increase in such placements. Thus, the Dunston Administration continued the trend of the Hall Administration of looking to the private, voluntary agencies to handle increasing numbers of DFY youths deemed suitable for a community-based setting.

Political Issues

During 1984, several private groups once again began to examine the Juvenile Offender issue. The Citizens' Committee for Children of New York conducted an extensive study of processing under the Juvenile Offender Law and issued a report critical of the law and calling for its repeal. Additionally, the New York City Bar Association's Committee on Juvenile Justice held hearings and released a report critical of the law and calling for repeal (though a minority report in favor of the law was also released). Other advocacy groups concurred in these findings and continued to express dissatisfaction with the law. However, as was the case with initial attempts to repeal the law in the year or two following passage, no active political support for repeal was found; indeed, clear political opposition to such attempts existed.

Figure 7.4 indicates that the same basic configuration of groups were involved in 1984 as was the case in the years immediately following the law's passage. If one were to compare the tactics utilized by those seeking to repeal the Juvenile Offender Law with those who originally sought the law's passage, one would find the same basic tactics were employed (studies of the system, criticism of the law, news releases, meetings with key politicians). The main distinction is that those seeking to pass the law were led by members of the legislature, i.e., formal decisionmakers, while those seeking repeal were all outside the formal political decisionmaking group. Additionally, a number of respondents noted that the easing of population pressures within secure facilities and the perception that the law had been "less draconian" (in terms of the number of youths sentenced as Juvenile Offenders) than expected, diminished pressure to question or examine the law. Thus, despite the attempts of these groups to press for change, the lack of political support precluded change in the law.

One other issue that continues since the Hall years is the question of PINS diversion. Advocacy groups continued to push for legislation promoting PINS diversion. Several state agencies conducted studies on local level processing of PINS and administrators from a number of state agencies, including DFY, the Division of Probation, the Council on Children and Families, and the Division of Criminal Justice Services, as well as staff from the governor's office and key legislators and their staffs, have been engaged in negotiations over legislation that seeks to promote diversion and the provision of community-oriented services while answering the objections to previous bills concerning denial of access to the Family Courts. As of the close of the 1984 legislative session, the issue remains unresolved. However, advocates and opponents of the proposed bills both stated that a compromise appeared to be imminent. On the other hand, the potential impact on DFY appears limited because of the already low number of status offenders placed with DFY (1984, N=100). This may prove to be a case of legislation merely codifying existing practice.

Thus, the Dunston years have witnessed an apparent end to the growth of secure facilities, a slight decline in community-based populations, and a rise in placements with voluntary agencies. Although attempts have been made to reconsider the Juvenile Offender Law, no apparent political support is found to do so. Finally, the PINS diversion issue continued to be debated.

Analysis

The post-1978 years thus saw DFY move in a new policy direction. Through most of the 1970s, DFY's primary focus had been to move away

Figure 7.3 Influence patterns related to increased use of private, voluntary facilities for DFY referred youths, New York State, 1976, 1979-1984

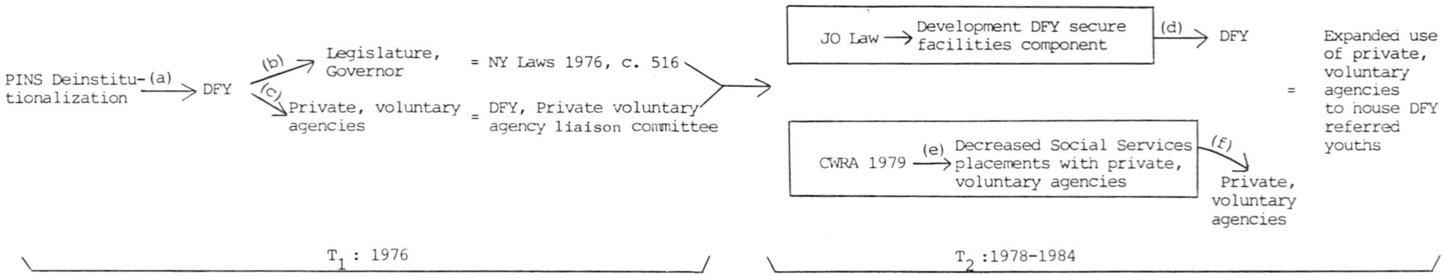

Policy Network

Link	Who (Initiator)	Influencing Whom (Target)	To Do What (Goals)	Tactics	Outcome
(b)	DFY/Edelman	Legislature, Governor	Pass bill making DFY youth placed in private, voluntary agencies eligible for ADC-FC funding	Enlist governor's support	Bill passed; Effect on voluntary population mixed - slight increase but established mechanism
(c)	DFY/Edelman	Private, voluntary agencies	Increase placements of DFY referred youths to private, voluntary agencies	Exchange - established joint committee to encourage mutually advantageous placements	Mixed - slight increase voluntary population, but established mechanism

Related Factors

Link	What	Influencing Whom	To Do What	How Influencing	Outcome
(a)	PINS Deinstitu-tionalization	DFY	Look for alternative community-based settings	Mandate to remove PINS youths from training schools meant had to find community-based settings	Developed DFY community-based settings and worked to increase placements in private, voluntary agencies

Figure 7.3 (Continued)

Link	What	Influencing Whom	To Do What	How Influencing	Outcome
(d)	JO Law and subsequent development of secure facilities	DFY	Look for alternative placements for PINS youth and juvenile delinquents	Expansion of secure facilities forced DFY to look for alternative placements for youths in nonsecure population	Increased placements of DFY referred youths in private, voluntary agencies
(e)	Child Welfare Reform Act (CWRA) of 1979	Local DSS units	Decrease foster care placements in private, voluntary agencies	CWRA legislatively creates disincentive to place foster care placements in private, voluntary agencies	Drop of DSS placements in private, voluntary agencies
(f)	Decreased DSS placements with private, voluntary agencies	Private, voluntary agencies	Accept DFY referred youths	Decreased DSS placements create openings and incentive to accept DFY referred youths	Increased placements of DFY referred youths in private, voluntary agencies

CWRA - Child Welfare Reform Act of 1979

Figure 7.4 Influence patterns related to attempts to repeal Juvenile Offender Law, New York State, 1979-1981, 1984

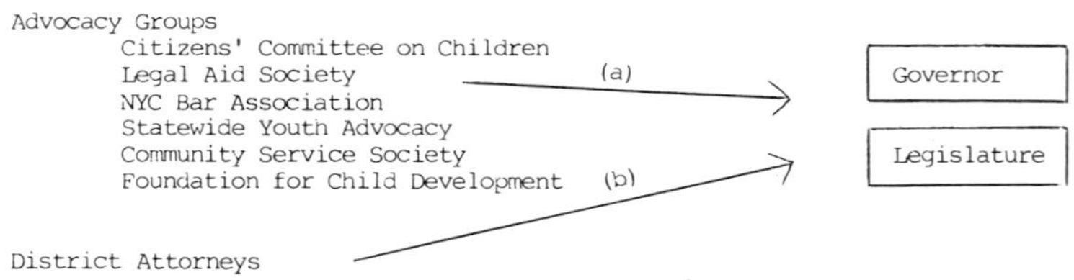

Advocacy Groups
    Citizens' Committee on Children
    Legal Aid Society   (a)
    NYC Bar Association
    Statewide Youth Advocacy
    Community Service Society
    Foundation for Child Development   (b)

District Attorneys

T_1 : 1979-1981 T_2: 1984 (same basic configuration of actors during each period

Policy Network

Link	Who (Initiator)	Influencing Whom (Target)	To Do What (Goals)	Tactics	Outcome
(a)	Advocacy Groups	Formal Decisionmaking Group - Governor, Legislature	Repeal Juvenile Offender Law	Mandates - meetings with formal decision-makers, press releases; Investigation of and information about implementation and effects of law; criticize law	No apparent desire to repeal among Formal Decisionmaking Group
(b)	District Attorneys	Formal Decisionmaking Group - Governor, Legislature	Retain Juvenile Offender Law	Ad hoc, individual support of law expressed in opposition to critics of law	Law retained

from the traditional training schools and to develop a community-based system. The period from 1978 to 1984 saw a renewed emphasis on institutional programming and a reversal in the trend toward increased reliance on community-based programs. The Hall Administration entered the policy arena in 1979 with the clear mandate to build the secure center component required by the Juvenile Offender Law. By 1983, when Leonard Dunston became DFY director, sufficient secure beds had been opened to meet the now slightly declining demand for such settings. The Hall and Dunston Administrations were similar in that both directors assumed the role of administrator rather than policymaker (as had Luger and Edelman). Both accepted the broad contours of the system as established by the governor and the legislature and sought to do "what's best for kids" within this context. For Hall, it meant building the secure component with a juvenile justice orientation and fighting the emasculation of other DFY programs. For Dunston, it meant strengthening internal administration and making prevention services DFY's top priority.

Theoretical Principles

As noted, the major changes that occurred in the juvenile corrections system during the period from 1979 to 1984 involved the expansion of the secure centers, the growth in the noncommunity-based population, and the decline in the utilization of community-based programs. Figure 7.5 illustrates the key factors leading to these changes. The two primary elements were the actual passage of the Juvenile Offender Law and the rate of court processing. The law represented an external political shift in that lawmakers formally established policy that select juveniles committing the more serious offenses would be subject to long sentences in secure facilities. The law also created an internal economic shift in that it changed DFY technology. With respect to youths sentenced under Juvenile Offender provisions, DFY lost its traditional discretion over placement and transfer decisions, and its control over release. This meant that the size of the secure center population was determined by an external economic factor, the rate of placement of youths sentenced under the Juvenile Offender Law. Consequently, the secure center population increased from 1978 to 1982 as the number of Juvenile Offender sentenced youths increased, and decreased in 1983 and 1984 as the number of Juvenile Offender sentenced youths decreased and at least a portion of those sentenced received shorter maximum sentences. The actual shape of the secure center component was largely dictated by the Hall Administration's commitment to a number of small facilities (versus one or two large centers) and Hall's ability to enlist the support of the governor and key legislators for this structure.

The overall growth in the noncommunity-based population and the decline in the community-based population were also the products of these wide-ranging factors. To meet the demands of the Juvenile Offender Law, there was some reallocation of resources from community-based programs to the secure centers. In addition, the number and proportion of juvenile delinquents placed with DFY by the Family Courts increased. This led to an internal political and technological shift in that DFY considered community-based placements as inappropriate for a growing proportion of its clientele.

Figure 7.5 classifies these factors according to the internal-external, political-economic dimensions and clearly indicates that a full range of such factors were influencing the system. Thus, the sequencing principle, which states that fundamental change is the product of a full range of internal and external, political and economic factors, is supported.

Several external political changes had a limited effect on the growth of the secure care centers. Court intervention led to the provision of Youthful Offender status and the development of a temporary release program. Youthful Offender status provided criminal court judges with the option of a probation sentence for certain youths processed under the Juvenile Offender Law. Indeed, 65 percent of the youths convicted under the Juvenile Offender statute have been granted Youthful Offender status, with 39 percent receiving a probation sentence (Division of Criminal Justice Services, 1984:16). However, assessing the effect of this provision on the secure center population is impossible because it is unclear whether these cases would have been sentenced under the Juvenile Offender Law or whether they would have been returned to Family Court in the absence of such provisions. The development of the temporary release program affected internal technology by creating some flexibility to move youths sentenced as Juvenile Offenders to a nonsecure, temporary release facility prior to release. However, the program consisted of only one facility with a twenty-youth capacity and thus did not have a major impact on the population of secure centers. The two proposals that would have had more fundamental impact by affecting both internal and external dimensions, the proposals to repeal the law and to allow transfer to nonsecure facilities, received no external political support.

The other major change that occurred during these years, the growth in the number of DFY youths placed in private, voluntary agency care, also provides support for the sequencing principle. The Juvenile Offender Law (external, political) and the consequent building of the secure care component forced DFY to look to the private, voluntary agencies as an alternative

Figure 7.5 Categorization of factors influencing New York State's juvenile corrections system according to political economy model, 1979-1984

	External		Internal	
	Political	Economic	Political	Economic
Increased use non-community-based facilities/decreased use community-based facilities				
Development and growth of secure centers	JO Law mandates secure care for certain youths. Governor and key legislators support Hall plan for shape of secure facilities. Court cases require DFY to accept sentenced youths within time limits	Actual court processing of youths under JO Law (as affected by demographics, youth offending rates, police and court practices). DOB places fiscal constraints of DFY	Hall commitment to relatively small, heavily staffed facilities	JO Law changes DFY technology in relation to youths sentenced under law. No discretion to move youths to non-secure facilities and release decision placed in hands of Parole Board
Proportional increase in placement youths in noncommunity-based facilities		Increase in Family Court placements of juvenile delinquents, decrease in placements of status offenders	Hall and Dunston Administrations respond to changes in placement practices by viewing more youths as inappropriate for community-based programming; some reallocation of resources from community-based to non-community-based programming	Technology shifts to expanded use of noncommunity-based programming
Growth in placements of DFY youths in private, voluntary agency programs	JO Law CWRA	DOB places fiscal constraints on DFY. Private agencies more willing to accept DFY youths due to drop in placements from local DSS units (effect of demogrpahic and CWRA)	DFY reallocates some resources from community-based to noncommunity-based programs; looks to private voluntary agencies to handle some youths previously placed in DFY community-based programs	Cut-back in DFY community-based facilities; private, voluntary agencies increasingly seen as alternative placement option

placement option (internal, political and economic). Declining placement of youths by local DSS units to the private, voluntary agencies forced these agencies to accept more DFY youths (external, economic) (see Figure 7.5).

The crisis principle and the key swing group principle remain largely untested by the developments occurring during the Hall and Dunston years. The changes that occurred during these years were largely the product of working through the ramifications of the Juvenile Offender Law and then consolidating the newly configured system. There were no other major changes from which either of these principles could be examined.[13]

There is limited support for Miller, Ohlin, and Coates's (1977) fourth principle that the Conservative and Liberal Interest Coalitions will be responsive to changes in the juvenile corrections system. Recall that there are three aspects of this principle. The first is that groups whose interests are not reflected in current practice will respond by becoming increasingly active and critical of the system. Indeed, a number of advocacy groups responded to the Juvenile Offender Law with investigations, issuance of critical reports and news releases, and lobbying of the legislature and the governor's office. However, there was no active involvement of either the DFY director, the governor and his staff, or legislators. No one within the political system responded to the conservative policy trend by leading counterreform efforts.

The second aspect of the principle holds that the coalition whose policies are reflected in currect practice is likely to become less politically active, even to the extent of letting its defenses down. Conservative interest groups did become less active in the sense of no longer conducting formal investigations of the system. However, this seems primarily due to the fact that the passage of the Juvenile Offender Law represented the accomplishment of their main objective and because their interests were never truly threatened. That is, despite the efforts of the advocacy groups, the Juvenile Offender Law has never truly been questioned at the political decisionmaking level. It seems clear to all involved in the juvenile justice policy arena that the conservative groups maintain a latent interest which would quickly mobilize to prevent emasculation of the Juvenile Offender Law. Because of this recognition and because of the lack of political leadership in opposition to the law, advocacy groups have tended to view repeal or modification of the Juvenile Offender Law as a losing proposition and have moved to other issues.

Finally, in relation to the third aspect of this principle, the Conservative Interest Coalition did not view their position in relation to the juvenile corrections system as threatened. Thus, the proposition that interest coalitions will respond to threatened loss of control over policy with extreme tactics was untested.

The fifth principle raises the issue of short- and long-run effects of extreme tactics. Chapter Six noted that conservative interests had used extreme tactics following the passage of the JJRA. They had denounced the supposed bipartisan compromise agreement embodied by the JJRA, and had continued to investigate and criticize the system, introduce bills for criminal court jurisdiction for juveniles, and attack the governor's position on juvenile waiver. Furthermore, they worked to make juvenile crime an issue in the 1978 election. The tactics proved successful with the adoption of the Juvenile Offender Law.

Although these tactics were successful, the repudiation of the Formal Decisionmaking Group's compromise agreement (i.e., JJRA) probably would have long-term negative consequences for the Conservative Interest Coalition. However, this does not appear to be the case. The secure care system was developed and the policy move towards increased noncommunity-based programming became consolidated. Thus, in this instance, extreme tactics proved successful in the short-term without apparent long-term negative consequences.

Summary

The Hall and Dunston Administrations represented a profound change for DFY. In contrast with the Luger and Edelman Administrations, DFY was no longer the key initiator of change and reform. During the period between 1978 and 1984, the key forces of change came from DFY's environment, primarily from legislative mandate and the courts. Whereas under Luger and Edelman, DFY established the basic shape and direction of the juvenile corrections system (abetted by external factors), under Hall and Dunston, DFY accepted the context of the system as established by legislative and gubernatorial dictate. Consequently, as these groups have mandated the control of serious juvenile offenders as the primary goal of the system, DFY's residential component moved towards an increased reliance on secure and noncommunity-based facilities.

Figure 7.6 summarizes the changes in the key set of relationships resulting from the above-described processes.

Figure 7.6 Summary of changes in key relationships of juvenile corrections arena, Hall and Dunston years

Relationship	Beginning period (1979-1982)	Ending period (1983-1984)
People Processing Relationship	Reversal in trends witnessed through 1970-1978 period. Expansion of secure care and noncommunity-based programs.	Slight decline in number of youths in secure facilities and non-community-based programs. Community-based programs stable. Increased number of youths in private, voluntary agencies.
Relationship among Interest groups	Governor and legislature adopt laissez-faire posture. Hall delegates control over building of secure component. DFY administration adopts administrator versus policymaker role. Consequently, not seeking major change but responding to external demands.	Governor and legislature continue laissez-faire posture and Dunston continues administrator versus policymaker role. Focuses on improving administration of agency and delinquency prevention programs.
Conservative Interest Coalition	Conservative interests less active. Seen as latent force precluding major reform.	Conservative interests maintain posture of opposition to major reform.
Liberal Interest Coalition	Advocacy groups respond to JO Law with investigations, criticism expressed in news releases and reports, and lobbying for repeal. No active support within political system.	Advocacy groups respond with same tactics but once again receive no political support. Tendency to move to other issues-- procedural reform, legal representation of upstate youths, PINS diversion.

Chapter Eight

The Overall Change Process:
Findings, Implications, and Conclusions

The previous three chapters provided an intensive examination of the key developments that seemed to shape the process of change in New York State's juvenile corrections system. At each chapter's end the degree of support for each of the empirical principles was assessed. At this point, the analysis focuses on the process of change over the entire period. This approach provides insight into the structure of state -level decisionmaking and allows final assessment of the theoretical principles. In addition, the final sections of the chapter move beyond the confines of the New York State analysis and attempt to place the study within the context of theoretical and policy issues raised by contemporary trends in juvenile justice.

Findings

The Structure of State-Level Juvenile Policy Making

The structure of state-level decisionmaking in New York State's juvenile justice system generally conforms to political scientists' descriptions of policy communities and policy subsystems (Cobb and Elder, 1983; Milward, 1982). The policy community is comprised of two sets of actors: those who seek to influence policy and those who ultimately make policy decisions. The first group consists of interest groups; the second, of formal decisionmakers. The policy subsystem, a subset of the policy community, is comprised of the group of formal decisionmakers.

As suggested by the studies reviewed in Chapter Two, a number of interest groups were involved in the policy process. These groups could be characterized according to the permanency of their involvement in juvenile justice issues and whether they were internal or external to the state political system. Several interest groups remained permanently involved in juvenile justice policy issues. These tended to be citizen advocacy groups such as the Citizens' Committee for Children of New York, Statewide Youth Advocacy, the New York State Coalition on Juvenile Justice, the Community Service Society, and the Foundation for Child Development. Another permanent interest group was the Legal Aid Society, a professional group providing legal services for New York City juveniles. Several other groups had recurrent involvement in issues that affected group interests. These included state agencies such as the Department of Social Services, Department of Corrections, Division of Parole, Division of Probation, Council on Children and Families, and the Division of Criminal Justice Services. Other groups with recurrent interests included several federal agencies, the New York City Department of Juvenile Justice (within the mayor's office), the Detention Administrators' Association, and the New York City and New York State Bar Associations. Others with recurrent interests were the district attorneys, however, these actors tended to act individually rather than collectively. Finally, several *ad hoc* community groups arose in relation to plans to locate secure centers in their communities.

Furthermore, based on the data presented in Chapter Six, the media may have played a recurrent interest group role. Then, too, several individuals played dual roles. These individuals, including the DFY director and several legislative committee chairs, acted as interest group partisans at some times and formal decisionmakers at other times. Further, these actors and the state agencies mentioned above, acted as internal interest groups. The advocacy groups, legal associations, community groups, and the media represented external interest groups.

As in previous research on criminal lawmaking and correctional policy formation, these interest groups tended to form two loose oppositional coalitions in relation to any specific issue (Berk, Brackman, and Lesser, 1977; Messinger and Johnson, 1978). These coalitions roughly conformed to labels such as treatment-punishment, civil rights-law enforcement, and Miller, Ohlin, and Coates's (1977) Liberal and Conservative Interest Coalitions. However, while these oppositional groups could be identified in relation to any specific issue, the use of the labels should not be taken as an indication of two unchanging groups driven by well-established ideological positions. Rather these are fluid coalitions, for whom labels such as treatment-punishment may mask diversity both within the coalition and over time. For instance, groups comprising the Liberal Interest Coalition in the late 1960s were primarily concerned with the lack of treatment within the training schools. In the mid-1970s, groups within the Liberal Interest Coalition focused on civil rights issues such as the lack of distinction between status offenders and delinquents. As another example, the Liberal Interest Coalition advocating passage of the Juvenile Justice Reform Act of 1976 consisted of two distinct sets of groups. The first included those who favored offense-based distinctions in Family Court. The second included groups and individuals actually opposed to such legal distinctions but who considered this preferable to criminal court jurisdiction. The point is that while labels such as treatment-punishment and liberal-conservative are helpful in "sorting out the players," they also tend to oversimplify diverse attitudes and policy preferences.

The other group comprising the policy community are formal decision-makers whom the interest groups are attempting to influence. As noted, this group has been termed the policy subsystem or decision network. Previous research indicates that a small group of actors, the governor and key staff, chairs of relevant legislative committees, legislative party leaders, and correctional administrators tend to control policy decisions in an issue area such as juvenile justice (Heinz, Gettleman, and Seeskin, 1969; Berk and Rossi, 1977). The present study supports this basic picture but also indicates that the structure of the policy subsystem varies over time and issue.

For some issues, the DFY director was able to implement policies by enlisting the support of the other key decisionmakers. This control was true not only for routine, incremental policy decisions but also for several key policy decisions. For example, both Luger and Edelman were able to secure the support of the governor's office and key legislators for the general policy of closing training schools and opening community-based programs. Edelman was also the prime figure in removing status offenders from the training schools. In all these cases, the director's success in enlisting political support was dependent on external political and economic factors but the key point is that the director drove policy.

At other times and for other issues, this structure changed with control over policy clearly in the hands of the governor and key legislators. One example of gubernatorial control occurred in relation to the transfer of the training schools. Staff members within the governor's office responsible for the reorganization of DSS decided that the training schools should be transferred to DFY. The governor then *told* Luger that DFY would be assuming control over the administration of the training schools.

In the passage of the JJRA, the governor delegated authority to Edelman who then clearly influenced policy. In the case of the Juvenile Offender Law, however, the governor and key legislators dictated policy excluding Edelman from meaningful participation. Policymaking, in terms of the structure of the policy subsystem, thus varied between an administrative controlled mode of decisionmaking (DFY director, working with gubernatorial and legislative staff) and a politician controlled mode of decisionmaking (governor and key legislators).

In viewing these two modes of decisionmaking the power differential between these two groups must be noted. The DFY director's control over policy was clearly subservient to that of the governor and legislative leaders. The director had control where it was delegated, consciously or unconsciously, by the key politicians. The director could not dictate policy over the objections of the governor and the legislature. On the other hand, the governor and key legislators could and did dictate policy over the DFY director's objections.

Finally, at certain times other groups became involved in formulating policy. Of particular importance were state courts through decisions such as those mandating separate confinement of status offenders and delinquents, and providing Youthful Offender status for Juvenile Offenders. Other state agencies, such as DOB, also became involved in subsystem decisionmaking in relation to certain issues. However, unlike the courts, these agencies did not exert control over decisionmaking.

The recognition of the subsystem control over state-level policymaking and the variation in the structure of this subsystem are important concepts in understanding policy change. This importance is due to the fact that, as Heinz, Gettleman, and Seeskin (1969) noted, issues are framed at this level and options are set. For example, in the post-1978 years, a number of proposals were made to repeal or modify the Juvenile Offender Law. These proposals never went beyond the subsystem level, i.e., the consideration of gubernatorial and legislative committee staff. The failure to bring these proposals to full consideration was due not so much on the basis of fundamental opposition on the part of actors within the subsystem, but because of the judgment that such an effort would be futile due to the strong opposition within the larger political system.

On the other hand, once support at the subsystem level was secured, more general and consensual political support was assured. As a consequence, by the time a bill reached the floor of the legislature, support was virtually ensured (see also Fairchild, 1981).[1] The subsystem, both in bottling-up legislation and in sending agreed-upon legislation to the entire legislature, thus played a key gatekeeping role.

Thus, the structure of state-level juvenile correctional decisionmaking consists of a policy community of interest groups and formal decisionmakers. The interest groups are comprised of groups with permanent, recurrent, and *ad hoc* interests in juvenile justice, and groups internal and external to the state's political system. The formal decisionmakers, comprising the policy subsystem, consist of the DFY director, the governor and his or her staff, and legislative committee chairs and party leaders. Control over policy within the group of formal decisionmakers varies among the administrative mode, the typical subsystem structure, and the politician mode controlled by the governor and party leaders. Understanding this structure is key to understanding state-level decisionmaking. In subsequent sections, issues of the way this structure changes and issues concerning the process of decisionmaking will be discussed.

Theoretical Principles

SEQUENCING AND THE POLITICAL ECONOMY OF JUVENILE CORRECTIONS

The key principle identified in Miller, Ohlin, and Coates's (1977; see also Miller and Ohlin, 1985) work, and that which receives the strongest empirical support in this study, is the sequencing principle. In the initial theoretical model this principle emphasized the importance of congruence between internal and external forces of change. The later formulation stressed congruence between aspired choices and available choices. The emphasis on internal and external dimensions, and aspired and available choices places the Miller, Ohlin, and Coates theory within what has been termed the political economy model of public organizations (Wamsley and Zald, 1973; see also Benson, 1975; Hasenfeld, 1983; Hasenfeld and Cheung, 1985).

The political economy model states that the structure and process of a public organization and change within a public organization are the products of political and economic forces operating at internal and external levels. The synthesis of Miller, Ohlin, and Coates's sequencing principle and the political economy model provides a way to structure the juvenile corrections arena (internal and external, political and economic dimensions) and to understand the process of change. The utility of such an approach is strongly suggested herein. Throughout the course of the study, all major changes in the juvenile corrections system were shown to be the product of a combination of internal and external, political and economic forces. While merely repeating the findings presented in each of the three preceding chapters would be redundant, further examination of these forces appears warranted.

Figure 8.1 summarizes the key political and economic forces influencing New York State's juvenile corrections system. At the external political level the key forces relate to power relationships and value or sentiment distributions among the formal decisionmakers. Wamsley and Zald (1973) emphasize the importance of power and values, and they correspond to Miller, Ohlin, and Coates's (1977) distributions of power, responsibility, and reward, and focal concerns. In New York State, the power dimension was determined by whether the formal decisionmakers, i.e., the governor and legislative leaders, assumed control over an issue or delegated to the policy subsystem. The value dimension refers to the ends sought in any particular policy. Both power relationships and value distributions appeared to be driven by other external political forces such as broad social and ideological shifts (civil rights movement, social science criticism of rehabilitative ideal), interest group activity (investigations and criticism of system, media attention), and political crises (fiscal crises of 1971 and 1975).

At the external economic level, the two key variables are client flow from the courts and fiscal support. Client flow was shown to be important in the late 1960s and early 1970s as the decline in Family Court placements provided impetus for the deinstitutionalization movement. The rise in the secure center population in the early 1980s reflected the in-flow of youths under the Juvenile Offender Law and illustrated the combined impact of client flow and changes in internal technology (restrictions on placement and release). The role of external funding has obvious impact and was most clearly reflected in the use of federal funds for the expansion of community-based programs. Both Luger and Edelman also used declining fiscal support to legitimize closing several training schools. One additional external economic factor that proved important during the Hall and Dunston years was the availability of alternative placements with the private, voluntary agencies (see also Lerman, 1984).

The internal political dimension is very similar to external polity with the exception that the key decisionmaker is the agency director. Clearly, values (ideology and goals) and control over policy were key to Luger's and Edelman's deinstitutionalization efforts. On the other hand, director ideology was of little importance in the mid-1970s when the governor wrested control over policy from Edelman.

Figure 8.1 Summary of factors influencing New York's juvenile corrections system catgorized according to political economy model

External		Internal	
Political	Economic	Political	Economic
Distribution power and value choices among agency super-ordinates (Governor, Legislature, courts)	Client flow	Distribution power and value choices among agency leadership	Costs
-Set policy vs. delegate -Policy choices	Fiscal support	-Director control over policy -Director ideology and goals	Available alternative technologies
	Alternative service providers		
As affected by: -Broad cultural and ideological shifts -Interest group activity -Political crises			

Finally, key aspects of internal economy are available technology and costs. One aspect of technology relates to control over placement and release decisions. When a correctional agency loses control over these decisions, as was the case in relation to youths processed under the Juvenile Offender Law, then program decisions begin to be driven by external demand.

Wamsley and Zald (1973) make the additional points that the lines between these dimensions are often blurred and that the relationships between dimensions are dynamic. These points are supported herein. For example, both Luger and Edelman responded to a state fiscal crisis by closing training schools. Similarly, a shift in the external economy, declining placements in the training schools, caused a change in the internal economy, increased per diem costs of the training schools. This, in turn, caused an external political shift as the governor and legislature supported DFY's deinstitutionalization effort. Of course, the recognition of these interrelationships once again points to the utility of the sequencing principle.

CRISIS

The notion of crises as *necessary* ingredients for change was not supported in this study. For instance, the PINS deinstitutionalization effort was accomplished in the absence of a political crisis. On the other hand, support was evidenced for a more limited view of the crisis principle. According to this view, crises may be important as representing political or economic shifts in themselves or by causing political or economic shifts. Thus, the legitimacy crisis in the juvenile justice system during the mid-1970s led to a political change as the governor assumed control over the issue of serious juvenile crime and changed the executive policy choice toward a position favoring criminal court jurisdiction for select juveniles. Likewise, the fiscal crises of 1971 and 1975 represented external economic shifts which led to external political shifts (support for DFY deinstitutionalization initiatives). Thus, on the basis of this study, the crisis principle can be stated as follows: Crises, either within the juvenile corrections system or at related levels of state government, may be important factors in system change to the extent they represent, or lead to, changes at the political and/or economic levels.

KEY SWING GROUPS

The key swing groups principle is empirically supported herein. However, as was the case with the crisis principle, this principle seems most appropriately viewed in relation to the sequencing principle. In each of the

major policy shifts, the transfer decision and the early deinstitutionalization movement, the removal of status offenders from the training schools,
and the adoption of the Juvenile Offender Law, either the governor, legislative
leaders, or the DFY director played a key swing role. In the case of the
governor and legislative leaders, the change in position represented a shift
in power relationships and value choices at the external political level. In
the case of Edelman's succession of Luger and the subsequent removal of
PINS from the training schools, this represented an internal political shift
(with external decisionmakers delegating control).

RESPONSIVENESS OF INTEREST COALITIONS

As noted in earlier chapters, this principle has three aspects. First, groups
whose interests are not reflected in policy and programs are likely to attempt
to discredit the system through investigation and criticism. This was supported
as both conservative groups, who saw their interests thwarted during the Luger
and early Edelman years, and liberal advocacy groups, following passage
of the Juvenile Offender Law, responded with investigations, critical reports,
and attempts to build political support for change.

Second, once a coalition gains control over policy it is likely to become
less politically active and to let its defenses down. This was not supported,
however. Luger's control over policy after transferring the training schools
was never threatened and Edelman did not seem to become less politically
active following his initial successes in PINS deinstitutionalization and
ratifying the JJRA. Rather, he continued to work to build political support
as evidenced by his efforts to secure federal funds for the community-based
programs and to maintain the coalition opposed to criminal court jurisdiction.
The governor's change in position destroyed the coalition, but it did not appear
to be the product of the Liberal Interest Coalition having let down its defenses.

Finally, neither of the groups who lost control over juvenile corrections
policy during the study period responded with extreme tactics as predicted
by the third aspect of this principle.

SHORT- AND LONG-RUN EFFECTS OF EXTREME TACTICS

In Chapter Three, two questions addressed extreme tactics. Are extreme
tactics necessary for change? Do such tactics carry long-term negative consequences? The change process in New York State suggests that extreme
tactics, in the sense of a partisan seizing control over policy and repudiating
the Formal Decisionmaking Group, are not necessary change tactics. Indeed,

the only instance of such tactics was the repudiation of the JJRA by conservative legislative interests. Further, these tactics did not seem to carry long-term negative consequences. Thus, this principle was not supported.

At least three potential explanations are plausible for the lack of support for these last two principles. First, the findings on which the principles were developed may have been idiosyncratic to the Massachusetts experience and lack generalizability. Second, the lack of use of extreme change tactics and the more gradual change process in New York State may have precluded an adequate test of the principles. Third, the retrospective approach may not have been sufficiently sensitive to structural changes in the coalitions. In any case, it may be that prospective and/or comparative analysis would provide a more adequate test of these principles.

Internal and External Polity and Agenda Setting

In the earlier discussion it was noted that the structure of state-level decisionmaking tended to vary between an administrative mode and a politician mode. In the administrative mode, the DFY director, at least during the Luger and Edelman years, tended to control policy. The director would work with a small group of actors, principally key staff within the governor's office, chairs of relevant legislative committees, and key staff within the party leader's office of both houses of the legislature. During the Hall and Dunston years, this same basic configuration of actors was in place, although neither Hall nor Dunston played as visible a leadership role in setting policy as had Luger and Edelman. Regardless, this small group of actors formed the policy subsystem in the juvenile corrections area and can be considered the usual or typical subsystem decisionmaking structure.

Similar points were made in the discussion of the sequencing principle where key political shifts were shown to involve either external political control or delegation of decisionmaking authority.

The distinction between these two modes of decisionmaking seems to conform to the distinction between the policy subsystem and the formal agenda made by political scientists who study what is termed the agenda-setting process (Cobb and Elder, 1983; Anderson, 1984). Consideration of some of the key points made by students of the agenda-setting process can help clarify the movement between these two modes of decisionmaking and clarify the overall policymaking process.

The notion of agenda setting as a key process in policymaking is based on the premise that because the universe of issues facing policymakers exceeds that which can be dealt with, only a sample of issues can be addressed by lawmakers at any given time. Because of this situation, control over an issue area such as juvenile corrections is typically delegated to a small group of decisionmakers, the policy subsystem. Policy then tends to be dominated by this small and relatively stable group of actors who are considered the experts in the given issue area. In New York State, in relation to juvenile corrections issues, this network consisted of the DFY director, legislative chairs of relevant committees, and key staff within the governor's office and the legislative party leader's offices.

Cobb and Elder (1983) note that decisionmaking at the subsystem level tends to be incremental. However, while this held true during the Hall and Dunston years, this was not the case during the Luger and Edelman years. During these years, significant innovation occurred based on decisionmaking at the subsystem level.

Despite this point of difference, because subsystem decisionmaking tends toward incremental policymaking, much of the focus of agenda-setting research is on the way issues move from the subsystem level to the formal agenda of decisionmakers such as the governor and legislature. This issue is key because fundamental policy change is considered more likely at the formal agenda level. Several factors are considered crucial in the movement of an issue from the subsystem level to the formal agenda level. These include crises or scandals, shifts in leadership, media attention, the mobilization of public concern, and the efforts of moral crusaders (Cobb and Elder, 1983; Anderson, 1984).

Reflection on those issues observed herein in which policy control moved from the subsystem level to the formal agenda, indicates that these types of factors were crucial in this "issue expansion" process. The governor's decision to transfer the training schools in 1971 was most immediately the product of the crisis in the state's social welfare system. In 1978, the governor's change in position on the issue of criminal court processing of juveniles was the product of the efforts of conservative moral crusaders, media attention, and the legitimacy crisis in the state's juvenile justice system. In both instances, these factors elevated juvenile justice issues from the pool of public policy issues to a matter of immediate concern to the governor and other state lawmakers. At such time, these issues were deemed too important to be left at the subsystem level.

Relating the findings herein to these concepts on agenda setting serves several purposes. First, the theoretical principles on crises and key swing groups and the findings of variation in decisionmaking structure gain added empirical and theoretical support from these more general studies of policymaking. Second, and very similarly, the points made about the factors leading to significant political shifts gain added support when viewed in light of agenda-setting research.

Implications

This study has approached the analysis of change in New York State's juvenile corrections system through the use of the political economy model of public organizations (Wamsley and Zald, 1973) and the theory of social reform developed in studies of change in the Massachusetts juvenile corrections system (Miller, Ohlin, and Coates, 1977; Miller and Ohlin, 1985). Both of these models are attempts to integrate theoretical and empirical findings from several fields of study. The justification for joining the two models is based on the premise that Miller, Ohlin, and Coates's emphasis on internal and external dimensions, and aspired (political) and available (economic) choices naturally links their model to the political economy model. The advantage of doing so is that it links a theory developed in the study of juvenile corrections to a general model of public organizations. The approach employed herein, to use the political economy categorization as a way of structuring the analysis and the Miller, Ohlin, and Coates principles as a way of examining the change process, has proven useful for understanding change in New York State's juvenile system.

Wamsley and Zald (1973), as well as researchers who have attempted to use the model (Hasenfeld and Cheung, 1985), offer the political economy approach as a framework rather than a fully developed theory. However, despite the model being at an initial stage of theoretical development, the approach offers at least two key advantages. As indicated in this study, the structure and process of an organization and the course of change in an organization, are affected by a wide range of factors, including developments at the national, state, and local levels, and the actions of numerous individuals, groups, and organizations. Recognition of this array of influences is apt to leave the analyst with an "everything affects everything" type explanation. One key advantage of the political economy framework is that it provides a means for categorizing these forces in a theoretically meaningful way. The second key advantage is that because it is an integrative model, an abundance of literature exists from which to explicate the theory. Political scientists have long-studied external polity, and economists, external economy. Similarly, organizational theorists and students of public administration have studied internal power relationships and organizational structure. Furthermore, researchers from different areas of specialization have considered technology issues, e.g., criminological and correctional research. In addition, theorists and researchers taking an open-systems approach and studying interorganizational relationships offer insights concerning the interrelationships among these dimensions. The attempt herein to relate shifts in external polity and the crisis and key swing group principles to the agenda-setting literature illustrates the utility of the model for integrating diverse theoretical and research findings.

The theoretical principles developed in the Massachusetts study and examined herein, provide an initial step toward moving from the framework level to the theory level. Also, these two studies help to isolate the key political and economic variables for juvenile corrections systems. Figure 8.1 represents an attempt to focus on these dimensions. However, this is an initial attempt and further research is needed to isolate and clarify key concepts and operationalize and validate key variables. This study suggests such research is warranted.

The findings of the importance of wide-ranging factors and of variation in decisionmaking structure also has implications for research design. This study suggests that study of isolated change incidents might result in misleading conclusions. For instance, examining the decision to close several training schools in the early 1970s might lead to the conclusion that funding drives policy. On the other hand, the fact that the attempt by the advocacy groups to enlist support for modification of the Juvenile Offender Law was unsuccessful, despite the massive budget appropriations required to build the secure centers, suggests that political considerations outweigh fiscal considerations. One of the main findings of this study is that examining several issues over a longer timeframe indicates that *both* political and economic forces drive policy and system change (see subsequent sections).

Similarly, the finding of variation in the decisionmaking structure governing state-level juvenile corrections policy formation calls into question the generalizability of descriptions of this structure based on cross sectional studies. For example, was Berk and Rossi's (1977) finding of an administrative coalition in Florida and Washington and a legislative coalition in Illinois due to long-term differences between the states or due to the cross-sectional nature of the study which identified the coalition currently controlling policy? Clearly, longitudinal studies could help in addressing such an issue.

Despite the advantages of longitudinal approaches, difficulties also arise. Because longitudinal analyses tend to be restricted to a single site, isolating the key political and economic variables is difficult. Comparative state studies have the advantage of holding constant national developments, such as broad social changes and federal funding programs. An example of such an approach is Downs's (1976) study of juvenile deinstitutionalization following passage of the JJDPA. By focusing on this issue Downs held national political (goals) and economic (funds) forces constant. This allowed a focus on state-level factors that determined the way states responded to national policy. The finding that director ideology and autonomy were related to rates of deinstitutionalization illustrates the ability to focus in on key proximate causes. The advantage of a longitudinal analysis such as the present study, is that it suggests that a concept like director autonomy is likely to vary over time and issue.

Cross sectional comparative studies have the further advantage of more adequately addressing questions of generalizability than has been possible herein. Thus, a need for a combination of intensive, longitudinal analyses and comparative analyses of different state systems seems apparent.

These findings also provide some tentative implications for those seeking to change the system. At a general level, the political economy framework provides a means to analyze the forces promoting and inhibiting change. Using this framework to structure the juvenile corrections arena, the sequencing, crisis, and key swing group principles and the findings on the structure of decisionmaking may then suggest appropriate strategies for targeting change efforts.

The sequencing principle suggests the need to promote change at both political and economic levels, and within and outside the organization. Such wide-ranging change may be beyond the means of the change agent. Further, factors such as general public attitudes, broad social shifts, and economic changes are unlikely to be influenced by the change agent. However, by being aware of these types of forces, the change agent may be able to take advantage of shifts at either the political or economic levels by then focusing efforts at complementary levels. Examples of such an approach were Luger's and Edelman's responses to fiscal crises. They capitalized on the crisis by enlisting external political support for desired program changes (deinstitutionalization).

The key swing group principle suggests that for many issues it may not be necessary to influence a majority of policymakers, but rather to influence a select member of the key decisionmaking group. This principle might suggest focusing efforts during campaign elections. Such a strategy might target an incumbent, as proponents of criminal court jurisdiction did in relation to Governor Carey in 1978, or a challenger (in the event the challenger wins the election). Similarly, crisis periods may be a time to attempt to influence key decisionmakers who might play a swing role.

Finally, recognition of the variation in the decisionmaking structure of state-level policy formation has practical implications. During most periods, the small group of actors labelled the policy subsystem is the key group to deal with in change efforts. As noted, they play a gatekeeping role in determining what initiatives are likely to be supported. However, this study, and studies of policymaking in other issue areas, indicates that a second level of decisionmaking exists: the formal agenda. Consequently, where the subsystem proves to be an obstacle to change, those seeking change might wish to gear their efforts toward expanding the issue to the level of the formal agenda. Questions can be raised concerning the extent to which such an agenda building strategy is an available option for a group seeking change. However, to the extent such groups can either promote, or capitalize on, crises, scandals, and/or media attention, such an attempt may prove effective.

Broader Issues

Despite the fact that this study has covered approximately twenty years of juvenile correctional change, in some respects it is rather narrow. It is a case study of one state that attempts to test the applicability of a theory of social reform and change. The issues raised in the study, deinstitutionalization and the rejection of the *parens patriae* doctrine, however, go to the core of the study of social control. I now turn to these issues, albeit in a rather tentative and speculative fashion. The intent is to place this study in the context of theoretical debates concerning social control and in the perspective of nationwide trends in juvenile justice policy and practice.

Deinstitutionalization

As evidenced in the present study of New York State, the early 1970s witnessed a nationwide decline in the population of public juvenile correctional facilities. Furthermore, the years following passage of the federal JJDPA, witnessed significant drops in the numbers of status offenders in secure detention centers, jails, and training schools (Handler and Zatz, 1982; Kobrin and Klein, 1983; Krisberg and Schwartz, 1983). However, despite these shifts and despite the apparent support for deinstitutionalization in the late 1960s and early 1970s,[2] the number of juveniles incarcerated in public juvenile correctional facilities has risen since 1974. Paradoxically, the rise in institutionalization has occurred at a time when juvenile arrests have declined (Krisberg *et al.*, 1986). One apparent explanation for these divergent trends appears to lie in the rejection of the traditional *parens patriae* philosophy for certain categories of youths.

Get Tough Movement

Perhaps the most dramatic rejection of the *parens patriae* principle is New York State's Juvenile Offender Law. Indeed, the law's provisions of automatic placement in criminal court, long sentences, mandated secure confinement, low age jurisdiction, and overall community protection emphasis, appear to be the antitheses of the *parens patriae* philosophy.

Although the Juvenile Offender Law may be extreme, it appears to be representative of a general and nationwide "get tough" movement in relation to juvenile crime and juvenile justice. As Chapter One notes, this movement has led to legislative changes in a number of states since the late 1970s. Included are laws that make it easier to waive cases to criminal court, that lower the age for waiver, that exclude certain offenses from juvenile court jurisdiction, and that mandate minimum periods of incarceration (see Chapter One). Further, since 1980, the federal role in juvenile justice reform has significantly changed as the Reagan Administration has opposed federal deinstitutionalization initiatives and endorsed policies focusing on punishment of serious or repeat juvenile offenders.

That this get tough movement has influenced the juvenile justice system seems apparent in Krisberg *et al.'s* (1986) review. They found that the increase in juvenile correctional populations at a time of declining arrests could be explained in the rather simple equation of increasing numbers of youths being incarcerated for increasing periods of time.

Thus, the last two decades have been a time of apparently divergent trends in juvenile justice policy and procedure. Although the deinstitutionalization movement and the get tough movement appear contradictory, these two policy directions are ultimately intertwined.

Explaining Divergent Trends

These divergent policy trends lend a degree of support, but also raise questions about some explanations of the deinstitutionalization movement. For instance, Scull (1977) related long-term decarceration of mental health, juvenile justice, and correctional institutions to the fiscal crisis experienced by Western capitalist nations following World War II. Scull argued that structural pressures generated by the fiscal crisis led to the move away from costly institutions and toward increased reliance on cheaper, but control-oriented, community-based programs. The present finding that New York

State's fiscal crises, described as the state's first in modern times, led to the closing of training schools, lends support to Scull's thesis.

Lerman's (1984) study of deinstitutionalization in the mental health, mental retardation, child welfare, and juvenile corrections sectors, also tied the movement into economic forces. Deinstitutionalization was seen as the product of changing federal welfare funding patterns in the post-New Deal era. In brief, the availability of federal funds for nontraditional programs led to a move away from traditional state and local supported institutions and the expansion of alternative, often private, programs. In addition, Lerman tied these economic shifts into shifts in ideology ("anti-institutional"). The New York State study lends support to the Lerman thesis as the availability of federal funds was crucial in closing training schools and opening community-based programs. Further, federal funds from the AFDC-FC program have been used to purchase placement in private foster care institutions.

When the analysis moves away from the deinstitutionalization efforts of the early 1970s, however, and focuses on the rising rates of juvenile incarceration, the economic analysis appears incomplete. Clearly, the policy shifts of the get tough movement have not been guided by concerns for reducing institutional costs. Indeed, in New York State, the new secure centers are much more expensive than either traditional training schools or community-based alternatives and have been developed at tremendous fiscal expense.

Thus, economics alone does not provide a sufficient explanation for these dual policy directions.[3] Rather, Lerman's emphasis on both economics and ideology appears to offer a more complete explanation. This dual emphasis gains added credence when considered in relation to the unique characteristics of the juvenile justice system.

Juvenile Justice as an Interstitial System

The juvenile justice system has always existed in a rather ill-defined, fuzzy area between the social welfare system and the criminal justice system (Schultz and Cohen, 1976). This interstitial setting is evidenced by the juvenile court's traditional jurisdiction over dependent and neglected youths, status offenders, and youths committing criminal acts. This in-between character is further highlighted by the traditional failure to even distinguish among these categories of youths. Through the years, a growing tendency has been to separate these categories of youths (Rubin, 1985). The separation process culminated in the 1970s with the deinstitutionalization of status offenders.

Deinstitutionalization has had the most impact on the mentally ill and mentally retarded populations (Lerman, 1984). It has had the least impact in the area of adult corrections. In keeping with the theme of juvenile justice as an interstitial system, deinstitutionalization has had a less dramatic impact on juvenile justice when compared to institutions for the mentally ill and retarded, but more of an impact than on adult prisons.[4] The reason seems to be due to the mixed clientele of the juvenile justice system.[5] As noted, the same economic forces driving deinstitutionalization in the mental health area were also influencing juvenile justice. Thus, dependent and neglected youths and status offenders were removed from the traditional juvenile corrections system. However, deinstitutionalization was ideologically acceptable only for these "deserving" categories of youths. The movement stopped at the point of lawbreakers, be they juveniles or adults.

This bifurcation of the juvenile justice system's clientele also paved the way for the get tough movement (see also Cohen, 1985). It did not make sense to speak of deserved punishment when addressing the undifferentiated clientele of the juvenile court. However, once dependent, neglected, and acting out (status offenders) youths were separated, confronting those youths who, according to the dominant ideology, needed and deserved punishment was then possible. What the purely economic analysis seemed to neglect was the apparent ingrained cultural fixation on punishment (i.e., incarceration) for lawbreakers (Scheingold, 1984).[6]

Contemporary Juvenile Justice

The last two decades have thus seen the juvenile corrections system shaped by the deinstitutionalization movement in relation to status offenders, and the get tough movement in relation to juveniles committing what would be crimes for adults. However, to end the story with only this broad brush picture of change would miss several corollary trends of contemporary juvenile justice.

As the public juvenile corrections system has expanded since 1974, its clientele has changed. Unless relabelled as delinquents (Klein, 1979; Schneider,1984), status offenders are rarely confined in public training schools. A more troubling shift, however, is the growing overrepresentation of Black, Hispanic, and Native American youths in the public juvenile corrections system (Krisberg *et al.*, 1987). This has been observed in New York State's new secure centers and is evident nationally.

At the same time, deinstitutionalization of status offenders has not necessarily meant noninstitutionalization. Rather, in a number of jurisdictions it has meant incarceration in private facilities (Krisberg *et al.*, 1986; Lerman, 1984; Schwartz, Jackson-Beeck, and Anderson, 1984). Just as private group foster care programs have increasingly handled DFY clientele in New York, so have private institutional programs expanded nationwide (Lerman, 1984; Krisberg *et al.*, 1986). Furthermore, one of the key distinctions between placement in a public versus private institution appears to be racially based with minority youths going to public facilities and white youths going to private facilities (Krisberg *et al.*, 1987).[7]

Conclusion

The growth in both public and private juvenile corrections indicates that the end result of the change processes described in this book is an expansion of the net of social control (Austin and Krisberg, 1981; Cohen, 1979). In New York State, and nationally, not only are stronger nets for those identified as delinquent found, but wider nets for those considered in danger of becoming delinquent are found as well.[8]

This expanded social control system appears to be the product of the crisis of legitimacy facing juvenile justice during the past two decades. This crisis surfaced in the deinstitutionalization movement (and related efforts to divert and provide due process) and culminated in the get tough movement of the late 1970s and 1980s. The fascinating feature of the resolution of this crisis is the connection between these seemingly contradictory policy directions. Further, the resolution appears very similar to the resolution of the policy debate that produced a separate juvenile court and juvenile justice system during the nineteenth and early twentieth centuries. That is, just as the juvenile court was the product of the rational separation of juveniles (troubled youths) from adults (evil criminals), so contemporary developments seem to be the product of rational attempts to separate status offenders (troubled youths) from lawbreaking youths (evil criminals). That this apparently rational approach would produce an expanding and increasingly racially segregated control system, although perhaps predictable to some theorists,[9] raises fundamental questions about our notions of juvenile justice reform.

Finally, the resolution of this crisis suggests a paradigm shift (Lemert, 1970) in the area of juvenile justice. That is, this study suggests that one of the fundamental changes occurring in the last two decades is that the terms of policy debate have shifted. Thus, current and future debate over juvenile justice policy and procedure is less likely to ask the traditional question: How should juveniles in trouble with the law be treated in comparison to adult lawbreakers. Rather, the new question is likely to be: How should certain categories of youths in trouble with the law be treated in comparison to other categories of youths in trouble with the law. The answers to this latter question will probably shape the future directions of juvenile corrections policy and procedure.

Notes

Chapter One

1. This movement from revisionist conspiracy accounts to a focus on structural forces can perhaps best be seen as part of a shift from instrumental Marxist theories to structuralist Marxist theories (Beirne, 1979; see also Chambliss and Seidman, 1982; Hall *et al.*, 1978).

2. Mennel (1983) and Ignatieff (1981) comment on the paucity of literature on the development of correctional institutions in the twentieth century and call for the extension of historical analysis to this era.

3. For example, see the studies of the Highfields, Provo, and Silverlake projects (McKorkle, Bixby, and Elias, 1958; Empey and Erickson, 1972; Empey and Lubeck, 1971).

4. See California Stats. 1961, c.1616; N. Y. Laws 1962, c. 686; *Kent v. United States,* 383 U. S. 541 (1966); *In Re Gault,* 387 U.S. 1(1967); *In Re Winship,* 397 U. S. 358 (1970).

5. Public Law 87–274 (1961), U. S. Statutes at Large, LXXV, 572–574.

6. Massachusetts closed its training schools in the early 1970s (Coates, Miller, and Ohlin, 1978); Washington eliminated juvenile court jurisdiction over status offenders in the late 1970s (Castellano, 1986).

7. Several scholars have questioned the persuasiveness of the data, the logic of the argument and the validity of the techniques used to demonstrate the nothing works doctrine (Sechrest, 1979; Gottfredson, 1979).

8. This statement should not be interpreted as an endorsement of orthodox interpretations emphasizing humanitarian reform. Rather, the argument is that as structural forces have created the need for altered social control responses, the debate within correctional and juvenile correctional circles has focused on successive technological reforms.

Chapter Two

1. Studies of the attempted revision of the federal criminal code support the view of extensive interest group involvement in the criminal lawmaking process (see Melone and Slagter, 1983; Stolz, 1984).

2. Although the Determinate Sentencing Law was revolutionary in terms of sentencing philosophy, Messinger and Johnson (1978:57) recognized that the implementation of the law reflected a much less drastic change in justice system processing.

3. Note, however, that Berk, Brackman, and Lesser (1977) found that when the structure of accommodation broke down in California, the contest between law and order and civil rights coalitions tended to lead to legislative stalemates. It may be that these conflictual periods open the system to change but do not guarantee that such change will occur.

Chapter Three

1. These studies are presented in Feld (1977); McEwen (1978); Coates, Miller, and Ohlin (1978); Miller, Ohlin, and Coates (1977); and Miller and Ohlin (1985).

2. For an example of similar use of the *New York Times Annual Index* in other issue domains, see Jenkins and Perrow (1977).

3. Although the final sample did not include all individuals named in the snowball procedure, at least one key actor from each of the groups identified as active in the policymaking process was included.

Chapter Four

1. This historical account is partially based on review of New York State statutes. This section also draws heavily on the following sources: Pickett, 1969; Sobie, 1981; Mennel, 1973.

2. N. Y. Laws 1824, c. 126.

3. The legislation included N. Y. Laws 1840, c. 100. Facilities opened included the Western House of Refuge and the Dobbs Ferry Juvenile Asylum.

4. N. Y. Laws 1922, c. 547.

5. N. Y. Laws 1962, c. 686.

6. One of the limitations of this study is the rather crude distinction between noncommunity-based and community-based programs. These two program categories are distinguished on the basis of DFY formal labels and descriptions.

Community-based programs are those in which youths remain in or near their home communities and participate daily in community activities such as school and work. Noncommunity-based facilities are programs dealing with youths who have been removed from their community, are typically located in rural areas, and are more self-contained in terms of provision of services. The problem with such distinctions is that previous research has indicated that formal program labels such as *community-based* and *institutional* can be misleading (Coates, Miller, and Ohlin, 1978). Such labels do not necessarily translate into differences at the service-delivery level. On the other hand, the fact that the programs labelled *community-based* tended to be located within the urban areas from which their clients were drawn and that the programs utilized community educational and work services, lends a certain degree of face validity to the distinction. Further, the provision of such programs structurally changes the juvenile corrections system in the sense that the presence of these community-based programs, at the very least, provides the opportunity for increased engagement of youths in the community (above that available in a system relying principally on rural, self-contained, training schools).

7. An exception to the eighteen-month placement were provisions allowing fifteen-year-olds charged with class A or B felonies to be placed in the adult reception center at Elmira (for offenders aged sixteen to twenty-one) for a period up to three years. N. Y. Family Court Act, sec. 758 (McKinney 1975) (repealed 1976).

8. The correlation between percent noncommunity-based population and the percent noncommunity-based budgetary allocations is .90. For percent community-based population and percent community-based budgetary allocation, the correlation is .70. Percents are used to adjust for the effects of inflation on budgetary allocations.

9. The U.S. Department of Justice, through its Children in Custody series (U.S. Department of Justice, Office of Juvenile Justice and Delinquency Prevention, 1984), has collected nationwide data on juvenile correctional facilities since 1971. Included in its reports are state by state data on juvenile incarceration rates. Meaningful comparisons are virtually impossible, however, due to state variation in age jurisdiction, use of private facilities, and use of detention facilities. The Children in Custody series attempts to adjust for the variation in age jurisdiction by basing rates on the number of youths in the general population eligible for juvenile court processing in each state. The problem remains, however, that the rates still reflect comparisons of systems that handle ten- to fifteen-year-olds with systems that handle ten- to seventeen-year-olds.

Krisberg *et al.* (1984) have attempted to adjust for many of these problems by including incarceration rates of juveniles in detention centers, adult jails, training schools, and adult prisons and then examining overall rates of juvenile incarceration. However, at least two problems remain. First, there is no measure of incarceration in private facilities, which for many states may be a major source of state variation. Second, the data on incarceration of juveniles in adult prisons may be unreliable. Krisberg *et al.* use prison data from a nationwide survey conducted by the National Center on Institutions and Alternatives (Lowell and McNabb, 1980:14). For New York State, they report that 321 youths younger than age eighteen were held in the adult prison system on January 1, 1979. Another national survey reported that on March 31, 1978, New York State housed 2,067 youths younger than age eighteen in the adult prison system (Carlson, 1980:121, 122). Review of the two reports reveals no obvious reason for the discrepancy. New York State's overall rate of juvenile incarceration fluctuates dramatically depending on which of the above figures are used.

Thus, although Krisberg *et al.* show the need to consider age and jurisdiction distinctions when comparing states, the data are not yet available to allow for reliable comparisons.

10. Because we are primarily interested in arrest and court statistics as indicators of caseflow into the juvenile corrections system, these data are presented in raw form and are not adjusted for changes in the population of youths ages fifteen and younger.

Chapter Five

1. From April 1970 to July 1971, Milton Luger acted as chairman of the Narcotics Addiction Control Commission. During this period, Roslyn McDonald was the DFY's acting director.

2. *Kent v. United States* 383 U. S. 541 (1966); *In Re Gault* 387 U. S. 1 (1967); *In Re Winship* 397 U. S. 358 (1970).

3. Reports criticizing the training schools included Citizens' Committee for Children of New York (1969); Committee on Mental Health Services Inside and Outside the Family Court in the city of New York (1972) (report submitted in 1971); Report of Joint Legislative Committee on Protection of Children and Youth and Drug Abuse (1970); Hopewell and Kernohan (1968). The lawsuits included *Lollis v. New York State Department of Social Services; Pena v. New York State Department of Social Services* 322 F. Supp. 473 (SDNY 1970).

4. The discrepancy between Family Court placement data (Table 5.1) and training school admission data (Table 5.4) is accounted for by the inclusion of parole violators and returned absconders in the admission data. For example, in 1970 there were 415 youths returned to the training schools for parole revocations (Goddard, 1977).

5. N. Y. Laws 1971, c. 947.

6. It should be noted that 1974 witnessed an increase in the noncommunity-based population. This seems to be due to increased number of placements from Family Court. There were 170 more youths placed in DFY in 1973 than 1972 (see Table 5.1). Court data for 1974 are problematic because the state switched its reporting period from July to June to the calendar year.

Chapter Six

1. *Ellery C. v. Redlich* 32 N. Y. 2d 588 (1973).

2. Luger's prediction of racially segregated facilities appears to have been borne out, at least with respect to the secure centers. In 1983, 38 percent of youths admitted to DFY care were white and 61 percent were Black and Hispanic (1 percent unknown or other). In admissions to secure centers, 10 percent were white, 88 percent were Black and Hispanic (New York State Division For Youth, *Masterplan 84,* 1984).

3. N. Y. Laws 1976, c. 515, 516.

4. In the following sections dealing with legislative changes, it is instructive to note that New York State has a two-house legislature. During the years 1974–1978, the Assembly was controlled by the Democrats and the Senate by the Republicans. Governor Carey was a Democrat.

5. N. Y. Laws 1976, c. 878.

6. N. Y. Laws 1978, c. 481. The original list of targeted offenses included: murder 2, kidnapping 1, arson 1 and 2, manslaughter 1, rape 1, sodomy 1, burglary 1 and 2, robbery 1 and 2, attempted murder 2, attempted kidnapping 1, and assault 1.

7. For example, for murder 2, a maximum sentence of life and a minimum sentence of five to nine years; for kidnapping 1 and arson 1, a maximum twelve to fifteen years and a minimum four to six years. For class B felonies (manslaughter 1, rape 1, sodomy 1, burglary 1, robbery 1, arson 2, attempted murder 2, and attempted kidnapping 1) a maximum three to ten years, minimum one-third of maximum. For class C felonies (assault 1, robbery 2, and burglary 2) a maximum three to seven years, minimum one-third of maximum. (N. Y. Penal Law 70.05 (McKinney Supp. 1983)).

8. The following categories of the *Annual Index* were searched for articles of potential relevance: Assaults; Children and Youth; Courts; Crime and Criminals; Murders; New York State Department of Social Services and Division for Youth; Prisons; Robberies and Burglaries; Sex Crimes. Several other categories were reviewed but ultimately excluded because they did not seem to present articles on juvenile crime or juvenile justice.

9. Variables coded included the following dichotomous variables (yes = article mentions, no = article does not mention): juvenile crime; policy recommendation; criticism of juvenile justice system. Articles making a policy recommendation or criticizing the system were also coded as either "youth rights" oriented, "crime control" oriented, "mixed," or "ambiguous."
Using the traditional coefficient of reliability of the ratio of coding agreements to total coding decisions, reliability estimates ranged from .85 to .99. Scott's pi, a conservative estimate of reliability that takes into account the skewed distribution of response categories, was .77 for criticism and .85 or above for all the other variables (see Holsti, 1969: 140).
Further information on the content analysis is available from the author.

10. At first glance, the decline appears to begin in 1978. Closer examination reveals that it began after the Juvenile Offender Law was passed in July 1978. From

January 1, 1978 to July 31, 1978, eighty articles appeared. This is a rate of 11.4 per month which projects to 137 articles per year. From August 1, 1978 to December 31, 1978, 34 articles appeared. This is a rate of 6.8 per month which projects to eighty-two articles per year. Thus, the decline in the *New York Times's* coverage occurred after the Juvenile Offender Law was passed in July 1978.

11. The crime control and youth rights orientations proved empirically to be mutually exclusive as there were no articles that expressed crime control recommendations and youth rights criticisms or youth rights recommendations and crime control criticisms.

Chapter Seven

1. Eighty-eight percent of the placements to DFY secure facilities in 1983 were youths sentenced in criminal court under the Juvenile Offender Law (New York State Division for Youth, *Masterplan 84,* 1984).

2. As noted in Chapter Six, existing data do not indicate whether these changes in placement practices reflect changes in youth behavior, changes in police and judicial practices, or relabelling of status offense behavior as delinquent behavior.

3. For example, the 1984 per diem budgetary rate for secure centers was twenty-two percent higher than for limited secure centers, seventy-five percent higher than for noncommunity-based programs, and 104 percent higher than for urban homes (data provided by New York State Division for Youth). See also Figure 4.3.

4. The case dealing with reception of juvenile delinquents was *Ronald W. and Eric M. v. Hall,* the case dealing with reception of Juvenile Offenders was *Crespo v. Hall,* 56 N. Y. 2d 856, 453 N. Y. S. 2d 392 (1982).

5. The figures cited refer only to placements with voluntary agencies that are actually DFY cases. A large number of Family Court cases are placed with voluntary agencies without being referred to DFY.

Two types of cases are referred to DFY and placed in voluntary agencies. The first involves cases in which the Family Court places a youth in a private, voluntary agency but administratively assigns jurisdiction of the case with DFY. The second are cases referred to DFY in which it decides to place a youth with a private, voluntary agency. Only in these latter cases does DFY actually make the discretionary choice to place in the voluntary agency.

6. N. Y. Laws 1978, c. 721, 722.

7. N. Y. Laws 1979, c. 411.

8. *People v. Michael D.,* 99 Misc. 2d 816, 417 N. Y. S. 2d 604 (1979).

9. Of 1,608 New York City youths sentenced under the Juvenile Offender Law between 1979 and 1983, 664 or 41.3 percent were granted Youthful Offender status

and sentenced to probation (New York State Division of Criminal Justice Services, "Juvenile Offenders in New York State: 1983 Report," 1984).

10. *Santiago v. Coughlin, Hammock and Hall; Dorsey v. Coughlin, Hammock and Hall.*

11. N. Y.Laws 1983, c. 308.

12. Other issues addressed during these years included the revision of procedural requirements in juvenile delinquency hearings and several budgetary matters. The issue of procedural requirements was resolved in 1982, when after several years of debate and negotiation, a new code of procedure for juvenile delinquency hearings was passed (N. Y. Laws 1982, c. 920).

One of the budgetary issues of particular significance in the juvenile corrections area involved the cut of funds for DFY's ombudsman program. This program, begun by Milton Luger during the early 1970s, comprises a group of attorneys who visit DFY facilities and receive and investigate youth's complaints. The 1983–84 fiscal year executive budget did not include funds for this program. Advocacy groups rallied around restoration of funds for this program and the legislature restored funds with no real opposition. Other funding issues raised by several advocacy groups have centered on periodic cuts in the areas of aftercare, foster care, mental health services, staff training, and educational and vocational programming.

13. The back-up of sentenced juveniles in the Spofford detention center in the early 1980s represented a crisis for DFY and the detention center's administrators. DFY was forced to violate its own standards for certification of detention standards because it did not have sufficient secure center beds to accept these youths. DFY then found itself the subject of several lawsuits. While this was a crisis for DFY and New York City detention administrators, the issue did not become a major concern within the larger political system and thus did not generate pressure to examine the merits of the Juvenile Offender Law. The drop in the number of youths sentenced under Juvenile Offender provisions and the subsequent drop in the secure care population in 1983 and 1984 further deflated pressure to examine the law.

Chapter Eight

1. For example, the bill which enacted the JJRA was passed by votes of 136-to-8 in the Assembly and 55–2 in the Senate. The bill which enacted the Juvenile Offender Law of 1978 was passed by a vote of 125- to -10 in the Assembly and 46-to-2 in the Senate. The fact that these two bills, embodying distinct approaches to serious juvenile crime and enacted within two years of each other, could gather such support, reflects this process in which a small group of key actors decide on a specific approach and then enlist the support of the rest of the legislature.

2. Evidence of this support is found in the recommendations of the President's Commission (1967b) and the National Advisory Commission (1973). Further evidence

comes from the overwhelming and bipartisan Congressional support for the JJDPA (Krisberg *et al.*, 1986).

3. This is not to deny that the fiscal crisis may have influenced the get tough movement. Indeed, the fact that Great Britain experienced a very similar "moral panic" as that described in Chapter Six may lend support to explanations that view get tough policies as elements of the further extension of state control over the powerless classes (Hall *et al.*, 1978). This interpretation gains support in findings of increasing overrepresentation of minority youths in public juvenile corrections systems (see subsequent discussion; see also Duster's (1987) discussion of a growing urban underclass and their overrepresentation in the justice system).

4. This statement is based on the fact that even combining the growth in public and private juvenile correctional facilities, this expansion is still less than the explosion in the adult prison population that has occurred since the early 1970s (Flanagan and McGarrell, 1986: 517, 531).

5. Indeed in his second edition, Scull (1984) has attributed the growth in adult and juvenile correctional institutions to their unique clientele.

6. Pepinsky (1987) has made the analogy between incarceration trends and warfare. The tremendous fiscal resources devoted to defense, prisons, and juvenile corrections supports the analogy. In the current political *zeitgeist*, just as we must spare no expense for national defense, neither must we spare funds for domestic defense. Indeed, New York State's liberal Governor Cuomo describes the state's criminal justice system as its department of defense.

7. Some will argue that the public-private placement distinction is not based on race but on culpability. They are likely to point to the "rational" deserts and deterrence based sentencing revisions that now focus on prior record and seriousness versus individual characteristics. However, the data on the racial disproportionality of public correctional facilities and recent findings on racial disparity and the accumulation of prior records (e.g., Huizinga and Elliott, 1987; Fagan, Slaughter, and Hartstone, 1987) bring us back to Wilkins's (1984) question of whether the individual and the act can ever be disentagled in assessments of culpability.

8. The expanded use of probation, intensive supervision, restitution, community service, shock probation, etc., in addition to the growth of private and public institutions reinforces this picture of an expanded net of social control (Austin and Krisberg, 1981; Cohen, 1979).

9. For instance, Marxist theorists might point to Poulantzas's (1973) discussion of the hidden class structure behind rational legal formalism. For application of these ideas to the emergence of the justice model, see Paternoster and Bynum (1982).

References

Aldrich, Howard E. 1979. *Organizations and Environments.* Englewood Cliffs, N. J.: Prentice-Hall.

American Friends Service Committee. 1971. *Struggle for Justice.* New York: Hill and Wang.

Anderson, James E. 1984. *Public Policy-Making* (3rd ed.). New York: Holt, Rinehart and Winston.

Austin, James and Barry Krisberg. 1981. "Wider, Stronger, and Different Nets: The Dialectics of Criminal Justice Reform." *Journal of Research in Crime and Delinquency* 18:165–196.

Bailey, Walter C. 1966. "Correctional Outcome: An Evaluation of 100 Reports." *Journal of Criminal Law, Criminology and Police Science* 57:153–160.

Bakal, Yitzhak and Howard W. Polsky. 1979. *Reforming Corrections for Juvenile Offenders.* Lexington, Mass.: Lexington Books.

Bartollas, Clemens, Stuart J. Miller, and Simon Dinitz. 1976. *Juvenile Victimization: The Institutional Paradox.* New York: John Wiley and Sons.

Beccaria, Cesare. (1764) 1963. *On Crimes and Punishments.* Indianapolis: Bobbs-Merrill.

Becker, Howard S. 1963. *Outsiders.* New York: Free Press

Beirne, Piers. 1979. "Empiricism and the Critique of Marxism on Law and Crime." *Social Problems* 26:374–385.

Benson, J. Kenneth. 1975. "The Interorganizational Network as a Political Economy." *Administrative Science Quarterly* 20:229–249.

Bentham, Jeremy. (1789) 1973. *An Introduction to the Principles of Morals and Legislation.* Garden City, N. Y.: Anchor Books.

Berk, Richard A., Harold Brackman, and Selma Lesser. 1977. *A Measure of Justice: An Empirical Study of Changes in the California Penal Code, 1955-1971*. New York: Academic Press.

Berk, Richard A. and Peter H. Rossi. 1977. *Prison Reform and State Elites*. Cambridge, Mass.: Ballinger.

Berman, Paul. 1978. "The Study of Macro- and Micro- Implementation." *Public Policy* 26:157-184.

Blau, Peter M. 1955. *The Dynamics of Bureaucracy*. Chicago: University of Chicago Press.

Boland, Barbara and James Q. Wilson. 1978. "Age, Crime, and Punishment." *The Public Interest* 51:22-34.

Campbell, Donald T. 1979. " 'Degrees of Freedom' and the Case Study." Pp. 49-67 in *Qualitative and Quantitative Methods in Evaluation Research*, edited by Thomas D. Cook and Charles S. Reichardt. Beverly Hills, Calif.: Sage.

Carlson, Kenneth. 1980. *American Prisons and Jails Volume Two: Population Trends and Projections*. Washington, D. C.:U. S. Department of Justice, National Institute of Justice.

Castellano, Thomas C. 1986. "The Justice Model in the Juvenile Justice System: Washington State's Experience." *Law and Policy* 8:479-506.

Chambliss, William and Robert Seidman. 1982. *Law, Order, and Power* (2nd ed.). Reading, Mass.: Addison-Wesley.

Churchman, C. West. 1968. *The Systems Approach*. New York: Dell.

Clemmer, Donald. 1958. *The Prison Community*. New York: Holt, Rinehart and Winston.

Cloward, Richard A., et al. 1960. *Theoretical Studies in Social Organization of the Prison*. New York: Social Science Research Council.

Cloward, Richard A. and Lloyd E. Ohlin. 1960. *Delinquency and Opportunity: A Theory of Delinquent Gangs*. New York: Free Press.

Coates, Robert B., Alden D. Miller, and Lloyd E. Ohlin. 1978. *Diversity in a Youth Correctional System: Handling Delinquents in Massachusetts*. Cambridge, Mass.: Ballinger.

Cobb, Roger W. and Charles D. Elder. 1983. *Participation in American Politics: The Dynamics of Agenda-Building* (2nd ed.). Baltimore, Md.: John Hopkins University Press.

Cohen, Albert K. 1955. *Delinquent Boys: The Culture of the Gang*. New York: Free Press.

Cohen, Stanley. 1979. "The Punitive City: Notes on the Dispersal of Social Control." *Contemporary Crises* 3:339-363.

________. 1985. *Visions of Social Control: Crime, Punishment and Classification.* Cambridge, U.K.: Polity Press.

Cook, Fay Lomax. 1981. "Crime and the Elderly: The Emergence of a Policy Issue." Pp. 123–147 in *Reactions to Crime,* edited by Dan A. Lewis. Beverly Hills, Calif.: Sage.

Cressey, Donald R. 1960. "Limitations on Organization of Treatment in the Modern Prison." Pp. 78–110 *Theoretical Studies in Social Organization of the Prison,* by Richard A. Cloward et al. New York: Social Science Research Council.

Downs, George W. 1976. *Bureaucracy, Innovation, and Public Policy.* Lexington, Mass.: D. C. Heath.

Duffee, David. 1975. *Correctional Policy and Prison Organization.* Beverly Hills, Calif.: Sage-Halsted.

________. 1980a. *Correctional Management: Change and Control in Correctional Organizations.* Englewood Cliffs, N. J.: Prentice-Hall.

________. 1980b. *Explaining Criminal Justice.* Cambridge, Mass.: Oelgeschlager, Gunn and Hain.

Duffee, David E. and John Klofas. 1983. "Organizational Mandates and Client Careers: An Examination of Penal Policy." Pp. 197–210 in *Organizational Theory and Public Policy,* edited by Richard H. Hall and Robert E. Quinn. Beverly Hills, Calif.: Sage.

Dunford, Franklyn W. 1977. "Police Diversion: An Illusion?" *Criminology* 15:335–352.

Duster, Troy. 1987. "Crime, Youth Unemployment, and the Black Urban Underclass." *Crime and Delinquency* 33:300–316.

Elmore, Richard F. 1978. "Organizational Models of Social Program Implementation." *Public Policy* 26:185–228.

________. 1979–80. "Backward Mapping: Implementation Research and Policy Decisions." *Political Science Quarterly* 94:601–616.

Empey, LaMar. 1979. "Introduction: The Social Construction of Childhood and Juvenile Justice." Pp. 1–34 in *The Future of Childhood and Juvenile Justice,* edited by LaMar T. Empey. Charlottesville, Va.: University Press of Virginia.

________. 1982. *American Delinquency.* Homewood, Ill.: Dorsey Press.

Empey, LaMar T. and Maynard L. Erickson. 1972. *The Provo Experiment: Evaluating Community Control of Delinquency.* Lexington, Mass.: Lexington Books.

Empey, LaMar T. and Steven G. Lubeck. 1971. *The Silverlake Experiment: Testing Delinquency Theory and Community Intervention.* Chicago: Aldine.

Erickson, Maynard L. 1979. "Some Empirical Questions Concerning the Current Revolution in Juvenile Justice." Pp. 277–311 in *The Future of Childhood and*

Juvenile Justice, edited by LaMar T. Empey. Charlottesville, Va.: University Press of Virginia.

Fagan, Jeffrey, Ellen Slaughter, and Eliot Hartstone. 1987. "Blind Justice? The Impact of Race on the Juvenile Process." *Crime and Delinquency* 33:224–258.

Fairchild, Erika S. 1981. "Interest Groups in the Criminal Justice Process." *Journal of Criminal Justice* 9:181–194.

Faust, Frederic L. and Paul J. Brantingham. 1979. *Juvenile Justice Philosophy.* St. Paul, Minn.: West Publishing.

Feld, Barry. 1977. *Neutralizing Inmate Violence: Juvenile Offenders in Institutions.* Cambridge, Mass.: Ballinger.

Fishman, Mark. 1978. "Crime Waves as Ideology." *Social Problems* 25:531–543.

Flanagan, Timothy J. and Edmund F. McGarrell, eds. 1986. *Sourcebook of Criminal Justice Statistics–1985.* U. S. Department of Justice, Bureau of Justice Statistics. Washington, D. C.: U. S. Government Printing Office.

Fogel, David. 1975. *We Are the Living Proof: The Justice Model for Corrections.* Cincinnati, Ohio: Anderson.

Foucault, Michel. 1979. *Discipline and Punish.* New York: Vintage Books.

Fox, Sanford. 1970. "Juvenile Justice Reform: An Historical Perspective." *Stanford Law Review* 22:1187–1239.

————. 1974. "The Reform of Juvenile Justice: The Child's Right to Punishment." *Juvenile Justice* 25:2–9.

Galliher, John F. and Linda Basilick. 1979. "Utah's Liberal Drug Laws: Structural Foundations and Triggering Events." *Social Problems* 26:284–297.

Glaser, Barney G. and Anselm L. Strauss. 1967. *The Discovery of Grounded Theory: Strategies for Qualitative Research.* Chicago: Aldine.

Goffman, Erving. 1961. *Asylums.* Garden City, N. Y.: Anchor Books.

Gottfredson, Michael. 1979. "Treatment Destruction Techniques." *Journal of Research in Crime and Delinquency* 16:39–54.

Gottlieb, Barbara. 1985. *Public Danger as a Factor in Pretrial Release: The Dynamics of State Law Development.* Washington, D. C.: Toborg Associates.

Hagan, John. 1980. "The Legislation of Crime and Delinquency: A Review of Theory, Method, and Research." *Law and Society Review* 14:603–628.

Hagan, John and Jeffrey Leon. 1977. "Rediscovering Delinquency: Social History, Political Ideology and the Sociology of Law." *American Sociological Review* 42:587–598.

Hall, Richard H. 1982. *Organizations: Structure and Process.* Englewood Cliffs, N. J.: Prentice-Hall.

Hall, Stuart, Chas Critcher, Tony Jefferson, John Clarke, and Brian Roberts. 1978. *Policing the Crisis: Mugging, the State, and Law and Order.* New York: Holmes and Meier.

Hamparian, Donna M., *et al.* 1982. *Major Issues in Juvenile Justice Information and Training, Youth in Adult Courts: Between Two Worlds, Northeast Region.* Columbus, Ohio: Academy for Contemporary Problems.

Handler, Joel F. and Julie Zatz, eds. 1982. *Neither Angels Nor Thieves: Studies in Deinstitutionalization of Status Offenders.* Washington, D. C.: National Academy Press.

Hannan, Michael T. and John H. Freeman. 1977. "The Population Ecology of Organizations." *American Journal of Sociology* 82:929–964.

Hasenfeld, Yeheskel. 1983. *Human Service Organizations.* Englewood Cliffs, N. J.: Prentice-Hall.

Hasenfeld, Yeheskel and Paul P. L. Cheung. 1985. "The Juvenile Court as a People-Processing Organization: A Political Economy Perspective." *American Journal of Sociology* 90:801–824.

Hawes, Joseph M. 1971. *Children in Urban Society: Juvenile Delinquency in Nineteenth-Century America.* New York: Oxford University Press.

Heinz, John R., Robert W. Gettleman, and Morris A. Seeskin. 1969. "Legislative Politics and the Criminal Law." *Northwestern Law Review* 64:277–358.

Holsti, Ole R. 1969. *Content Analysis for the Social Sciences and Humanities.* Reading, Mass.: Addison-Wesley.

Huizinga, David and Delbert S. Elliott. 1987. "Juvenile Offenders: Prevalence, Offender Incidence, and Arrest Rates by Race." *Crime and Delinquency* 33:206–223.

Ignatieff, Michael. 1978. *A Just Measure of Pain: The Penitentiary in the Industrial Revolution, 1750–1850.* New York: Pantheon Books.

______. 1981. "State, Civil Society, and Total Institutions: A Critique of Recent Social Histories of Punishment." Pp. 153–192 in *Crime and Justice: Annual Review of Research Volume 3,* edited by Michael Tonry and Norval Morris. Chicago: University of Chicago Press.

Ingraham, Barton L. 1980. "Reforming Criminal Procedure." Pp. 23–38 in *Improving Management in Criminal Justice,* edited by Alvin W. Cohn and Benjamin Ward. Beverly Hills, Calif.: Sage.

Institute of Judicial Administration – American Bar Association Juvenile Justice Standards Project. 1977a. *Standards Relating to Juvenile Delinquency and Sanctions.* Cambridge, Mass.: Ballinger.

______. 1977b. *Standards Relating to Transfer Between Courts.* Cambridge, Mass.: Ballinger.

Jenkins, J. Craig and Charles Perrow. 1977. "Insurgency of the Powerless: Farm Worker Movements (1946–1972)." *American Sociological Review* 42:249–268.

Kassebaum, Gene, David Ward, and Daniel Wilner. 1971. *Prison Treatment and Parole Survival.* New York: John Wiley.

Katz, Daniel and Robert L. Kahn. 1966. *The Social Psychology of Organizations.* New York: John Wiley.

Kaufman, Herbert. 1971. *The Limits of Organizational Change.* University, Ala.: University of Alabama Press.

Kemp, Kathleen A. 1984. "Accidents, Scandals, and Political Support for Regulatory Agencies." *The Journal of Politics* 46:401–427.

Klein, Malcolm W. 1979. "Deinstitutionalization and Diversion of Juvenile Offenders: A Litany of Impediments." Pp. 145–201 in *Crime and Justice: An Annual Review of Research Volume 1,* edited by Norval Morris and Michael Tonry. Chicago: University of Chicago Press.

Kobrin, Solomon. 1959. "The Chicago Area Project — a 25-Year Assessment." *The Annals of the American Academy of Political and Social Science* 322:20–29.

Kobrin, Solomon and Malcolm W. Klein. 1983. *Community Treatment of Offenders: The DSO Experiments.* Beverly Hills, Calif.: Sage.

Krisberg, Barry and Ira Schwartz. 1983. "Rethinking Juvenile Justice." *Crime and Delinquency 29:333–364.*

Krisberg, Barry, Paul Litsky, and Ira Schwartz. 1984. "Youth in Confinement: Justice by Geography." *Journal of Research in Crime and Delinquency* 21:153–181.

Krisberg, Barry, Ira M. Schwartz, Paul Litsky, and James Austin. 1986. "The Watershed of Juvenile Justice Reform." *Crime and Delinquency* 32:5–38.

Krisberg, Barry, Ira M. Schwartz, Gideon Fishman, Zvi Eisikovits, Edna Guttman, and Karen Joe. 1987. "The Incarceration of Minority Youth." *Crime and Delinquency* 33:173–205.

Kuhn, Thomas S. 1970. *The Structure of Scientific Revolutions* (2nd ed.). Chicago: University of Chicago Press.

Lemert, Edwin M. 1967. "The Juvenile Court — Quest and Realities." Pp. 91–106 in The President's Commission on Law Enforcement and Administration of Justice, *Task Force Report: Juvenile Delinquency and Youth Crime.* Washington, D. C.: U. S. Government Printing Office.

———. 1970. *Social Action and Legal Change.* Chicago: Aldine.

———. 1981. "Diversion in Juvenile Justice: What Hath Been Wrought." *Journal of Research in Crime and Delinquency* 18:34–46.

Lerman, Paul. 1984. *Deinstitutionalization and the Welfare State.* New Brunswick, N. J.: Rutgers University Press.

Lipton, Douglas, Robert Martinson, and Judith Wilks. 1975. *The Effectiveness of Correctional Treatment.* New York: Praeger.

Lowell, Harvey D. and Margaret McNabb. 1980. *Sentenced Prisoners Under 18 Years of Age in Adult Correctional Facilities: A National Survey.* Washington, D.C.: National Center on Institutions and Alternatives.

Mack, Julian W. 1909. "The Juvenile Court." *Harvard Law Review* 23:104–122.

Martinson, Robert. 1974. "What Works? Questions and Answers about Prison Reform." *The Public Interest* 35:22–54.

McCarthy, John D. and Mayer N. Zald. 1977. "Resource Mobilization and Social Movements: A Partial Theory." *American Journal of Sociology* 82:1212–1241.

McCleery, Richard. 1960. "Communication Patterns as Bases of Systems of Authority and Power." Pp. 49–77 in *Theoretical Studies in Social Organization of the Prison,* by Richard Cloward et al. New York: Social Science Research Council.

———. 1968. "Correctional Administration and Political Change." Pp. 113–149 in *Prison Within Society,* edited by Lawrence E. Hazelrigg. New York: Doubleday.

McCorkle, Lloyd W., Albert Elias, and F. Lovell Bixby. 1958. *The Highfields Story.* New York: Holt, Rinehart and Winston.

McEwen, Craig A. 1978. *Designing Correctional Organizations for Youth: Dilemmas of Subcultural Development.* Cambridge, Mass.: Ballinger.

McGregor, Douglas. 1960. *The Human Side of Enterprise.* New York: McGraw–Hill.

Melone, Albert P. and Robert Slagter. 1983. "Interest Group Politics and the Reform of the Federal Criminal Code." Pp. 41–55 in *The Political Science of Criminal Justice,* edited by Stuart Nagel, Erika Fairchild, and Anthony Champagne. Springfield, Ill.: Charles C. Thomas.

Mennel, Robert M. 1973. *Thorns and Thistles: Juvenile Delinquents in the United States, 1825–1940.* Hanover, N. H.: University Press of New England.

———. 1983. "Attitudes and Policies toward Juvenile Delinquency in the United States: A Historiographical Review." Pp. 191–224 in *Crime and Justice: An Annual Review of Research Volume 4,* edited by Michael Tonry and Norval Morris. Chicago: University of Chicago Press.

Messinger, Sheldon L. and Phillip E. Johnson. 1978. "California's Determinate Sentencing Statute: History and Issues." Pp. 13–58 in *Determinate Sentencing: Reform or Regression?* U. S. Department of Justice. Washington, D. C.: U. S. Government Printing Office.

Miles, Matthew B. and A. Michael Huberman. 1984. *Qualitative Data Analysis: A Sourcebook of New Methods.* Beverly Hills, Calif.: Sage.

Miller, Alden D. 1983. "Technical Appendix on the Network Mapping Study." Mimeograph. Cambridge, Mass.: Center for Criminal Justice, Harvard Law School.

Miller, Alden D., Lloyd E. Ohlin, and Robert B. Coates. 1977. *A Theory of Social Reform: Correctional Change Processes in Two States.* Cambridge, Mass.: Ballinger.

Miller, Alden D., Robert B. Coates, and Lloyd E. Ohlin. 1980. "Evaluating Correctional Systems Under Normalcy and Change." Pp. 593–610 in *Handbook of Criminal Justice Evaluation,* edited by Malcolm W. Klein and Katherine S. Teilmann. Beverly Hills, Calif.: Sage.

Miller, Alden D. and Lloyd E. Ohlin. 1985. *Delinquency and Community: Creating Opportunities and Controls.* Beverly Hills, Calif.: Sage.

Milward, H. Brinton. 1982. "Interorganizational Policy Systems and Research on Public Organizations." *Administration and Society* 13:457–478.

Morris, Norval. 1974. *The Future of Imprisonment.* Chicago: University of Chicago Press.

Nagel, Stuart, Erika Fairchild, and Anthony Champagne. 1983. *The Political Science of Criminal Justice.* Springfield, Ill.: Charles C. Thomas.

National Advisory Commission on Criminal Justice Standards and Goals. 1973. *A National Strategy to Reduce Crime.* Washington, D. C.: U. S. Government Printing Office.

National Advisory Committee on Criminal Justice Standards and Goals. 1976. *Juvenile Justice and Delinquency Prevention.* Washington, D. C.: U. S. Government Printing Office.

National Commission on Law Observance and Enforcement. 1931. *The Child Offender in the Federal System of Justice.* Washington, D. C.: U. S. Government Printing Office.

O'Brien, David J. 1975. *Neighborhood Organization and Interest-Group Processes.* Princeton, N. J.: Princeton University Press.

Ohlin, Lloyd E. 1960. "Conflicting Interests in Correctional Objectives." Pp. 111–129 in *Theoretical Studies in Social Organization of the Prison,* by Richard A. Cloward et al. New York: Social Science Research Council.

———. 1974. "Organizational Reform in Correctional Agencies." Pp. 995–1020 in *Handbook of Criminology,* edited by Daniel Glaser. Chicago: Rand McNally.

———. 1983. "The Future of Juvenile Justice Policy and Research." *Crime and Delinquency* 29:463–472.

Ohlin, Lloyd E. and William C. Lawrence. 1959. "Social Interaction Among Clients as a Treatment Problem." *Social Work* 4:3–14.

"OJJDP Project Offers States 'Just Deserts' Juvenile Code." 1986. *Criminal Justice Newsletter* 17, 10:1–3.

Paternoster, Raymond and Tim Bynum. 1982. "The Justice Model as Ideology: A Critical Look at the Impetus for Sentencing Reform." *Contemporary Crises* 6:7–24.

Pepinsky, Harold E. 1987. "Information Sharing as a Human Right." *Humanity and Society* 11:189–211.

Platt, Anthony M. 1969. *The Child Savers: The Invention of Delinquency.* Chicago: University of Chicago Press.

______. 1974. "The Triumph of Benevolence: The Origins of the Juvenile Justice System in the United States." Pp. 366–389 in *Criminal Justice in America,* edited by Richard Quinney. Boston: Little, Brown.

Polsky, Howard W. 1962. *Cottage Six.* New York: Russell Sage Foundation.

Poulantzas, Nicos. 1973. *Political Power and Social Classes.* London: NLB and Sheed and Ward.

President's Commission on Law Enforcement and Administration of Justice. 1967a. *Task Force Report: Juvenile Delinquency and Youth Crime.* Washington, D. C.: U. S. Government Printing Office.

______. 1967b. *The Challenge of Crime in a Free Society* Washington, D. C.: U. S. Government Printing Office.

Pressman, Jeffrey L. and Aaron B. Wildavsky. 1973. *Implementation.* Berkeley, Calif.: University of California Press.

Regnery, Alfred S. 1985. "Getting Away with Murder: Why the Juvenile Justice System Needs an Overhaul." *Policy Review* 34:1–4.

Rendleman, Douglas R. 1971. "Parens Patriae: From Chancery to the Juvenile Court." *South Carolina Law Review* 23:205–259.

Rieselbach, Leroy N. 1983. "Legislative Change, Reform, and Public Policy." Pp. 359–394 in *Encyclopedia of Policy Studies,* edited by Stuart Nagel. New York: Marcel Dekker.

Robison, James and Gerald Smith. 1971. "The Effectiveness of Correctional Programs." *Crime and Delinquency* 17:67–80.

Roby, Pamela A. 1969. "Politics and Criminal Law: Revision of the New York State Penal Law on Prostitution." *Social Problems* 17:83–109.

Rose, Gordon. 1959. "Status and Grouping in a Borstal Institution." *British Journal of Delinquency* 9:258–275.

Rose, Stephen M. 1972. *Betrayal of the Poor.* Cambridge, Mass.: Schenkman.

Rothman, David, J. 1971. *The Discovery of the Asylum: Social Order and Disorder in the New Republic.* Boston: Little, Brown.

________. 1980. *Conscience and Convenience: The Asylum and its Alternatives in Progressive America.* Boston: Little, Brown.

Rubin, H. Ted. 1985. *Juvenile Justice: Policy, Practice, and Law.* New York: Random House.

Sarri, Rosemary C. and Robert D. Vinter. 1976. "Justice for Whom? Varieties of Juvenile Correctional Approaches." Pp. 161–200 in *The Juvenile Justice System,* edited by Malcolm W. Klein. Beverly Hills, Calif.: Sage.

Scheingold, Stuart A. 1984. *The Politics of Law and Order: Street Crime and Public Policy.* New York: Longman.

Schlossman, Steven L. 1977. *Love and the American Delinquent.* Chicago: University of Chicago Press.

Schneider, Anne Larason. 1984. "Divesting Status Offenses from Juvenile Court Jurisdiction." *Crime and Delinquency* 30:347–370.

Schrag, Clarence. 1954. "Leadership Among Prison Inmates." *American Sociological Review* 19:37–42.

Schultz, J. L. and F. Cohen. 1976. "Isolationism in Juvenile Court Jurisprudence." Pp. 20–41 in *Pursuing Justice for the Child,* edited by M. K. Rosenheim. Chicago: University of Chicago Press.

Schwartz, Ira M., Marilyn Jackson-Beeck, and Roger Anderson. 1984. "The 'Hidden' System of Juvenile Control." *Crime and Delinquency* 30:371–385.

Scull, Andrew. 1977. *Decarceration: Community Treatment and the Deviant — a Radical View.* Englewood Cliffs, N. J.: Prentice-Hall.

________. 1984. *Decarceration: Community Treatment and the Deviant — a Radical View* (2nd ed.). New Brunswick, N. J.: Rutgers University Press.

Schur, Edwin M. 1971. *Labeling Deviant Behavior.* New York: Harper and Row.

Sechrest, Lee, Susan O. White, and Elizabeth Brown, eds. 1979. *The Rehabilitation, of Criminal Offenders: Problems and Prospects.* Washington, D.C.: National Academy of Sciences.

Seidman, Edward. 1983. "Introduction." Pp. 11–17 in *Handbook of Social Intervention,* edited by Edward Seidman. Beverly Hills, Calif.: Sage.

Selznick, Philip. 1949. *T. V. A. and the Grassroots.* Berkeley, Calif.: University of California Press.

________. 1957. *Leadership in Administration: A Sociological Interpretation.* New York: Harper and Row.

Serrill, Michael S. 1980. "Washington's New Juvenile Code." *Corrections Magazine* 6, 1:36–41.

Shaw, Clifford R. and Henry D. McKay. 1942. *Juvenile Delinquency and Urban Areas*. Chicago: University of Chicago Press.

Sherman, Lawrence W. 1983. "Reducing Police Gun Use: Critical Events, Administrative Policy and Organizational Change." Pp. 98–125 in *Control in the Police Organization*, edited by Maurice Punch. Cambridge, Mass.: MIT Press.

Shichor, David. 1980. "Some Issues of Social Policy in the Field of Juvenile Delinquency." Pp. 317–334 in *Critical Issues in Juvenile Delinquency*, edited by David Shichor and Delos H. Kelly. Lexington, Mass.: Lexington Books.

Smith, Charles P., Paul S. Alexander, Garry L. Kemp, and Edwin M. Lemert, 1980. *A National Assessment of Serious Juvenile Crime and the Juvenile Justice System: The Need for a Rational Response. Volume III*. U. S. Department of Justice. Washington, D. C.: U. S. Government Printing Office.

Spergel, Irving A. 1976. "Interactions Between Community Structure, Delinquency, and Social Policy in the Inner City." Pp. 55–99 in *The Juvenile Justice System*, edited by Malcolm W. Klein. Beverly Hills, Calif.: Sage.

Steinberg, Ronnie. 1982. *Wages and Hours: Labor and Reform in Twentieth-Century America*. New Brunswick, N. J.: Rutgers University Press.

Stinchcombe, Arthur L. 1965. "Social Structure and Organization." Pp. 153–193 in *Handbook of Organizations,* edited by James G. March. Chicago: Rand McNally.

Stolz, Barbara Ann. 1984. "Interest Groups and Criminal Law: The Case of Federal Criminal Code Revision." *Crime and Delinquency* 30:91–106.

Strasburg, Paul A. 1984. "Recent National Trends in Serious Juvenile Crime." Pp. 5–30 in *Violent Juvenile Offenders,* edited by Paul DeMuro and Richard S. Allinson. San Francisco: National Council on Crime and Delinquency.

Street, David, Robert D. Vinter, and Charles Perrow. 1966. *Organization for Treatment*. New York: Free Press.

Sykes, Gresham M. 1958. *The Society of Captives*. Princeton, N. J.: Princeton University Press.

Sykes, Gresham M. and Sheldon Messinger. 1960. "The Inmate Social System." Pp. 5–19 in *Theoretical Studies in the Social Organization of the Prison,* by Richard Cloward, *et al*. New York: Social Science Research Council.

Taylor, Frederick W. 1911. *The Principles of Scientific Management*. New York: Harper and Row.

Terreberry, Shirley. 1968. "The Evolution of Organizational Environments." *Administrative Science Quarterly* 12:590–613.

Thompson, James D. and William J. McEwen. 1958. "Organizational Goals and Environment: Goal–Setting as an Interaction Process." *American Sociological Review* 23:23–31.

Travis Lawrence F. 1982. "The Politics of Sentencing Reform." In *Sentencing Reform,* edited by Martin L. Forst. Beverly Hills, Calif.: Sage.

Trist, E.L. 1961. "On Socio–Technical Systems." Pp. 269–282 in *The Planning of Change,* edited by Warren G. Bennis, Kenneth D. Benne, and Robert Chin. New York: Holt, Rinehart and Winston.

Twentieth Century Fund, Task Force on Sentencing Policy Toward Young Offenders. 1978. *Confronting Youth Crime.* New York: Holmes and Meier.

U. S. Department of Justice, Office of Juvenile Justice and Delinquency Prevention. 1984. *Children in Custody: Advance Report on the 1982 Census of Public Juvenile Facilities.* Washington, D. C.: U. S. Government Printing Office.

van den Haag, Ernest. 1975. *Punishing Criminals: Concerning a Very Old and Painful Question.* New York: Basic Books.

Vinter, Robert D., George Downs, and John Hall. 1975. *Juvenile Corrections in the States: Residential Programs and Deinstitutionalization.* Ann Arbor: Institute of Continuing Legal Education, University of Michigan.

von Hirsch, Andrew. 1976. *Doing Justice: The Choice of Punishments.* New York: Hill and Wang.

Wamsley, Gary L. and Mayer N. Zald. 1973. *The Political Economy of Public Organizations.* Lexington, Mass.: Lexington Books.

Wilkins, Leslie T. 1984. *Consumerist Criminology.* London: Heinemann Educational Books.

Wilson, James Q. 1975. *Thinking About Crime.* New York: Vintage.

Wright, Kevin N. 1981. "The Desirability of Goal Conflict Within the Criminal Justice System." *Journal of Criminal Justice* 9:209–218.

Zald, Mayer N. 1968. "The Correctional Institution for Juvenile Offenders: An Analysis of Organizational 'Character'." Pp. 229–246 in *Prison Within Society,* edited by Lawrence E. Hazelrigg. Garden City, N. Y.: Anchor Books.

―――――. 1970. *Organizational Change: The Political Economy of the YMCA.* Chicago: University of Chicago Press.

Bibliography of New York State Specific References

Allinson, Richard. 1983. "Is New York's Tough Juvenile Law a Charade?" *Corrections Magazine* 9:40–45.

Association of the Bar of the City of New York. 1983. *Report of the Juvenile Justice Committee of the Association of the Bar of the City of New York.* New York: Association of the Bar of the City of New York.

Baaklini, Abdo I. and Charles S. Dawson. 1979. *The Politics of Legislation in New York State: How a Bill Becomes a Law.* Albany, NY: Comparative Development Studies Center, Graduate School of Public Affairs, State University of New York at Albany; and New York State Assembly.

Bedell, Frederick D. 1984. *Persons in Need of Supervision—A Study of the Origins and Controversies Surrounding the Status Offender Jurisdiction in New York State.* Ph.D. dissertation, Amherst, Mass., University of Massachusetts.

Caloff, Judy. 1974. *Status Offenders and the Juvenile Court.* Albany, N. Y.: New York State Division for Youth.

Cammarata, Frank A. and Michael William R. Stott. 1977. "Judicial Administration of Mental Health Services for Juvenile Offenders." *Juvenile Justice* 28:3–7.

Carew, Donald K., et al. 1977. "New York State Division for Youth: A Collaborative Approach to the Implementation of Structural Change in a Public Bureaucracy." *Journal of Applied Behavioral Science* 13:327–339.

Carey, Hugh L. 1979. "Juvenile Justice Reform: A Positive Perspective." *Trial* 15:31–33.

Citizens' Committee for Children of New York. 1969. *The New York State Training School System: Findings and Recommendations December 15, 1969.* New York: Citizens' Committee for Children of New York, Inc.

————. 1979. *In Search of Juvenile Justice: An Interim Report on the 1978 New York Juvenile Offender Law.* New York: Citizens' Committee for Children of New York, Inc.

————. 1982. *Last Chance: Juveniles Behind Bars.* New York: Citizens' Committee for Children of New York, Inc.

————. 1982. *Lost Opportunities: A Study of the Promise and Practices of The Department of Probation's Family Court Services in New York City.* New York: Citizens' Committee for Children of New York, Inc.

————. 1984. *The Experiment that Failed: The New York State Juvenile Offender Law.* New York: Citizens' Committee for Children of New York, Inc.

Cohen, Fred. 1977. "Juvenile Justice: New York's Act is Hard to Follow." *Trial* 13:28–35.

Cole, Larry. 1972. *Our Children's Keepers: Inside America's Kid Prisons.* New York: Grossman.

Committee on Mental Health Services Inside and Outside the Family Court in the City of New York. 1972. *Juvenile Justice Confounded: Pretensions and Realities of Treatment Services.* Paramus, NJ: National Council on Crime and Delinquency.

Community Service Society of New York, Committee on Youth and Correction. 1970. *Highlights of 1970 Youth and Correction Legislation in New York State.* New York: Community Service Society of New York.

————. 1974. *Youth and Correction Legislation in New York State: A Review of Key Issues in 1974.* New York: Community Service Society of New York.

Community Service Society of New York. 1981. *An Agenda for New York's Forgotten Millions: An Appeal to the 204th Legislature.* New York: Community Service Society of New York.

Council of State Governments. Eastern Office. 1975. *Criminal Justice '75: Summary of the Fall Meeting.* New York: Council of State Governments, Eastern Office.

Crime and Justice in New York. n.d. Proceedings of the Governor's Conference on Crime. Held at John Jay College of Criminal Justice, New York, June 14–16, 1982.

Edelman, Peter B. 1976. *Progress Report on Placement Diversification in the Division for Youth.* Report Presented to the Association of Judges of the Family Court of the State of New York, Inc. Albany, N. Y.: New York State Division for Youth.

————. 1977. "Overview of the New York State Division for Youth." In *Children: In Pursuit of Justice.* Rockefeller Foundation Conference, February 1977. Working Papers. New York: The Rockefeller Foundation.

Fabricant, Michael. 1983. *Juveniles in the Family Courts*. Lexington, Mass.: Lexington Books.

Gettinger, Steve. 1976. "Profile/Juvenile Justice in New York City." *Corrections Magazine* 2,4:51–57.

Goddard, Malcolm S. 1976. "The Role of Legal Services in the Evolution of the State Training Schools." *New York State Bar Journal* 48:49–54.

______. 1977. "Juvenile Parole Revocation Hearings: The New York State Experience." *Criminal Law Bulletin* 13:552–573.

Gottfried, Richard N., Simon K. Barsky, and Helayne L. Baron. 1976. *Juvenile Crime: Report of Recommendations and Summary of Findings on Juvenile Justice, Based on the Legislative Investigations and Hearings of the New York State Assembly Standing Committee on Child Care*. Albany, N.Y.: New York State Assembly Standing Committee on Child Care.

Governor's Conference on Children and Youth. 1963. *New Yorkers Look to the Future*. Albany, N. Y.: New York State Division for Youth.

______. 1963. *Report of Youth and Adult Workshops to the Statewide Meeting, Albany, N. Y., November 15, 1963*. Albany, N. Y.: New York State Division for Youth.

Governor Rockefeller's Conference on Crime, April 21–22, 1966. n.d. Albany, N. Y.

Guggenheim, Martin. 1976. "Juvenile Justice and the 'Violent' Juvenile Offender." *New York State Bar Journal* 48:550–555.

Hairston, George E. 1981. "Black Crime and the New York State Juvenile Offender Law: A Consideration of the Effects of Lowering the Age of Criminal Responsibility." In *Major Issues in Juvenile Justice Information and Training: Readings in Public Policy*, edited by John C. Hall et al. Columbus, OH: Academy for Contemporary Problems.

Harris, L. 1978. "A Reporter at Large: Persons in Need of Supervision." *New Yorker Magazine* 54,26:55–89.

Hopewell, John A. and Frances K. Kernohan. 1968. *Out of Sight—Out of Mind: A Report on an Examination of the New York State Training Schools in the Downstate Complex January–May 1967*. New York: Community Service Society of New York.

Institute of Judicial Administration. 1975. *The Ellery C. Decision: A Case Study of Judicial Regulation of Juvenile Status Offenders*. New York: Institute of Judicial Administration, Inc.

Judicial Conference of the State of New York, Office of Childrens' Services. 1973. *Juvenile Injustice*. New York: Judicial Conference of the State of New York.

Knitzer, Jane and Merril Sobie. 1984. *Law Guardians in New York State: A Study of the Legal Representation of Children, Executive Summary.* New York: New York State Bar Association.

Lash, Trude W., Heide Sigal, and Deanna Dudzinski. 1980. *State of the Child: New York City II.* New York: Foundation for Child Development.

Levy, Harlan A. 1979. "Violent Juveniles: The New York Courts and the Constitution." *Columbia Human Rights Law Review* 11:51–62.

Luger, Milton. 1969. "Innovations in the Treatment of Juvenile Offenders." *Annals of the American Academy of Political and Social Science* 381:61–70.

__________. 1973. "Tomorrow's Training Schools: Problems, Progress, and Challenges." *Crime and Delinquency* 19:545–550.

Marino, Ralph J. 1977. "New York's Juvenile Criminals: A Call for Trial by Adult Courts." *Trial* 13:25–27.

McGarrell, Edmund F. 1985. "Change in New York's Juvenile Corrections System." Rockefeller Institute Working Paper No. 22. Albany, NY: The Nelson A. Rockefeller Institute of Government.

Morgan, Ted. 1975. "They Think, 'I Can Kill Because I'm 14' : A Case Study in a Juvenile Justice System that Neither Protects the Victims Nor Helps the Rising Number of Violent Youth." *New York Times Magazine* January 19:9–34.

Mullen, J. Thomas and Sidney Zirin. 1981."Death of a Training School." *Corrections Today* 43,5:52–57.

New York City Criminal Justice Agency. 1979. *The Processing of Juvenile Offenders in New York City: The Early Effects of Extending Criminal Responsibility to 13 to 15 Year Olds.* New York: New York City Criminal Justice Agency.

New York Senate Research Service. Task Force on Critical Problems. 1977. *Family Court. . .The System that Fails All: A Report on Probation Intake, Family Court, and Juvenile Justice.* Albany, N. Y.: New York Senate Research Service.

New York State Assembly Subcommittee on the Family Court. 1974. *The Resurgence of Youth Gangs in New York City.* Albany, N. Y.: New York State Assembly Subcommittee on the Family Court.

__________. 1974. *Armies of the Streets: A Report on the Structure, Membership and Activities of Youth Gangs in the City of New York.* Albany, N. Y.: New York State Assembly Subcommittee on the Family Court.

New York State Council on Children and Families. 1983. *Coordinated Planning: An Approach to Improving Services for Court-Related Youths.* Albany, N. Y.: New York State Council on Children and Families.

__________. 1983. "Juvenile Justice in New York State." *Trends: A Statistical Bulletin on the Status of Children and Families in New York State.* 1,3:1–8.

________. 1984. *Characteristics of Children in Out of Home Care.* Albany, N. Y.: New York State Council on Children and Families.

New York State Crime Control Council. 1967. *Governor Rockefeller's Conference on Crime.* Albany, N. Y.

New York State Department of Social Services. 1984. "The Changing Characteristics of Children in Social Services Funded Group Residential Programs, 1983." Albany, NY: New York State Department of Social Services, Division of Family and Children's Services.

New York State Division for Youth. 1972. *Youth and Work Training Programs: An Evaluation Study.* Albany, N. Y.: New York State Division for Youth.

________. 1973. "Documents Reflecting Legal Issues Confronting the Division for Youth as a Result of the Ellery C. Decision . . . From the Files of the Division for Youth, General Counsel, Malcolm S. Goddard." Albany, N. Y.: New York State Division for Youth.

________. 1974. *Statement to the New York State Assembly Judiciary Committee.* Presented by Malcolm S. Goddard, General Counsel, New York State Division for Youth. March 28, 1974.

________. 1975. *Goals and Objectives for the Division for Youth: A Planning Model.* Albany, N. Y.: New York State Division for Youth.

________. 1977. *Report of the Investigation of the New York State Agricultural and Industrial School at Industry, New York by the Division for Youth Investigative Team.* Albany, N. Y.: New York State Division for Youth.

________. 1978. *An Agency in Transition: An Issue Paper.* Albany, N. Y.: New York State Division for Youth.

________. 1982. *Gubernatorial Decision Papers Agency Action Reports.* Albany, N.Y.: New York State Division for Youth.

________. 1983. "Population Growth in DFY Level I Programs: 1983 (Fall) Projection Executive Summary." Albany, N. Y.: New York State Division for Youth, Bureau of Program Analysis and Information Services, Analysis Group.

________. 1984. "Population Growth in DFY Level I Programs: 1984 (Spring) Projection Executive Summary." Albany, N. Y.: New York State Division for Youth, Bureau of Program Analysis and Information Services, Analysis Group.

________. 1984. *Masterplan 84.* Albany, N. Y.: New York State Division for Youth.

________. (1979, 1980.) *Annual Plan.* Albany, N. Y.: New York State Division for Youth.

________. (1971, 1972, 1974.) *Annual Report.* Albany, N. Y.: New York State Division for Youth.

________. (1979–1981.) *Annual Statistical Report.* Albany, N. Y.: New York State Division for Youth.

————. (1966–1974.) *Linkup.* Albany, N. Y.: New York State Division for Youth.

————. n.d. *Three-Part Article Relating to Right to Treatment and the Impact of Those Cases upon the Division for Youth.* Albany, N. Y.: New York State Division for Youth.

New York State Division for Youth and Division of Probation Juvenile Justice Planning Committee. 1981. *Joint Policy and Program Initiatives for Juvenile Services in New York State.* Albany, N. Y.: State of New York, Executive Department.

New York State Division of the Budget. 1981. *The Executive Budget in New York State: A Half-Century Perspective.* Albany, N. Y.: New York State Division of the Budget.

New York State Division of Criminal Justice Services. 1982. *Juvenile Offenders in New York State: September 1, 1978 – December 31, 1981.* Albany, N. Y.: New York State Division of Criminal Justice Services.

————. 1982. *Juvenile Offenders in New York State 1982 Mid-Year Report.* New York: New York State Division of Criminal Justice Services, Major Violent Offense Trial Program.

————. 1984. *Juvenile Offenders in New York State: 1983 Report.* Albany, N. Y.: New York State Division of Criminal Justice Services, Office of Policy Analysis, Research and Statistical Services.

New York State Division of Criminal Justice Services. (1975–1984.) *Crime and Justice, Annual Report.* Albany, N. Y.: New York State Division of Criminal Justice Services.

New York State Division of Criminal Justice Services and New York City Criminal Justice Agency. 1979. *Juvenile Offenders in New York City: Their Characteristics and the Course of Case Processing.* New York: New York State Division of Criminal Justice Services and New York City Criminal Justice Agency.

New York State Executive Budget. Albany, N. Y. (1967–68—1984–85.)

New York State Judicial Conference. (1965–1985.) *Report of the Administrative Board of the Judicial Conference of the State of New York.* Albany, N. Y.: New York State Judicial Conference.

New York State Legislative Commission on Expenditure Review. 1972. *State of New York Legislative Commission on Expenditure Review, New York Division for Youth Programs, April 21, 1972.* Albany, N. Y.: Legislative Commission on Expenditure Review.

————. 1982. *Impact of Youth Rehabilitation Programs.* Albany, N. Y.: Legislative Commission on Expenditure Review.

————. 1982. *Management of Youth Rehabilitation Programs.* Albany, N. Y.: Legislative Commission on Expenditure Review.

New York State Legislature. Assembly Ways and Means Committee. 1973. *The Costs of Institutional Care for Delinquent Adolescents in New York State: Crisis and Legislative Remedies*. Albany, N. Y.: A Report Prepared by the Assembly Ways and Means Committee.

New York State Legislature. Senate Committee on Crime and Correction. 1977. *Delinquency? The Juvenile Justice System and the New Delinquent*. Albany, N. Y.: Report of the New York State Senate Committee on Crime and Correction and the New York State Select Committee on Crime.

New York State Temporary Commission on Child Welfare. 1975. *Children of the State I: A Time for Change in Child Care. The Preliminary Report*. Albany, N. Y.: Report Prepared by the Temporary Commission on Child Welfare.

________. 1976. *Children of the State II*. Albany, N. Y.: Report Prepared by the Temporary Commission on Child Welfare.

________. 1980. *Children of the State III*. Albany, N. Y.: Report Prepared by the Temporary Commission on Child Welfare.

New York State Temporary State Commission to Recodify the Family Court Act. 1980. *Initial Report of the Temporary State Commission to Recodify the Family Court Act*. Albany, N. Y.: New York State Legislature.

Note. 1976 "The New York Juvenile Justice Reform Act of 1976: Restrictive Placement — An Answer to the Problem of the Seriously Violent Youth?" *Fordham Law Review* 45:408–426.

Note. 1981. "The Juvenile Offender Laws of New York." *Albany Law Review* 45:436.

Note. 1981. "Post-Conviction Proceedings Under New York's Juvenile Offender Laws: A Due Process Critique." *New York Law School Law Review* 26:773–818.

Paquin, Henry and Frederick Foster-Clark. 1980. *Delinquency Intervention in New York's Division for Youth: A Look at the Youngsters, Programs, and Outcomes*. Albany, N. Y.: New York State Division for Youth.

Paulsen, Monrad, G. 1963. "The New York Family Court Act." *Buffalo Law Review* 12:420–441.

Pickett, Robert S. 1969. *House of Refuge: Origins of Juvenile Reform in New York State, 1815-1857*. Syracuse, N. Y.: Syracuse University Press.

Polier, Justine Wise. 1964. *A View From the Bench: The Juvenile Court*. New York: National Council on Crime and Delinquency.

Preliminary Report of the Governor's Special Committee on Criminal Offenders. 1968. New York.

Problems Related to Detention and Placement of Children. A Report Prepared by the Subcommittee on Detention and Placement of Children for the Subcommittee on Liaison with Public and Private Agencies of the Departmental Committees of the Appellate Divisions First and Second Departments, March 1973.

Report to the Governor from Kevin M. Cahill, M.D., Special Assistant to the Governor on Health Affairs, New York State: Governor's Panel on Juvenile Violence. Albany, N. Y.: Submitted to Governor Carey, January 5, 1976.

A Report on the Governor's Conference on Youth, April 5, 1968. Albany, N. Y.

Report of the Joint Legislative Committee on Protection of Children and Youth and Drug Abuse. 1970. *What Chance for Children? A Report on What Happens in New York State to the Young in Trouble.* Albany, N. Y.: New York State Legislative Document No. 19.

Roysher, Martin and Peter Edelman. 1981. "Treating Juveniles as Adults in New York: What Does it Mean and How is it Working?" In *Major Issues in Juvenile Justice Information and Training: Readings in Public Policy,* edited by John C. Hall *et al.* Columbus, Ohio: Academy for Contemporary Problems.

Salken, Barbara. 1981. "Down the Up Staircase: Due Process and Removal from Criminal Court." *New York Law School Law Review* 26:643–675.

Schackman, Walter M. 1980. "New York's New Juvenile Felony Law." *Judges Journal* 19:33,55–56.

Schinitsky, Charles. 1962. "The Role of the Lawyer in Children's Court." *The Record* (New York City Bar Association) 17:10–26.

Silbert, James D. and Alan N. Sussman. 1974. "The Rights of Juveniles Confined in Training Schools and the Experience of a Training School Ombudsman." *Brooklyn Law Review* 40:605–633.

Silver, Martin T. 1972. "The New York City Family Court: A Law Guardian's Overview." *Crime and Delinquency* 18:93–98.

Singer, Simon I. 1985. "Relocating Juvenile Crime: The Shift from Juvenile to Criminal Justice." Rockefeller Institute Special Report. Albany, N. Y.: The Nelson A. Rockefeller Institute of Government.

Sobie, Merril. 1981. "The Juvenile Offender Act: Effectiveness and Impact on the New York Juvenile Justice System." *New York Law School Review* 26:677–722.

State of New York. Joint Legislative Committee on Penal Institutions. n.d. *Report on Youth House, New York City to the 1967 Session of the New York State Legislature.* Albany, N. Y.: Joint Legislative Committee on Penal Institutions.

Statewide Youth Advocacy. 1983. "The Effect of 1983–84 Budget Cuts and Freeze on the New York State Division for Youth." Rochester, N. Y.: Statewide Youth Advocacy, Inc.

______. 1984. *Preliminary Report for the New York State 1984–1985 Children's Budget.* Rochester, N. Y.: Statewide Youth Advocacy, Inc.

Sullivan, Mercer L. 1983. "Youth Crime: New York's Two Varieties." *New York Affairs* 8,1:31–48.

Thorpe, Mara T. 1979. "Juvenile Justice Reform: A Critical Perspective." *Trial* 15:27–30.

Whisenand, Lucia Beadel and Edward J. McLaughlin. 1982. "Completing the Cycle: Reality and the Juvenile Justice System in New York State." *Albany Law Review* 47:1–36.

Wilson, Rob. 1978. "Juvenile Inmates: The Long-Term Trend is Down." *Corrections Magazine* 4:3–11.

Woods, John P. 1980. "New York's Juvenile Offender Law: An Overview and Analysis." *Fordham Urban Law Journal* 9:1–50.

Zimmerman, Joseph F. 1981. *The Government and Politics of New York State.* New York: New York University Press.

Index